On Truth and Meaning

Also available from Continuum:

Epistemology: Key Concepts in Philosophy, Christopher Norris

Deconstruction and the 'Unfinished Project of Modernity', Christopher Norris

On Truth and Meaning: Language, Logic and the Grounds of Belief

Christopher Norris

continuum
LONDON • NEW YORK

For Terry Hawkes

Continuum International Publishing Group

The Tower Building   80 Maiden Lane
11 York Road   Suite 704
London   New York
SE1 7NX   NY 10038

www.continuumbooks.com

British Library Cataloguing-in-Publication Data
A catalogue record for this book is available from the British Library.

ISBN: 0-8264-9127-8 (hardback) 0-8264-9128-6(paperback)

Library of Congress Cataloging-in-Publication Data
Norris, Christopher, 1947-
    On truth and meaning : language, logic and the gounds of belief / Christopher Norris.
        p. cm.
    Includes index.
    ISBN 0-8264-9127-8 (hardback) – ISBN 0-8264-9128-6 (pbk.)
    1. Analysis (Philosophy) 2. Language and languages–Philosophy. 3. Knowledge, Theory of. I. Title.
    B808.5.N65 2006
    121–dc22   2006000667

Typeset by YHT Ltd, London
Printed and bound in Great Britain by MPG Books Ltd, Cornwall

Contents

Preface

This book explores a range of contiguous issues in epistemology, ethics and philosophy of mind, language, and logic. It marks a further stage in the author's project of developing a realist, truth-based approach that would point a way beyond the various unresolved dilemmas and dichotomies bequeathed by old-style logical empiricism. In a series of closely argued chapters Norris draws out the two chief kinds of deficit – normative and casual-explanatory – that have characterized much recent work in the mainstream analytic line of descent. He pinpoints their source in the various failed attempts, after Quine, to make good the promise of a naturalized epistemology that would somehow remedy those defects while not falling prey to the Quinean barrage of sceptical counter-arguments. Elsewhere – as in the debate around Kripke's reading of Wittgenstein on 'following a rule' – philosophers have sought to head off the threat of a yet more radical scepticism aimed at the very ground rules of logical thought. The opening chapter sets the issues in a longer historical perspective by examining Frege's objectivist conception of mathematics, logic and the formal sciences, his outright rejection of 'psychologism' in any guise, and the resultant (mistaken) idea among many analytic philosophers that this charge was justified in the case of Husserlian transcendental phenomenology. Hence, Norris argues, the rift that opened up between the 'two traditions' of contemporary philosophic thought, one consequence of which was the analytic failure to develop precisely those normative resources that were needed in order to break out of the post-Quinean impasse. His book then proceeds through critical engagement with the work of (among others) Donald Davidson, Saul Kripke, John McDowell, Hilary Putnam, Richard Rorty and Crispin Wright. It also mounts a vigorous challenge to the prominent strain of anti-realist thinking first espoused on logico-semantic and metaphysical grounds by Michael Dummett and more recently subject to revision and refinement by Neil Tennant. A chapter on 'Ethics, Autonomy, and the Grounds of Belief' pursues these issues into a different though germane area of enquiry. Altogether Norris' book provides a wide-ranging and distinctively angled perspective on some of the most challenging topics in current philosophical debate.

Introduction and Acknowledgements

This book has to do mainly with topics in epistemology and philosophy of language, although it does take a few parallel routes (I hope not detours or excursions) through various neighbouring terrains. Among its central themes are a number of much-rehearsed but as yet unresolved questions that have pre-occupied many analytic philosophers since the demise of old-style logical empiricism. They include the issue of priority between logic and psychology posed most forcefully by Frege and still a matter of dispute in some quarters; the problem of 'radical interpretation' across variant paradigms or conceptual schemes as raised by Quine, Kuhn, Davidson and others; the debate around realism and anti-realism that has lately assumed centre-stage in consequence of Dummett's logico-semantic recasting of earlier verificationist arguments; the issue as to what properly counts as 'following a rule', taken up by Saul Kripke with presumptive warrant from late Wittgenstein; the role of causal reasoning (or inference to the best explanation) in epistemology and philosophy of science; and the question whether one can wrest a viable conception of free will or autonomous human agency and choice from a causal-realist approach of this type when extended to philosophy of mind. Between them, these issues have pretty much defined the agenda of current debate, at least in the mainstream analytic journals and amongst the most prominent post-1970 arbiters of philosophic relevance and worth. Then there are various related topics such as the extent to which a middle-ground position – e.g., 'internal' (framework) realism or the response-dispositional approach – might offer what's needed by way of reply to the anti-realist challenge or the rule-following paradox.

Meanwhile some broadly 'analytic' philosophers (among them John McDowell and Robert Brandom) have shown an increased willingness to place such concerns within a wider cultural and a longer chronological perspective, looking back to Kant – even Hegel – for a better sense of where these problems first took hold and maybe for a glimpse of new horizons beyond them. So on the one hand it might plausibly be said that the present-day analytic scene is more diverse and less set in its ways than at any time since Russell and Moore famously announced their break with the discourse of German idealism, and Frege just as firmly signalled his objections to the project of Husserlian phe-nomenology. On the other hand it is likely to strike any reader with a more than passing knowledge of work in the post-Kantian mainland European tradition that these overtures from the analytic side of the fence are couched very much in terms of their own philosophical agenda – as summarized above – and are apt to draw upon these continental texts in a highly selective, not to say skewed and exegetically under-informed way. Thus Kant is typically brought in by way of a 'revisionist' reading that recruits certain aspects of his thought as a remedy for the problems and dilemmas bequeathed by old-style logical empiricism while conveniently shunting aside any others – like the whole elaborate and (for Kant) indispensable machinery of transcendental deduction – which happen not to fit with the analytic rules of the game. In Hegel's case, the revisionist strategies range from a 'linguistified' update of Hegel versus Kant on the limits of formal analysis and hence the need for a somewhat more holistic or context-sensitive mode of reasoning to full-fledged historicist or cultural-relativist attacks on the very idea of philosophy as a discipline with its own distinctive standards of validity and truth.

This is not to say – far from it – that the recent signs of a belated *rapprochement* between the 'two traditions' of post-Kantian philosophy are really nothing more than an ill-disguised takeover bid by those on the lookout for fresh grist to the analytic mill. To be sure, there is an element of that in the versions of Kant put forward by revisionists from Strawson to McDowell. It is also present in Brandom's distinctly selective retrieval of Kantian-Hegelian themes as back-up for his inferentialist argument concerning the 'myth of the given' and the fallacy of thinking that truth or knowledge could possibly have any grounds or justification apart from the fabric of our various, rationally connected beliefs-held-true. Then again, there is the Rortian neo-pragmatist take whereby that whole chapter of developments from Kant to the present becomes just a prelude to the realization that philosophy is in truth good for nothing save the burial of its old, overweening ambitions and the constant retelling of this cautionary tale in refurbished, more or less inventive or imaginative ways. Still it is a welcome development – conducive to the opening-up of intellectual channels blocked for too long by the silt of entrenched prejudice – that these 'continental' thinkers are now back on the agenda, even if by way of some highly partial or opportunist readings. Meanwhile, there is also much to be said (and some good work now being done) on the extent to which, *contra* the orthodox view, philosophers in the mainland-European line of descent from Husserl to Derrida have long been engaged with the same sorts of issue that typically preoccupy their analytic counterparts. Thus, for instance, the best recent commentaries on Derrida have made a strong point of engaging with those early texts where he raises distinctly 'analytical' questions – often *via* a meticulous close-reading of Husserl – about the objectivity of truth, the status (and possible revisability) of classical or bivalent logic, and the role of linguistic representation *vis-à-vis* propositional content or such abstract mathematical entities as numbers, sets, and classes. My point in all this is partly to explain how the chapters that follow, with their strongly analytic bent, can nonetheless be seen as growing out of my attempt over the past two decades to chip away at the barriers erected by successive generations of Anglophone philosophers against successive waves of continental (mainly French) thought.

As I say, this volume is very largely concerned with debates within the analytic camp, and makes reference to thinkers like Husserl and Derrida chiefly in order to point up certain contrasts or communities of interest. Even so I should perhaps acknowledge by way of fair warning to the reader that, at least by comparison with most current work in that tradition, my book tends toward the synoptic approach rather than the kind of intensive concentration on sharply defined topic-areas that typifies the mainstream analytic mode. More precisely: I take it that the range of issues outlined in my opening paragraph can best be understood as variations on a common underlying theme, namely the debate between realists and anti-realists with regard to those otherwise discrete topic-areas. Analytic philosophy is nowadays a specialized sort of business – too much so by half, opponents often say – and it is likely that the range of topics here dealt with will strike some practitioners as diverse to the point of intellectual promiscuity or worse. To other, e.g., 'continentally' inclined types it will more likely seem just a further example of the bias toward narrowly technical concerns which prevents philosophy from earning its keep as a socially responsive, culturally relevant, and (not least) a publicly accountable since tax-funded academic discourse.

At risk of being thought to pin my colours firmly to both sides of the fence (and mixing metaphors with reckless abandon) let me say that I am in something of a cleft stick here. A great deal of current analytic work strikes me as self-absorbed and overly preoccupied with intra-professional debates while the attacks come very often from ill-informed middlebrow broadsheet journalists or from 'post-analytic' philosophers (along with cultural and literary theorists) who clearly have their own axes to grind. Perhaps I can lay some claim to a view atop these territorial squabbles, having spent a large part of the last twenty years trying to promote better relations and mutual understanding between the (so-called) 'two traditions'. Yet of course such good-willed ecumenical efforts are themselves liable to strike some observers – those with a strong attachment either way – as little more than a fudgy compromise. Still I would hope that this book, if it doesn't quite offer the best of both worlds, will be of interest to readers more used to 'continental' styles of philosophizing while nonetheless holding the attention of those with analytically trained habits of thought. At any rate the topics here discussed – in philosophy of mind, logic, and language – are also (as I have said) absolutely central to some main developments in continental thought from Husserl to Derrida. Besides, they are topics that must clearly find a place in any kind of philosophical enquiry meriting the name. That is, such issues are sure to arise whenever thinking declines to endorse Wittgenstein's quietist injunction that philosophy should leave everything as it is with our everyday, acculturated language-games and life-forms, or Rorty's kindred neo-pragmatist advice that we should leave off fretting about all those tedious pseudo-problems and allow philosophy to take its place as just one voice in the cultural conversation of humankind.

To be sure, some currently hot topics of analytical debate – like the Kripkean rule-following 'paradox' – might well be regarded as products of a hypercultivated sceptical mindset that invites a therapeutic or debunking response along these lines. However it is an irony which can scarcely escape notice that the whole debate about rule-following (along with sundry other variations on a sceptical or anti-realist theme) itself takes rise from just the kind of placidly communitarian appeal that Wittgenstein proffers as our last, best hope of escape from the travails of philosophic doubt. Thus Kripke's 'sceptical solution' to Wittgenstein's 'sceptical problem' really amounts to no more than a flat re-statement, in somewhat sharpened form, of the same (as I think it) false and misconceived dilemma. One might likewise suggest that anti-realism in its nowadays most prominent logico-semantic (Dummettian) form is a doctrine that could hardly have become the focus of so much intensive debate had it not combined the promise of a direct escape from all our epistemological woes with the curious appeal exerted by so strongly paradoxical or counter-intuitive a theory. Anyway this particular issue comes in for its share of detailed discussion in the following chapters so I shall say no more about it here. What I wish to emphasize, again for the benefit of readers trying to get their bearings, is that my book sets out to address these topics in such a way as to engage the attention of analytic philosophers while also – at times – adopting a more distanced, even diagnostic approach so as to place them in a broader philosophical perspective.

Meanwhile let me offer a few brief remarks about individual chapters in order to provide some signposts along the way. Chapter 1 ('Who's Afraid of Psychologism?') examines the often vexed and sometimes openly hostile rela-tionship between psychology and philosophy, in particular those disciplines – logic, epistemology, and philosophy of mind – that have been most anxious to disown any taint of subjective or 'psychologistic' content. I focus on the various forms that this quarrel has taken, most strikingly in Frege's objectivist con-ception of logical and mathematical truths, along with his well-known animadversions on the kinds of vulgar empiricist fallacy supposedly committed by thinkers like J. S. Mill. I go on to take stock of various opposing arguments, among them the project of naturalized epistemology advanced by W. V. Quine according to which even certain axioms of classical logic (bivalence or excluded middle) might have to be revised or abandoned under pressure of empirical counter-evidence. I maintain that this approach – especially when conjoined with Quine's doctrine of radical meaning-holism – gives rise to some strictly insoluble problems, not least the normativity-deficit induced by its failure to provide any adequate criteria for rational theory-choice. The same criticism applies even more strongly to full-scale assaults on the discipline, ethos and presumed authority of logic. One such assault is that mounted by the feminist philosopher Andrea Nye, who denounces 'malestream' logicians – Frege chief among them – for their inhumanly abstract and doctrinaire pursuit of objective (or quasi-objective) truths. Here again the argument fails on grounds of reflexive self-inconsistency, i.e., for want of any adequate standard by which to sustain or legitimize its own claims.

Nevertheless, this quarrel cannot be resolved in favour of either party since it is one that has its roots in the drastic bifurcation between formal (logico-semantic) and empirically based modes of reasoning which has characterized much analytic philosophy over the past half-century and more. What is required, I suggest, is an alternative approach that follows the example of philosophers like Philip Kitcher in developing a more refined, non-reductionist, and normatively adequate version of naturalized epistemology. A further beneficial result would be the shift of focus from that largely sterile debate between realist and anti-realist positions in philosophy of language, logic and science that has preoccupied so many thinkers in the wake of old-style logical empiricism. Otherwise there seems little hope of escaping what has become – after Dummett – just the latest, logico-semantic update on a range of well-worn sceptical themes and equally well-worn rejoinders. For this is also the product of a failure to acknowledge the strength of those counter-arguments put forward by advocates of causal realism plus inference to the best, most rational explanation as a means of avoiding the post-empiricist predicament. That is to say, there is no reason to go along with Quine's pithily expressed but philosophically dubious idea that 'the Humean condition is also the human condition'.

Chapter 2 ('Meaning, Truth and Causal Explanation') develops a similar line of argument with regard to some of the problems that have dogged epistemology and philosophy of language since the heyday of logical empiricism. I put the case that these problems can be traced back to Hume – to his radical disjunction between empirical 'matters of fact' and analytic 'truths of reason' – and that they took an even deeper hold through Kant's heroic but failed attempt to transcend the dichotomy between Hume's radically empiricist outlook and the rationalist 'way of ideas'. Moreover they have resurfaced with striking regularity in various post-1950 developments, among them (ironically) Quine's root-and-branch attack on the residual elements of Kantian thinking in the logical-empiricist programme and Davidson's critique of Quine for embracing the 'third dogma' of empiricism, namely the scheme/content distinction. This in turn led on to Quine's problematical claims concerning the topics of 'radical translation' and ontological relativity. In fact, as I show, that dualism is still very much present in Davidson's proposed combination of a Tarskian formalized or truth-theoretic approach with a strain of radical empiricism that claims to put us back in 'unmediated' touch with the objects of perceptual experience. It also re-emerges at various points in the effort of thinkers like John McDowell to come up with a revisionist ('naturalized' or 'de-transcendentalized') reading of Kant that would offer a welcome escape-route.

On my account the only way beyond these dilemmas is a realist approach that endorses the principle of inference to the best explanation as applied not only in epistemological (e.g., scientific) contexts but likewise in contexts of linguistic-communicative uptake. I therefore reject the currently widespread idea – with its chief sources in Frege and Wittgenstein – that issues in philosophy of language are logically or methodologically prior to other, more substantive issues of knowledge and truth. This 'language-first' argument can always be pressed toward an anti-realist (Dummett-type) conclusion, even when adopted by thinkers like Davidson who resist that conclusion on the grounds that truth (or the attitude of holding-true) is itself a precondition for all and any linguistic understanding. Thus on the one hand this chapter sets out to resist what I view as the negative, philosophically retrograde effects of the 'linguistic turn' in its various present-day manifestations. On the other, more constructively, it proposes an alternative realist approach whereby such questions can be seen to assume a properly subordinate role *vis-à-vis* the range of first-order epistemological and causal-explanatory issues.

Chapters 3 and 4 develop this case with particular reference to issues of scientific knowledge and natural-language interpretation. I examine various opposed lines of argument from an anti-realist, scheme-relativist, or sceptical quarter and conclude that they cannot be consistently maintained without contravening some basic suppositions regarding our epistemological placement and our powers of communicative grasp. Anti-realism in its current, logico-semantic form – as advanced most notably by Dummett – is a programme that generates just such problems, and is therefore best seen as a *reductio* of the idea that issues of linguistic understanding should be treated as methodologically prior to issues of substantive (rational or causal-explanatory) warrant. Those problems can again be traced back to Kant's (in my view) unsuccessful attempt to reconcile the claims of empirical realism and transcendental idealism. The consequences of that failure are still visible not only in the unresolved dichotomy of scheme and content inherited by logical empiricism but also in various later claims – by Quine, Davidson, and McDowell among others – to have shifted the debate on to different epistemological ground. Hence the ease with which anti-realists can turn this shared agenda to their own advantage and deploy the 'language-first' argument to bolster their case for a refined (but no less problematical) version of old-style verificationism. Not the least of its problems, in Dummett's case, is the conjunction of a Fregean compositional and logico-semantic approach with a Wittgensteinian holistic or contextualist appeal to 'language-games' and cultural 'forms of life'. I conclude that the linguistic turn in whichever guise is not at all the kind of epochal advance that Dummett proclaims but rather a distraction from other, philosophically prior concerns such as that of establishing adequate grounds for our various discipline-specific practices of inference to the best, most rational explanation.

Hence – to repeat – the various dilemmas (or, as I suggest, pseudo-dilemmas) that have left such a deep and often disfiguring mark on recent analytic philosophy. Hence also the continuing impact of Kant's failure to offer any plausible, explanatorily adequate account of the process whereby 'sensuous intuitions' were brought under 'concepts of understanding' through the joint (somewhat mysterious) agency of 'judgement' and 'imagination'. My argument proceeds, via Quine's (on the face of it) radically anti-dualist critique of logical empiricism, to more recent attempts – by Davidson and McDowell – to locate the residual dualism in Quine (that of scheme and content), and thus bring philosophy out on the far side of all these inherited problems. I suggest that the difficulty goes much deeper and re-emerges with full force both in Davidson's coupling of a formalized (Tarskian) truth-theoretic approach with a strain of radical empiricism and in McDowell's revisionist, supposedly 'naturalized', but nonetheless dualist reading of Kant on the twin powers of 'spontaneity' and 'receptivity'. Its ultimate source – once again – is the normative deficit, i.e., the lack of rational and justificatory values that has typified empiricist thinking from Hume to Quine, along with its attendant sceptical outlook concerning the existence of causal powers or the status and validity of causal explanations. Chapter 4 thus concludes with a survey of those alternative philosophical arguments that speak strongly for a realist approach and that might point a way beyond this long-standing impasse.

In chapter 5 I raise some related issues with regard to truth, knowledge and epistemic warrant but here in the context of a central concern with the question of doxastic responsibility, or whether we can properly be held accountable for the content and nature of our various beliefs. This discussion takes in a wide range of issues from philosophy of mind and cognitive science to epistemology, philosophical semantics, and – of course – ethical theory. It also goes some way toward fulfilling the promise that my book would engage on occasion with certain distinctly 'continental' themes. Here they show up via a comparative account of how the issue has been addressed by thinkers from Sartre to Derrida, and (resuming various lines of argument from previous chapters) how those who approach it from an analytic viewpoint might profit by reflecting on the challenge thus posed to their accustomed modes of thought. Without for one moment claiming to resolve what is undoubtedly one of the most difficult – maybe unresolvable – problems in philosophy I suggest that it has encountered a series of conceptual dead-ends in the mainstream analytic discourse and could do with just the kind of sharpened (if at times overly extreme or paradoxical) formulation brought to it by thinkers in the 'other' line of descent. My point is that the best way to conceive their relationship is not (as so often) in terms of downright antagonism but rather as a mutual interrogative exchange where the analytic impulse is one that exerts a constant restraining or moderating force while the continental impulse is one that tends often to challenge, unsettle, or problematize any such approach.

Chapter 6 ('Kripkenstein's Monsters') comes at its topic from an opposite angle since it concerns what I take to be a species of exorbitant sceptical doubt yet one that has arisen in the very heartland of recent analytic philosophy and can plausibly be seen as the inevitable upshot of those various developments noted above. Kripke's take on Wittgenstein's thoughts about 'private languages' and 'following a rule' is (on his own submission) bizarre, absurd, even unthinkable by commonsense or rational standards. Indeed it goes beyond anything that even Hume was willing to contemplate by way of undermining every last source of assurance with regard not only to our warrant for inductive reasoning on empirical evidence but also to our capacity for the most basic kinds of logical deduction or means of distinguishing valid from invalid modes of formal inference. There is no doubt that Kripke has here hit on a highly ingenious technique for raising such ultra-sceptical questions as concerns our knowledge of what we or other people have in mind when purportedly following a rule or performing a routine task in elementary arithmetic. Just as surely his argument must have gone off the rails at some point since we should otherwise be utterly deluded – or stuck for an adequate justification – if we believed that there existed any standard of truth or correctness in such matters beyond that of 'agreement in judgement' or whatever counts as true or correct within some shared (community-wide) practice or form of life. This is Kripke's 'sceptical solution' to Wittgenstein's 'sceptical problem', one that effectively declares the problem insoluble except by retreating to a flat restatement of Wittgenstein's communitarian view.

To be sure, Kripke goes out of his way to acknowledge how far this upshot strains credibility and how forcefully it strikes even him as a conclusion scarcely to be borne if one wishes to preserve any semblance of rational thought. Still it is hard to see how the demon of all-consuming sceptical doubt can possibly be kept at bay if Kripke's argument goes through. Thus the simplest recursive operations, like those of elementary arithmetic, must be thought of as lacking any standards of correctness – of objective, practice-transcendent truth or falsehood – save those that we deludedly suppose to possess that character in so far as they define what counts as correct according to the relevant communal norms. On Kripke's account, we can never be sure that other people who seem to come up with a wrong answer are trying (and failing) to apply the same rule, since they might always – if asked – offer an alternative, non-standard but (on its own terms) perfectly consistent explanation of what they were doing. More than that: we are none of us entitled to say – perhaps through some mode of privileged first-person epistemic access – that our present idea of what constitutes a correct rule-following move is the same idea that we applied on any number of previous occasions. Our situation *vis-à-vis* our own past self, whether when we last did some basic arithmetic or maybe just one stage back in the present calculation, is to this extent analogous with our situation *vis-à-vis* the other person who might always have come up with a 'wrong' (i.e., non-standard) answer by correctly applying some deviant rule rather than incorrectly applying the standard one. Quite simply, there is no deep further fact – no determinate or introspectible truth – about what we mean or intend in our various modes of rule-following behaviour, and hence no way of excluding the possibility that, given some simple instruction like 'Continue the series $n+2$', we have not switched from one interpretation to another at some stage in the sequence.

As I say, Kripke fully acknowledges the extreme, indeed barely thinkable consequences of a sceptical argument pressed so far as to embrace not only Humean 'matters of fact' (i.e., the grounds of inductive warrant or causal explanation) but also Humean 'truths of reason' (that is, those pertaining to arithmetic, logic, and the formal sciences). Still there is little sign that his treatment of the topic is meant as a *reductio ad absurdum* of this whole line of argument, or that his sceptical-communitarian 'solution' is advanced solely or mainly in order to show up its patent inadequacy. Rather it seems that, despite those express misgivings, Kripke intends his 'elementary exposition' of passages from late Wittgenstein as a straightforward lesson in the non-availability of any grounds or justification for our various kinds of rule-following procedure save those that find warrant in the appeal to some shared life-form or communal practice. Chapter 6 offers what I hope is a strong case for thinking that Kripke is wrong about this. More specifically, I argue that the sceptical problem and the sceptical (pseudo-)solution alike are products of a straw-man approach that starts out from the misconceived idea of truth, correctness, consistency, and so forth, as matters of first-person apodictic warrant and then – having raised all the usual objections to that idea – ends up embracing a communitarian doctrine which it takes to be the sole alternative on offer. What thus drops completely out of sight is the realist (or objectivist) view of truth and correctness in rule-following which no doubt needs defending against some familiar counter-arguments but which nonetheless offers – as I seek to demonstrate here – the only way of conceptualizing these issues that doesn't court charges of manifest absurdity.

Another chief reason for devoting so much space to this topic is that it shows up certain features of the analytic enterprise in a particularly sharp and revealing light. Among them is the strongly marked reactive tendency which began with the widespread turn against 'continental' thinking in whatever shape or guise, and which has since, I would argue, been largely responsible for the kinds of extreme position adopted by radicals of various persuasion, whether hard-line empiricists like Quine, committed anti-realists like Dummett, or out-and-out sceptics like Kripke. Indeed I put the case intermittently throughout this book that many of the problems and dilemmas confronted by analytic philosophy can be seen as resulting, at least in part, from the break with mainland-European thought that was first signalled by Russell and Moore in their renunciation of Hegelian idealism. This break was reinforced by those who followed Frege in rejecting the 'psychologism' falsely imputed to Husserlian transcendental phe-nomenology, as likewise by Ryle, who took an early interest in Husserl's work but subsequently came out against it on similar grounds. Only during the past decade or so have thinkers in the mainstream analytic tradition – Dummett among them – begun to take a different, more accommodating line and acknowledge the extent to which Husserl's philosophy of logic and language may be seen as an alternative (perhaps complementary) approach to issues of shared concern. Even so this new-found tolerance turns out to have sharp limits when it comes to the main point at issue, that is, the necessity (according to Husserl) or the strict irrelevance (according to Frege) of a phenomenological approach that would ground the truths of mathematics and logic in an adequate account of their discovery and genesis through various historically salient acts of human intuitive, cognitive or intellectual grasp.

I would suggest, moreover, that it is the resolute avoidance of just this phenomenological approach – together with the recourse to a Wittgensteinian conception of meaning-as-use – that has led Dummett to adopt an anti-realist stance so markedly at odds with the objectivist precepts of his other great mentor, Frege. Or again: it was Frege's misunderstanding of Husserl (like Ryle's and Dummett's after him) as practising what really amounted to just another version of subjective 'psychologism' decked out in dubious transcendental colours which led to all those chronic oscillations in the discourse of mainstream analytic philosophy that I have described briefly above. That is to say, this whole debate has been drastically skewed by the failure to grasp how a realist position might be maintained – despite the whole range of well-known rejoinders from a Wittgensteinian (or Kripkensteinian) quarter – by accepting the need that it should go by way of a critical reflection on the modes of experience, thought and judgement that characterize the process of human knowledge-acquisition. To the extent that analytic philosophy has set its face against any such genetic or phenomenological approach it can be seen to have engendered just the kinds of problem – or run into just the kinds of recurrent and, on its terms, strictly insoluble dilemma – that I examine in the following chapters. If this diagnosis is correct then the best way of viewing Kripke's sceptical paradox (along with his purported sceptical 'solution') is as the terminal stage in a history of thought – going back to Logical Positivism – that might well be described as having thrown the Husserlian baby out with the Heideggerian bathwater.

Hence, I suggest, the problems confronted by analytical revisionists who find themselves compelled to tread a tightrope walk between the sundry obligations of upholding some more or less qualified realist position, meeting the standard objections to it from various (e.g., Dummettian and Kripkean) quarters, somehow reaching an accommodation with Wittgenstein on terms that neither endorse nor explicitly reject his sceptical-communitarian approach, and – in McDowell's case – offering a suitably 'naturalized' (or de-transcendentalized) version of Kant that would redirect philosophy to a path not taken while making sure that it avoids the metaphysical quagmire into which a wrong turn along that path can so easily lead. Then there is the problem of explaining how all this can be accomplished without falling foul of the analytic veto on any approach that risks committing the genetic fallacy, that is, the typically 'continental' error of mistaking an account of how certain discoveries were made in logic, mathematics, or the physical sciences for an account of what constitutes their proper or legitimate claim to truth. At any rate there is good reason to conclude that the falling-out between the two traditions has done considerable harm and is long overdue for a more comprehensive and radical rethinking than anything attempted so far. However – as I argue in chapter 1 and at various points thereafter – this shouldn't obscure the range of alternative resources that exist within the analytic tradition, broadly construed, and that can also be marshalled in support of a realist approach with adequate normative provision. Thus a further source of that skewed perspective is the frequent failure to acknowledge that epistemology can be 'naturalized' in various ways, some of which (like Quine's) suffer from a marked and disabling normativity-deficit, while others – even when extended to philosophy of logic and mathematics – are liable to no such charge. Also I would suggest that these internal, i.e., intra-analytic sources of potential revitalization are perfectly consistent with a broadening of purview to take in various ideas and approaches from outside the analytic tradition, such as Husserlian phenomenology. Above all I would resist the facile notion that philosophy in the English-speaking world has now moved on – or had better move on as soon as possible – to a 'post-analytic' phase which marks the end of all that pointless fretting about issues that were really nothing more than a willed projection of its own self-image as a discipline specialized in resolving just such issues. As Jacques Derrida remarks in a different though related context, those who claim to 'turn the page' on philosophy are most often just 'philosophizing badly'.

So much for my aims and intentions in writing this book; now for the no less pleasurable business of acknowledging all those debts, intellectual and personal, that came to mind in the course of revising it for press. Many people have offered help, advice, and encouragement as the work went along. I should especially like to thank my colleagues and post-graduate students in the Philosophy Section at Cardiff, among them Robin Attfield, Andrew Belsey, Pat Clark, Andrew Edgar, Paul Gorton, Theo Grammenos, Richard Gray, Keith McDonald, Billy McMurtrie, Laurence Peddle, Robert Reay-Jones, Peter Sedgwick, Alessandra Tanesini, Alison Venables, Rea Wallden, Debbie Way and Barry Wilkins. Also – for taking my mind off these topics for the hour or so before closing-time – let me salute Gerald Gould, Terry Hawkes, Steve Latham, Scott Newton, Rob Stradling, and Robin Wood. I am grateful to the editors and publishers of *Copula*, *The Richmond Journal of Philosophy*, and *International Journal of Philosophical Studies* for permission to incorporate material that first appeared in their pages. Sarah Douglas at Continuum was unfailingly helpful and supportive while Tracey Smith and Slav Todorov did a fine job of proof reading and collation. Finally, to Alison, Clare and Jenny my love and apologies for yet more hundreds of hours spent at the word-processor.

Cardiff
September 2005

(Note: I have not provided bibliographical details for the various texts, authors and sources mentioned in this Introduction since they all receive more detailed treatment and adequate documentation in subsequent chapters.)

I

Who's Afraid of Psychologism? Normativity, Truth, and Epistemic Warrant

I

There is a long history of strained relations between philosophy and psychology, that is, between those (the philosophers) who invest a great deal in maintaining the validity of that distinction and those (the psychologists) who tend to regard it as just a product of philosophy's chronic proneness to delusions of episte-mological grandeur.[1] Thus philosophers from Plato to Descartes, Kant, Frege and Husserl have typically taken the view that theirs is a discipline concerned above all with matters of truth, reason, logic, a priori warrant, and so forth, rather than a merely 'psychologistic' enquiry into the way that people's minds just happen to work quite apart from such (supposedly) objective or veridical constraints. Of course some have seen less need for such a strict beating of the disciplinary bounds, whether because (like Aristotle) they were happy to grant psychology a place – along with rhetoric and the arts of persuasion – as a useful adjunct to the business of strict deductive reasoning or because (like pragmatists from James to Rorty) they were keen to talk philosophy down from its self-isolating specialist heights and restore it to a useful participant role in the ongoing 'cultural conversation'.[2] Still there is a sense in which philosophy takes its self-image from a steadfast refusal to accept any such claim that psychology provides everything needed for an adequate, i.e., rational and normative account of what constitutes a valid, truth-preserving, or properly *philosophical* mode of argument.

This refusal has been expressed in manifold ways and in diverse technical registers. They range from Plato's doctrine of transcendent forms to Descartes' rationalism, Kant's (purported) transcendental deduction from the conditions of possibility for knowledge and experience in general, or Frege's likewise cardinal distinction between subjective, merely psychological 'ideas' and the objective 'senses' of our various referring expressions and truth-apt statements.[3] It is also a crucial component of Husserlian transcendental phenomenology, whatever the arguments to contrary effect by philosophers in the analytic tradition – from Frege to Ryle and Dummett – who have regarded that project as ultimately lapsing into bad old 'psychologistic' habits of thought.[4] Hence the irony that this charge should still be brought despite Husserl's having made every effort – in the wake of Frege's critical review – to deflect such criticism by adopting a strictly a priori approach grounded in the certitudes of transcendental (as distinct from purely formal) logic.[5] What unites these parties despite and across their particular differences of view is the conviction that philosophy *can and must* be concerned with issues of truth, reason or logic that lie beyond the scope of any psychological enquiry, no matter how refined or (on its own terms) philosophically acute and self-aware. For there could otherwise be no holding the line against those various kinds of error – subjectivism, psychologism, and empiricism chief among them – which philosophers have often been quick to denounce as symptoms of naïve (= unphilosophical) thinking. No doubt there were those in the radical-empiricist line of descent from Hume to Quine who roundly rejected such claims and who argued the case for a naturalized epistemology which would take its cue from a study of how human beings actually thought and reasoned, as distinct from how they ought to think and reason according to certain purely notional (a priori) standards of validity and truth.[6] Still it can be argued on the one hand that these approaches suffer from a strongly marked normative deficit, and on the other – in Quine's case – that they seek to make up this deficit by appealing to criteria of rational judgement and scientifically informed theory-choice which tend to undercut their overt statements of radical-empiricist intent.[7]

Thus for all Quine's talk of revising logic under pressure from empirical counter-evidence (e.g., of suspending the principles of bivalence or excluded middle if required by certain quantum-physical results like superposition or wave/particle dualism) it can nonetheless be shown that he arrives at this verdict through a strict application of just those principles from stage to stage in his argument.[8] That is to say, what makes it a distinctively *philosophical* argument – one with a claim on our grasp of what counts as an instance of valid demonstrative reasoning – is precisely his adherence to the axioms of classical logic when advancing his revisionist case. Indeed this rejoinder (a 'transcendental *tu quoque*', as it is sometimes called) is among the most familiar forms of counter-argument deployed against claims for the empirically falsifiable character of logical axioms or – on a wider front – the framework-internal, culture-relative, or linguistically mediated character of 'truth' and 'knowledge'. Indeed it plays a basic, even a constitutive role in philosophy's prevailing self-image as a discipline equipped to address certain issues that lie beyond the remit of other, more empirically oriented modes of enquiry. This is nowhere more apparent than when philosophers (including some philosophers of psychology) run up against the notion that talk of truth, knowledge, a priori warrant, logical validity, and so forth, is really best regarded as just that, i.e., a form of talk whose main purpose – crudely expressed – is to keep philosophers in business.[9] Thus even those of a strongly marked psychoanalytic inclination manage somehow to convey their repugnance toward any such idea through certain philosophically distinctive turns of argument or phraseology. Wittgensteinians are the most adept at this, as might be expected given their need to maintain a firm distinction between psychoanalysis and that other version of the 'talking cure' – the therapeutic appeal to ordinary language as a means of deliverance from all our philosophic ills – which Wittgenstein likewise strove to keep clear of Freudian imputations.[10] What complicates such efforts, very often, is the ambivalence of philosophy's relationship on the one hand to an interpretative discourse such as that of psychoanalysis and, on the other, to those more empirically grounded (natural-scientific) disciplines, including some branches of psychology, from which it seeks to maintain a certain distance while not wishing to relinquish all claims to methodological rigour. Hence, to repeat, its tendency to veer between emulating science (or the best current notions of properly scientific method) and striving to establish its own criteria of rational-normative discourse.

As concerns the natural sciences, philosophers have sometimes assumed the right to specify standards – of truth, knowledge, evidential warrant, inference to the best explanation, and so forth – which either *typically do* or *ideally should* govern the conduct of scientific thought. Otherwise (as with empiricists from Locke to Quine) they have tended to renounce such lordly ambitions and adopt a decidedly scaled-down conception of philosophy's role *vis-à-vis* the methods and findings of the natural sciences. Hence Quine's well-known proposal that epistemology be treated as a sub-branch of empirical psychology, one whose task is best described (in behaviourist terms) as a study of how the 'meagre input' of ambient sensory stimuli is somehow transformed into the 'torrential output' of our various observations, theories, hypotheses, covering-law statements, and so on.[11] Even so – and despite its deflationary intent – this case involves a sequence of closely reasoned justificatory moves (i.e., the various stages of Quine's attack on the two last 'dogmas' of logical empiricism) that are themselves distinctly philosophical in character.[12] Thus Quine, like Locke before him, may wish to knock philosophy off its pedestal by adopting a more modest, psychologically informed, and scientifically oriented view of its operative scope and limits. However that purpose cannot be achieved by adopting a wholesale (behaviourist) version of naturalized epistemology which fails to meet the most basic normative criteria for rational choice among competing theories or belief-systems.

That is, if we take Quine at his word with regard to philosophy's come-uppance at the hands of a stimulus-response psychology then we must find his arguments conceptually flawed, while if we take those arguments at their phi-losophic worth then the psychology is apt to look remarkably crude and incapable of offering anything like an adequate epistemology. What this brings out to striking effect are the problems encountered by any attempt, like Quine's, to resolve the long-standing quarrel between those disciplines and to do so, moreover, on terms that reverse their traditional (philosophically sanctioned) order of priority. That is to say, the very process of arguing this case *on cogent and rational grounds* is one that will raise strictly unavoidable questions as concerns its philosophic cogency and conceptual justification. Still there is the issue as to whether philosophy can sustain the kinds of justificatory argument mounted on its own behalf by logicians, epistemologists, and others who take it that 'psychologism' is properly used as a pejorative term when it comes to issues of knowledge and truth. My point so far is that those (prototypically Frege) who take this line cannot be so easily distinguished from those (like Quine) who reject it as a matter of overt principle but who nonetheless implicitly acknowledge its force in their procedures of argumentation.

II

What I propose to do in the remainder of this chapter is look at some other, more controversial aspects of the long-standing quarrel (or disciplinary turf-war) between philosophy and psychology. Let me preface that discussion with a few disclaimers so as to avoid any possible misunderstanding. I don't for one moment wish to suggest that philosophers are wrong to maintain such cardinal distinctions as those between truth and the attitude of holding-true, knowledge and belief, reason and rhetoric, or – what is very often at stake when these issues arise – the proper domain of philosophical enquiry and that of psychological research. Indeed, as I have said, one lesson to be learned from Quine's thought-experiment in radical empiricism is that this case will run up against intractable problems – like the normativity deficit – if argued on terms that implicitly acknowledge the need for rational criteria which find no place in any such project of naturalized epistemology. However Quine's version of empiricism is one that has certain highly distinctive (and, I would argue, philosophically disabling) features. Chief among them is its having taken this approach to the point where any notional empiricist appeal to observational, perceptual, or other such (supposedly) first-order evidential data can count as such only when construed in relation to this or that favoured ontology or conceptual scheme. Hence Quine's famous – and no doubt shrewdly provocative – statements with regard to ontological relativity and the idea that such items as centaurs, Homer's gods, mathematical sets or classes, and brick houses on Elm Street should be thought of as strictly on a par as regards their scheme-relative (or framework-internal) claim to existence or reality.[13] What leads him to this conclusion is the espousal of a radically empiricist outlook devoid of rational-normative criteria along with a likewise deficient behaviourist psychology whose shortcomings have since been shown up by a great deal of jointly philosophical and cognitive-psychological enquiry.[14] From here it is no great distance to Quine's holistic view that truth-values are distributed across the entire 'fabric' or 'web' of belief to the point where no statement is in principle immune from revision, whether those at the observational 'periphery' or those in the presumed 'core' region of well-entrenched scientific theories or (albeit as a limiting case) the ground-rules of classical logic.

As a result philosophy has become hung up in some complex and even (be it said) some psychologically disabling ways on the kinds of dilemma that emerge with full force in Quine's project of naturalized epistemology. That is to say, it has lost sight of the very possibility that empiricism might be combined with a rational (normative) conception of truth-values and – contrary to Quine's claims – a conception of science that involves no such drastic split between the process of empirical knowledge-acquisition and the process of rational theory-formation. My case (briefly put) is that the strong analytic aversion to 'psychologism' in

whatever shape or form is the mirror-image of that 'post-analytic' approach –
one with its starting-point in Quine's 'Two Dogmas' – that rejects any notion of
philosophy as laying claim to objective standards of truth and rationality. What
they chiefly have in common is a failure to conceive that epistemology might be
naturalized – brought down from the heights of empirically unanchored speculative metaphysics – without, in the process, becoming just a form of applied
behaviourist psychology. Of course this latter strikes Quine as a thoroughly
desirable upshot and one that philosophers should be keen to embrace since it
holds out the prospect of a genuine (science-led) method for resolving otherwise
insoluble issues. To those of an opposite, e.g., Fregean persuasion it represents
nothing more than a collapse into downright 'psychologism' and a plain
inability to grasp the crucial distinction between logically articulated concepts,
propositions, and truth-values on the one hand and mere subjective mind-states
(Fregean 'ideas') on the other.[15]

Hence, as I have said, the widespread belief that empirical considerations can
have no place in logic, mathematics, or the formal sciences. Thus a thinker like
Mill is often assumed to have been completely off the track when he argued to
contrary effect, i.e., that those sciences were empirically grounded and *for just
that reason* possessed a whole range of well-proven scientific and everyday-
practical applications.[16] The resistance to such claims comes mainly from the
precept that to treat logic as in any way beholden to empirical considerations is
ipso facto to deny its special status as having to do with issues of objective, i.e.,
verification-transcendent validity and truth. Moreover, so it is held, this can
always lead on to the ultimate heretical conclusion, namely the 'psychologistic'
fallacy which confuses the realm of objective, truth-apt, logically articulated
Fregean 'thoughts' with mere ideas 'in the mind' of this or that individual
subject. Yet there is no reason – ingrained philosophical prejudice aside – to
suppose that the conception of logic as having its ground in certain processes of
empirical reasoning on the evidence must inevitably open the way to all manner
of subjectivist errors and illusions. On the contrary: what is apt to strike anyone
who has followed these debates over the past few decades is the extent to which a
narrowly logicist or truth-theoretic approach devoid of empirical content tends
to generate just those kinds of reactive, i.e., sceptical or psychologistic tendency.

One result is the problem that many anti-realists confront in squaring an
objectivist conception of truth in logic, mathematics, and the formal sciences
with an epistemology that brings such truth within the scope of human
knowledge.[17] That is to say, it then becomes hard to explain how the truth-value
of certain statements could be objective in the sense 'potentially transcending
our utmost means of proof or verification' yet also be grounded in various aspects
of our everyday practical-cognitive as well as our more specialized, e.g., scientific
dealing with the world. In the present context my main point is that these
thinkers have been over-impressed by such problems and led into some needless
philosophic quandaries through their failure to take an alternative route.[18]
Philip Kitcher puts this case in very forthright terms when he states that
'[m]athematical knowledge arises from rudimentary knowledge acquired by

perception'. More specifically: '[s]everal millennia ago, our ancestors, probably somewhere in Mesopotamia, set the enterprise in motion by learning through practical experience some elementary truths of arithmetic and geometry. From these humble beginnings mathematics has flowered into the impressive body of knowledge which we have been fortunate to inherit'.[19] His book goes on to develop this argument in detail and to offer a convincing naturalistic and also historically based (i.e., genetic-developmental) account of our knowledge of the growth of mathematical knowledge. Moreover, it does so expressly with a view to resolving those various conceptual problems – such as the problem of reconciling humanly attainable knowledge with objective (verification-transcendent) truth – which have dogged philosophy of mathematics in the hitherto dominant a priori mode. No doubt '[a]t first glance', as Kitcher concedes, 'the remoteness of contemporary mathematics from perceptual experience is so striking that it appears to doom any empiricist account' (Kitcher, p. 271). However the proponent of this latter approach should not be deterred by such well-worn objections but should rather 'respond by explaining how "higher" mathematics could emerge from those rudimentary parts of the subject that can be perceptually warranted' (ibid.). They can then make the point that philosophical concerns (like those of Frege) with regard to maintaining the absolute ideal objectivity of logic and mathematics against any taint of empiricist corruption have been largely misplaced and in any case strikingly out-of-touch with the major mathematical advances and discoveries of their time.

Thus, according to Kitcher, when Frege 'campaigned for major modifications in the language of mathematics and for research into the foundations of arithmetic' his plea went largely unheard by the community of practising mathematicians, who were 'unmoved by the epistemological considerations which Frege advanced' (p. 268). Not the least of their reasons for turning a deaf ear was Frege's espousal of an aprioristic approach that equated mathematical realism, objectivity and truth with a steadfast rejection of any idea that those values might possess (or require) any kind of empirical grounding or justification. Furthermore, Kitcher notes that as this lack of interest in his reformist programme continued so 'Frege's judgements became progressively harsher' (p. 268). He doesn't go so far as to suggest that there might have been some deeper, more than circumstantial or other-than-contingent link between Frege's unyieldingly objectivist approach to these issues in philosophy of logic and mathematics, his disappointment at their negative reception, and those strongly marked paranoid traits that have lately come in for some attention. Others – among them Andrea Nye in her book *Words of Power: A Feminist Reading of the History of Logic* – have been much less cautious in this regard.[20] That is to say, they have shown more willingness to flout the rule that enjoins a strict separation between work and life, or between those standards that properly apply in evaluating philosophic arguments and whatever is of merely anecdotal interest with regard to a thinker's biography, formative influences, personal opinions, political leanings, motivating interests, and so forth. Nowhere is this rule more strongly enforced than in the disciplines of logic and philosophy of logic, as might be expected given their claim to articulate the very conditions of valid argument quite apart from all merely extraneous concerns with the content of this or that sample case or whatever may occupy the place-filler roles of textbook premise and conclusion.

Hence Michael Dummett's reaction when he took time off from writing about Frege in order to work for the improvement of race relations in Britain – this at a time of resurgent right-wing extremism – only to discover the existence of a journal wherein Frege had confided some overtly racist and anti-Semitic thoughts.[21] Nevertheless Dummett resumed work on his book and did so (he asserts) with a clear moral and political conscience since, after all, Frege's contributions to the philosophy of logic and mathematics occupied a realm so utterly remote from his private opinions and political views as to suffer no possible guilt by contagion. And of course this is just what Frege maintains – especially in his essay 'The Thought' – with regard to the absolute ideal objectivity of truth and its having no truck with 'psychological' goings-on in the mind of this or that thinker.[22] Nothing could more grievously offend against those precepts than a notion that the very discipline of formal logic (as distinct from a certain type of mind-set attracted to it) might be viewed as symptomatic of various psychopathological disorders. Also there is a fairly obvious sense in which the study of logic – even at a high level of formal abstraction – still has to do with certain basic standards of truth, valid inference, and rational warrant that are presupposed in just about every field of human intellectual and practical activity. Were it not for our capacity to think, by and large, in accordance with such principles as bivalence and excluded middle – along with our regular (if informal) deployment of arguments like *modus ponens* and *modus tollens* – we should be wholly at loss to make sense of the world and our experience of it. Thus whatever the extent of disagreements concerning the scope, limits, and precise character of logic as a specialized discipline of thought it does play a strictly indispensable role in our sundry (everyday and scientific) processes of reasoning. Besides, there is the far from trivial fact that so much of the first-order quantified predicate calculus can be represented by means of Venn diagrams and other such strikingly graphic methods for bringing out the various co-implicated orders of logical negation, conjunction, disjunction, and so forth. And if mathematics has demonstrably played such a major role in the development of the physical sciences as to justify a realist conception of its object-domain – of numbers, sets, classes, etc. – then all the more must this apply to those above-cited basic principles of logic whose validity is assumed across some otherwise large divergences of scientific method and principle.

Still, one should recall Kitcher's point about the tendency of formal logic when conjoined with certain kinds of epistemological apriorism to become so divorced from the conditions of empirical applicability as to constitute a block to the advancement of mathematical thought. What is needed, he suggests, is an *alternative conception* of realism in philosophy of mathematics which no longer pins its faith to the existence of a Fregean 'third realm' wherein abstract entities such as thoughts, concepts, truth-values, and numbers would possess a full measure of objectivity (unlike merely psychological 'ideas') whilst of their very nature eluding any kind of perceptual or empirical warrant. Kitcher's proposal, to repeat, is that we drop this way of thinking along with all its deep-laid conceptual dilemmas and instead adopt the view that our entire existing body of often highly abstract mathematical knowledge has its source in certain basic, empirically grounded operations such as counting and grouping into sets. To this end he develops a theory of 'ecological realism' according to which our environment provides certain cognitive 'affordances', that is to say, standing opportunities of various kinds for organisms to grasp salient features or aspects of their physical life-world.[23] Such a theory would have the great advantage, from Kitcher's viewpoint, of allowing a direct (realist) account of our perceptual dealings with that world and hence a firm basis for his kindred claim with respect to the origins, growth and empirical pedigree of our acquired mathematical knowledge. 'What this means', he writes,

is that the idea of perception as a process in which the mind engages in complicated inferences and computations to construct a perception from scanty data is abandoned. Instead, ecological realists emphasize the richness of sensory information, claiming that questions about how we compute or construct to achieve awareness of intricate features of our environment only arise because the perceptual data have been misrepresented as impoverished. (Kitcher, p. 11)

In which case the empiricist about mathematics and logic can use this argument in order to block the first move of any a priori (e.g., Platonist or Fregean) epistemology, namely the move which declares it unthinkable − as in Frege's rejoinder to Mill − that so impressive a body of abstract yet objective truths could have its source in so conceptually 'impoverished' a realm as that of our empirical experience.

Hence Kitcher's claim that 'ecological realism' provides by far the best, most convincing alternative to those various aprioristic doctrines that have caused such a deal of philosophic trouble. On this account

mathematics is an idealized science of operations which we can perform on objects in our environment ... If we say that a *universal affordance* is an affordance which any environment offers to any human, then we may state [this] theory as the claim that mathematics is an idealized science of particular universal affordances. In this form, the theory expresses clearly the widespread utility of mathematics and, given the ecological realist claim that affordances are the objects of perception, it is also easy to see how mathematical knowledge is possible. (Kitcher, p. 12)

I have cited these two passages at length because they strike me as powerful statements of the case for a form of empirically based mathematical realism that avoids the conceptual dilemmas of a Platonist (or abstract realist) approach while yielding absolutely no ground to alternative, e.g., instrumentalist, fictionalist, or downright sceptical (Kripkean) positions.[24] Also they argue very forcefully against any outlook of Fregean apriorist disdain toward the notion that empirical methods or standards of evidential warrant might have their place in mathematics, logic and the formal sciences. Kitcher has his differences with Mill as regards the precise working-out of this claim and the extent to which the truth-value of certain complex mathematical statements or proofs can exceed the limits of direct empirical warrant. Nevertheless he agrees on the basic point: that without such a grounding in the kinds of perceptual 'affordance' provided by physical objects and their various possibilities of grouping, combination, numerical comparison, and so forth, it is simply impossible to explain how the 'abstract' discourse of mathematics could ever achieve any measure of proven scientific, let alone everyday, cognitive grasp.

As concerns geometry, this point can be made quite simply since geometrical reasoning started out as an applied science of measurement – in calculating areas of land – and thereafter moved through stages of increasingly formalized, axiomatized, and algebraic representation. Arithmetic – especially in its more advanced or speculative branches – seems a lot harder to explain by tracing its genesis back to some putative source in our practical dealing with aspects of the physical world. Yet the problem of offering a proof for Fermat's Last Theorem took rise from just such a challenge, first taken up by the ancient Egyptian geometers, then posed by Fermat in formal (proof-theoretic) terms, and now – as a matter of specialist agreement – resolved by Andrew Wiles through a hugely complex process of reasoning.[25] At any rate there is no good argument – Platonist or Fregean prejudice aside – for supposing that truth in mathematics, logic, or the formal sciences must accord with standards categorically distinct from those which apply to the evaluation of empirical hypotheses and truth-claims. Where the difference lies is not so much in their 'purely' analytic, a priori, or logically self-evident character as in the fact that they have resulted from various (relatively) high-level abstract or formal operations on the kinds of evidence empirically produced by counting, assembling into sets, comparing those sets in point of equinumerosity, and so forth. That is to say, if our basic mathematical knowledge can be treated as a matter of empirical (or perceptual) warrant then the same applies – albeit at a certain formal remove – to those theorems and conjectures that lie beyond the compass of direct empirical enquiry.

Of course this case requires a lot more detailed argument than can possibly be provided here. Any adequate account would involve a lengthy detour through debates in the field of naturalized yet normative, i.e., non-Quinean epistemology, in the causal (modal-logical) theory of naming and necessity, and in the empirically based philosophy of mathematics that Kitcher puts forward as the basis of an answer to all our aprioristically induced epistemic and ontological woes.[26] His main point is that empirical warrant, i.e., the deliverance of direct perceptual knowledge, can trump any kind of (supposedly) a priori truth-claim just so long as that knowledge is well grounded and subject to rigorous testing.

Thus it is an inbuilt assumption of the Fregean and other such anti-empiricist approaches that 'a priori warrants have to be able to discharge their warranting function, no matter what background of disruptive experience we may have' (Kitcher, p. 35). However this argument conspicuously trades on the self-vindicating premise that mathematical and logical truths simply *cannot* be subject to empirical disconfirmation since they belong to a realm of absolute ideal objectivity where perceptual evidence is completely beside the point. Still, Kitcher writes, 'the fact that a process is non-perceptual does not rule out the possibility that the ability of that process to warrant belief might be undermined by radically disruptive experiences' (ibid.). That is to say, it might always happen (however improbably) that some recalcitrant finding in the physical sciences turned out to controvert a whole range of hitherto accepted a priori truths, from those of elementary (Peano) arithmetic to those which have gained admittance at the most advanced levels of 'abstract' mathematical enquiry. For on this account the formal sciences retain their connection with – or dependence upon – certain basic standards of empirical warrant even where the process of increasing formalization or axiomatization appears to place them at the furthest remove from any such justificatory requirement.

All the same Kitcher is very far from endorsing the kind of radical empiricism conjoined with a strong revisionist outlook concerning the putative 'laws' of logic which has been such a prominent feature of post-Quinean developments in epistemology and philosophy of science. Where he differs most markedly with Quine, Putnam, and other advocates of this approach is in *not* contending that certain received though highly problematical theories in physical science – such as the 'orthodox' (Copenhagen) interpretation of quantum mechanics – may constitute a case for revising logic under pressure of empirical anomalies. I have discussed these issues at length elsewhere so will say no more than that the case is far from conclusively made out and runs into numerous problems as regards both its empirical credentials and its status as a matter of rational warrant or logical reasoning on the best available evidence.[27] Thus Kitcher's empiricism goes nothing like so far in a revisionist or anti-apriorist direction as those (like Quine and Putnam) who would maintain *on largely speculative grounds* that we might have to relinquish bivalence or excluded middle as a consequence of results thrown up by the physical sciences.[28] Rather he assumes – strongly counter to this post-Quinean trend – that we had much better go with the kind of theory which involves least conflict with those well-established principles of realism and inference to the best explanation that have up to now served as a reliable bridge between formal logic and the interests of empirical enquiry.[29]

This follows from Kitcher's 'ecological-realist' approach whereby (in the simplest terms) '[we] take as paradigms of constructive activity those familiar manipulations of physical objects in which we engage from childhood on' (Kitcher, p. 108). Or again,

[w]e might consider arithmetic to be true in virtue not of what we *can do* to the world but rather of what *the world* will let us do *to it*. To coin a

Millian phrase, arithmetic is about 'permanent possibilities of manipula-
tion'. More straightforwardly, arithmetic describes those structural features of the world in virtue of which we are able to segregate and to
recombine objects: the operations of segregation and recombination bring
about the manifestation of underlying dispositional traits. (ibid.)

This is a very different kind of proposal from the Quine-Putnam idea that logic
always stands open to refinement, correction, or (at the limit) wholesale revision
should its axioms come into conflict with this or that item of empirical evidence
as construed in accordance with our current best physical theory. To be sure,
Kitcher does adopt another, fairly strong version of the revisability thesis,
namely that in cases where a priori truth-claims are thrown into doubt by a
powerful body of jointly perceptual and well-informed scientific knowledge we
should do best to abandon the a priori claims rather than reject the empirical
evidence. However, he is much less ready than Quine or Putnam to suppose – on
the basis of certain highly speculative, e.g., quantum-theoretical results – that
such revision might extend to a radical rethinking of all those logic-based
methods, procedures, or forms of rational inference that have characterized the
history and development of mathematics and the physical sciences to date.[30]

This reluctance to accept such whole-hog revisionist arguments goes along
with Kitcher's main challenge to mathematical apriorism, that is to say, his
argument that any adequate philosophical approach must also provide a genetic
or historically grounded account of our knowledge of the growth of scientific
knowledge, from its earliest stages right up to its present, most advanced or
highly developed forms. After all, '[a]lthough philosophers of mathematics have
typically ignored the history of mathematics – and perhaps some have even
thought of that history as a sequence of benighted blunders – it would be
surprising if two millennia of haphazard development had bequeathed to us a
corpus of knowledge' (Kitcher, p. 100). In which case (ironically) the same
objection applies to apriorists and strong logical-revisionists alike, i.e., that they
are over-willing to discount such a large and historically cumulative body of
intertwined physical and mathematical knowledge in favour of a theory which
counts that history either irrelevant for its own purposes or (quite conceivably)
liable to overthrow through some startling new development in thought.
'Indeed, on apriorist grounds, the history of mathematics would be almost a
miracle . . . [since] it surely strains our credulity to suppose that a process which
was unsusceptible of rational reconstruction could produce a body of statements
which someone (Frege, Brouwer, or Gödel, for example) could transform into an
a priori science' (ibid.). Thus, on Kitcher's account, the chief virtue of a jointly
empirical and historically informed approach is its capacity to make adequate
sense of both the *genesis and structure* of mathematical knowledge, that is, the
various ways in which our present-best theories have developed on the basis of
previous episodes in the history of thought yet also attained a sufficient degree
of objective, free-standing rational warrant. In short, '[t]o adapt Newton's
famous figure, when giants continually stand on the shoulders of giants,

someone lucky enough to sit at the top can see a remarkably long way' (Kitcher, p. 271).

My main purpose in citing these arguments from Kitcher has been to emphasize the point – as developed previously with regard to Quine and Davidson – that epistemology and philosophy of science have much to gain from a genuine (as opposed to notional or ad hoc) mending of the rift that opened up in the wake of old-style logical empiricism. The case of mathematics is especially crucial in this regard since it tends to produce a regular stand-off between those (i.e., Platonists and Fregean objectivists) who take a strong a priori stance on the existence of absolute, ideal, recognition-transcendent mathematical truths and those (intuitionists or verificationists) who reject such a notion as plainly incoherent on epistemological grounds.[31] Hence (to repeat) the pyrrhic conclusion drawn by some philosophers: that this is an insoluble dilemma since if we opt for truth conceived in objectivist terms then it lies beyond our utmost cognitive reach, whereas if we adopt an epistemic conception based on the scope and limits of knowledge or effective provability then truth drops completely out of the picture.[32] To Kitcher's way of thinking, on the other hand, it is just the kind of pseudo-dilemma that typically results when philosophers recoil from one problematical or scepticism-inducing extreme to another with opposite but equally dire implications.

In the next section of this chapter I shall return to Nye's book *Words of Power* as a yet more striking example of this sharply reactive or Manichaean habit of thought. Thus Nye treats the discipline of formal logic – in particular Frege's work – as the expression of a deep-laid psychopathological and, beyond that, a widespread cultural and socio-political malaise. My point is not so much to endorse this remarkable verdict as to argue that it stems from a partially justified sense that philosophy of logic (at least in some of its present-day canonical forms) has become damagingly out-of-touch with matters of empirical warrant or perceptual grasp. That is to say, her book makes a plausible case – whatever its more dubious or ideologically driven claims – for reconsidering this whole issue of logic in relation to other, less formalized or 'regimented' modes of thought and knowledge.

III

'Logic in its final perfection is insane.' Thus Nye in the closing sentence of her essay 'A Thought Like a Hammer: The Logic of Totalitarianism', the penultimate chapter of a work devoted to just that arresting proposition.[33] I shall here be concerned mainly with the portions on Frege – leading up to her caustic summative remark – and not with the earlier chapters on Parmenides, Plato, Aristotle, Abelard, and others. For it is with the advent of Fregean logic, so Nye argues, that this tradition arrived at its final 'insane' stage of development, the stage at which logic perfected its ultra-formalized technique for rendering all else a matter of mere psychology, subjective ideas, or private-individual vagaries.

In the process there came about the marriage – the forced marriage, as Nye describes it – between language and mathematics, the former reduced to a skeletal structure purged of all extraneous (i.e., non-logical) content so as to provide the latter with an adequate, wholly perspicuous means of linguistic expression. 'To achieve this anorexic ideal', she writes, 'poeticism, tone, gesture, any intentions the speaker has, any attempt to speak for the understanding of the listener must be pared away' (Nye, p. 143). And again, in one of Nye's deliberately gruesome and (to logicians) offensive metaphors: '[t]here is nothing outside thought, nothing but prurient, seductive opinion, unreliable, shifting, fat with effeminate compassion, that must be cut off, reduced, not allowed to pollute the white bone of thought with its blackness, with its foreign stench' (ibid., p. 170). Here and elsewhere there is a constant claim that logic *by its very nature* – not just the preoccupation with logic among certain philosophers, Frege especially – is complicit with the exercise of male authority and power, to the point of a 'totalitarian' obsession with expunging all such alien residues. Indeed Nye purports to find a strong historical continuity between Parmenides' inaugural dream of a single, homogeneous, unified order of Being that excludes every form of negation or difference and the 'Nazi logic' which carries that programme to its ultimate, murderous conclusion. 'Those who do not think consistently with that logic do not think, do not exist, must not exist' (Nye, p. 170).

The book has received little notice from formal logicians or philosophers of logic, and a good deal more from cultural theorists, sociologists of knowledge, and those with an interest in knocking philosophy off its pedestal by attacking the supposed master-discipline on which its authority is taken to rest. Discussion has mostly been restricted to brief, dismissive, and often contemptuous comments by philosophers who regard Nye's entire line of argument as a gross impertinence and a flagrant example of the *ad hominem* fallacy. This reaction is scarcely surprising given that she treats their discipline as the inheritor of an age-old, male-dominated discourse which has functioned chiefly to exclude, devalue, or ruthlessly suppress the kinds of empathetic understanding that women – some few female philosophers among them – have typically valued above the claims of masculine 'phallocratic' reason.[34] Otherwise there seems to be a tacit consensus that her arguments stray so far beyond the bounds of academic (as well as logical) acceptability that they simply don't merit the effort of a serious or detailed response.

Again, one can see why this should be the case since if they are accorded such attention then they must be taken as raising at least the possibility that philosophy of logic – even logic itself – is open to challenge in socio-cultural, ideological, or gender-based dissident terms. From a logical point of view these are notions that involve such a basic failure of conceptual grasp (or such a stubborn refusal to abide by the norms of rational argumentation) as to stand altogether outside the sphere of competent philosophic debate. On the other hand Nye is then able to respond that her detractors – or those who loftily ignore her book – are showing yet again how they remain in thrall to a narrowly logicist or 'totalitarian' conception of truth. From Parmenides down, so the charge-sheet runs, this conception has worked to exclude or to marginalize any mode of knowledge (intuitive or experiential) that fails to satisfy its own strict criteria of truth, validity, or logical warrant. Such was the process that ultimately issued in Frege's 'insane' demand that logic be conceived as belonging to a realm of absolute ideal objectivity beyond the least taint of human psychology or subjective ideas 'in the mind' of this or that thinker. It is this programme that Frege sets out most clearly in his essay 'The Thought' and that Nye treats as a set-piece climax to her history of logic as an instrument of the self-promoting (yet also self-mutilating) masculine will-to-power which has characterized that discourse from the outset.[35]

The above brief synopsis will give some idea of how deliberately her book sets out to provoke, scandalize, and alienate the community of professional logicians. Thus it pays no heed to the standard (philosophical) distinction between 'context of discovery' and 'context of justification', treating it as just another handy technique for disguising the extent to which motives of social or sexual domination have masked behind a semblance of pure, truth-seeking objectivity and rigour. From the role of Diotima in Plato's *Symposium* to the mythicized student–master relationship between Eloise and Abelard the story that Nye has to tell is one which refuses on principle to separate 'life' and 'work' in the approved philosophical or doxographic manner. Even on its own terms this approach produces some politically and ethically skewed judgements. Among them is Nye's failure adequately to acknowledge how far the programme of 1930s' logical positivism – at least as advanced by thinkers like Neurath and Carnap – partook of a wider progressivist desire to clarify the thinking of social reformers and, just as urgently in that context, to expose the kinds of potent irrationalist or obscurantist language typified by Heidegger's 'jargon of authenticity'.[36] So far as Frege is concerned one may take her point about his racist, misogynist, and generally repugnant socio-political views and even accept that certain aspects of his work might have been affected – in terms of motivating interest – by those strongly marked psychotic traits that Nye is so relentlessly keen to expose. Still there is something wrong about any argument that reduces the logician's particular concern with issues of rational warrant or justification to a matter of subjective psychopathology or socio-political bias. Dummett takes an altogether more convincing – and not just 'philosophically' respectable – line when he agrees that Frege held some thoroughly abhorrent views yet maintains that his work in the philosophy of logic, mathematics and language was carried on at a level of conceptual abstraction so utterly remote from 'the life' that they cannot (or should not) influence our assessment of that work.

All the same I would suggest that there are aspects of Fregean logic that help to explain not only why it is capable of producing such an extreme adverse reaction but also why it has led – not least in the case of Dummett's anti-realist programme – to philosophical positions which themselves appear subject to certain (philosophically) extraneous motivating interests. That is to say, one is otherwise hard put to suggest why Dummett should espouse so drastically counter-intuitive a viewpoint with regard to the non-existence of objective (recognition-transcendent) mathematical truths, or the idea that any gaps in our historical knowledge must correspond to gaps in historical reality.[37] Then again, there is his claim that any well-formed (as it might seem truth-apt) statement concerning aspects of the physical world beyond our epistemic ken must *ipso facto* be regarded as belonging to the Dummettian 'disputed class' and hence as lacking a truth-value, albeit one unbeknown to us. Above all the issue arises as to why Dummett should quite seriously entertain the notion that any present or future change in our state of knowledge concerning past events might itself play a retroactive role in deciding whether or not those events occurred or how they transpired as a matter of (hitherto indefinite, now determinate) fact. Hence his idea – in essays like 'Bringing About the Past' – that there is nothing intrin-sically absurd about praying for a favourable outcome of some 'previous' occurrence, for instance, a father's prayer that his son should not have been killed in a battle that is known already to have taken place but the details of which have not yet reached home.[38] Here one can quite legitimately raise the question as to what kinds of, for example, theological commitment or motivating interest might have prompted his adoption of an anti-realist approach with such sharply paradoxical or downright bizarre consequences.[39] However any adequate response will need to set that question aside and engage Dummett's argument on its own metaphysical and logico-semantic terms. That is, it will need to address the main issue as to whether statements of the 'disputed class' – those that are well formed and (apparently) truth-apt yet for which we lack any means of proof or verification – can nonetheless properly be thought of as possessing an objective truth-value. For the realist it is nothing short of self-evident that this must indeed be the case for a vast range of such statements. Among them would be mathematical assertions like 'Goldbach's Conjecture is true (or false)', sci-entific hypotheses like 'There exists a duplicate solar system in some remote (radio-telescopically inaccessible) region of the expanding universe', or specific though unverifiable statements about historical events, such as 'Neville Cham-berlain coughed six times on his return flight from Munich in 1938'.[40] For the anti-realist, on the other hand, these all belong squarely within the Dummettian 'disputed class' since in each case their truth-value eludes our utmost capacities of proof, ascertainment, or cognitive grasp. To which the realist standardly responds that truth and knowledge are different things, that truth is objective or epistemically unconstrained, and that knowledge very often falls short of truth in every area of discourse.[41]

I shall not here enter into further discussion of a topic that has received much attention from thinkers on both sides of this issue during the past two decades. Sufficient to say, for present purposes, that anti-realism of the Dummettian (metaphysical and logico-semantic) variety is itself very much a product of those unresolved problems in the wake of logical empiricism which we have seen resurfacing in various forms despite Quine's claim to have laid them finally to rest. What is perhaps most striking about Dummett's programme is the fact that it derives very largely from Frege's work in philosophy of language, logic and mathematics while nonetheless rejecting the chief tenet of Fregean thought, i.e., the existence of objective truth-values that can always in principle transcend or outrun our best state of knowledge concerning them.[42] Thus Dummett goes along with Frege in adopting a compositional theory of logico-semantic content whereby the meaning of a sentence is given by its truth-conditions while these can be specified in turn through an analysis of its various component terms and their contributory role in the context of that particular sentence. On his account this strictly limited (sentence-relative) version of the context-principle is the only way to meet the three chief demands upon any theory of language. These are that it should offer an adequate explanation of (1) our capacity to *acquire* a grasp of the relevant meanings and truth-conditions which constitute linguistic understanding; (2) our ability to *manifest* that grasp by producing and correctly interpreting various well-formed expressions; and (3) our competence to *recognize* those sentences whose meaning (or whose compositional structure) is sufficiently determinate to render them apt for ascriptions of assertoric warrant. Failing that, Dummett argues, we should be completely at a loss to explain how language-users could ever make a start in the business of communicative utterance or uptake. For were it not for the compositionality of sentence-meaning, i.e., the two-way relation of dependence between component terms and their function within the sentence as a whole, then it is hard to explain how linguistic understanding could possibly get off the ground. Yet if this context-principle is over-extended – if it is pushed to a point where the meaning of any given term is relativized not just to the sentence in which it occurs but to its role in some entire language-game, life-form, discourse, or Quinean 'web' of beliefs-held-true – then the same problem arises. That is to say, without the kinds of interpretive constraint upon our powers of meaning-attribution provided by the sentence as a basic unit of logico-semantic structure or truth-functional grasp we should once again lack any theory of language that came close to meeting the above-mentioned three requirements.

Thus Dummett declares firmly against those versions of the context-principle which take it – following Quine in a well-known passage from 'Two Dogmas of Empiricism' – that Frege's was merely a halfway station on the path of retreat from the old, discredited 'term-by-term' conception of classical empiricist theories of knowledge to an outlook of full-fledged meaning-holism.[43] However it is far from clear that he (Dummett) can consistently sustain the alternative Fregean position, given his outright refusal to endorse what goes along with it in Frege's thinking, namely an objectivist approach to these issues in philosophy of language and logic which requires that the truth-value of any well-formed sentence, hypothesis, or theorem is fixed by the way things stand quite aside from our powers of proof or ascertainment. For there is an obvious tension between Frege's truth-based analysis of sentence meaning – construed in realist terms – and Dummett's verificationist proposal that truth-talk be replaced by talk of 'assertoric warrant', this latter coextensive with whatever can be known (i.e., acquired, manifested, or recognized) within our duly accredited powers of epistemic, conceptual, or logico-linguistic grasp. Once again the chief source of this tension can be traced back to problems in the legacy of logical empiricism. More specifically, it arises from Dummett's extension of the verification-principle beyond its previous delimited scope of application in matters of empirical warrant to areas of discourse (such as logic, mathematics, and the formal sciences) where it poses a far greater challenge to objectivist or realist theories of truth. This is why Dummett rejects the Fregean idea that we should best think of mathematical knowledge as advancing through a series of discoveries like those achieved by terrestrial explorers or astronomers, that is, as charting an ever more detailed and extensive range of (in this case) abstract though nonetheless objective realia. Rather we should think of it – on Dummett's intuitionist account – as having more in common with the kinds of inventive or creative thought that characterize the highest, most original artistic achievements.[44]

My point is that Dummett is led to this position by adopting a verificationist approach with its source in the doctrines of logical positivism/empiricism and applying the same principle (the notion of truth as epistemically or evidentially constrained) to regions of enquiry far beyond its original remit. Moreover, he is led to it *despite and against* those strongly marked Fregean elements in his thinking that would seem to demand a realist, verification-transcendent conception of truth in order to perform the kind of work required of them by Dummett's compositional theory of sentence-meaning. What emerges here, once again, is a version of that deep-laid dualist mind-set (still evident in Quine and Davidson) whereby the scheme/content distinction asserts itself in various disguised or surrogate forms whatever the claim to have left it behind in the progress through and beyond logical empiricism. In Dummett's case this dualism shows up in the curious conjunction of an anti-realist approach to issues of language, truth and logic still very much in hock to the old-style verificationist programme with a theory of propositional content that makes no sense unless construed on Fregean objectivist terms. That is to say: it is the clash between these rival conceptions (the impossibility of thinking how truth could meet the requirements of assertoric warrant, empirically or quasi-empirically construed) which drives Dummett to adopt his outlook of across-the-board anti-realism.

This is where Andrea Nye's critique of Fregean logic does have a certain force despite its (on occasion) grotesquely *ad hominem* character and its programmatic drive to reduce issues of validity and truth to issues of private (psychopatho-logical) motivation. As I have said, any adequate philosophic response to Dummettian anti-realism will have to discount such strictly extraneous matters and focus rather on the logico-semantic and metaphysical question of whether truth can transcend the limits of epistemic grasp or warranted assertibility. Still Nye's critique will surely ring true – at least in psycho-diagnostic terms – for anyone who has followed these debates in the recent specialist literature and then stood back to consider what could possibly have prompted or inspired such debates. For there is (to put it bluntly) something abnormal about the sheer amount of subtle argumentation expended on issues – such as whether truth might exceed the compass of human knowledge or whether there might exist objective standards of correctness in following a rule – to which the right answer (hypercultivated doubts apart) is plainly and self-evidently 'yes'.[45] According to the dominant conventions of analytic philosophy anyone who takes this line is falling into the worst, most vulgar of 'psychologistic' fallacies, or failing to observe the most basic principles of valid philosophical argument. Yet consider, if you will, the following passage from Dummett where he sets out the basic issue between realists and anti-realists concerning historical statements. For anyone subscribing to the former view

> [r]ealism about the past entails that there are numerous true propositions forever in principle unknowable. The effects of a past event may simply dissipate ... To the realist, this is just part of the human condition; the anti-realist feels unknowability in principle to be simply intolerable and prefers to view our evidence for and memory of the past as constitutive of it. For him, there cannot be a past fact no evidence of which exists to be discovered, because it is the existence of such evidence that would make it a fact, if it were one.[46]

Despite Dummett's keenness to present his approach as an even-handed treatment of the alternatives on offer across various disciplines or areas of discourse it is clear that he finds the realist position simply inconceivable and anti-realism the sole option for those au fait with the relevant metaphysical, epistemic, and logico-semantic issues. Yet any theory which renders such a viewpoint even halfway plausible is itself more than halfway along the path to a radical scepticism or constructivism concerning the 'reality' of past events – or the truth of statements concerning them – which entails (to say the least) some highly paradoxical conclusions.

Perhaps the most revealing passage in Dummett's work from a psychological or motivational viewpoint is the sentence cited above where he contrasts the realist's willingness to accept the existence of unknowable truths about the past with the anti-realist's refusal (or sheer inability) to tolerate any such thought. Thus the realist takes it as simply 'a part of the human condition' that our information sources are limited, that the historical evidence is often gappy or (in some cases) altogether lacking, that witnesses are fallible, memories partial, and hence that 'the effects of a past event may simply dissipate'. Moreover she will point to the fact – for such it is on her understanding of the matter – that there were vast periods of prehistory when human beings were around and witnessed various goings-on but for which, by definition, we possess no documentary evidence. And again, pushing back yet further, it is a truth scarcely deniable by any but the hard-line sceptic or (maybe) the convinced creationist that a great many cosmic and terrestrial events occurred during the far longer period of time before any human observers or other such sentient creatures had evolved to register the fact of their occurrence.

Of course the anti-realist can accept some of this – and even bring some fraction of those same events within the compass of 'knowability' or assertoric warrant – by appealing to the evidence of certain natural sciences such as archaeology, palaeontology and astrophysics. That is, those sciences offer rational grounds enough for asserting (to the anti-realist's satisfaction) that truth in such cases need not 'in principle' be taken to exceed the scope and limits of human epistemic or investigative grasp. Yet this concession is unlikely to impress the realist, who will be apt to remark that the scientific record is just as gappy, partial, or subject to effects of 'dissipation' as the record of humanly transmitted knowledge. At this point the anti-realist will again have to bite the bullet and maintain, in Dummett's words, that 'there cannot be a past fact no evidence of which exists to be discovered, because it is the existence of such evidence that would make it a fact, if it were one'.[47] After all, this thesis amounts to no more than another expression of his refusal to accept the existence of verification-transcendent truths, that is, the strong predisposition – be it temperamental or philosophically grounded – which 'feels unknowability in principle to be simply intolerable and prefers to view our evidence for and memory of the past as constitutive of it'. In which case, for him, there is just no avoiding the upshot of Dummett's anti-realist argument, namely the extreme version of that thesis which holds that any 'gaps in our knowledge' must also be construed as 'gaps in reality'.

IV

No doubt there are ways of toning such statements down or supplying an emollient gloss, as may be done with Kuhn's likewise (on the face of it) extreme ontological-relativist claim that scientists before and after some large-scale paradigm-change must be thought to 'live in different worlds'. Yet, as Davidson remarks about the 'heady and exotic' doctrine of conceptual relativism, '[t]he trouble is, as so often in philosophy, it is hard to improve intelligibility while retaining the excitement'.[48] In the case of Dummettian anti-realism one could take his paradoxical-sounding phrase 'gaps in reality' as bearing the weaker, epistemological sense 'gaps in the extent of knowable reality' or 'gaps in "reality" so far as we can make any well-informed or knowledgeable statement concerning it'. However this would render Dummett's thesis perfectly compatible with the realist view that truth, so far from being coextensive with the scope and limits of attainable knowledge, can always in principle transcend those limits and (moreover) fix the truth-value of our speculative statements quite unbeknown to us. That is to say, it would constitute not so much a revision, refinement, or qualification of that thesis as a downright abandonment of it.

So here, as with Kuhn's notorious sentence about scientists 'living in different worlds', one is obliged to take the doctrine at full strength – as making a metaphysical or ontological rather than a merely epistemological claim – if it is not to lose its provocative force and become just a trivial point about the psychology or sociology of belief. However this prompts the question as to why we should accord *philosophic* credence to a theory which expressly takes rise from a certain kind of temperamental bias (one that finds 'unknowability in principle simply intolerable') and which involves such a standing affront to our everyday-commonsense as well as scientific and historical modes of understanding. For there is nothing more basic to any truth-oriented branch of enquiry than the precept that truth may lie beyond our present-best (or even best-attainable) state of knowledge and hence that certain statements – precisely those of the Dummettian 'disputed class' – may be rendered true or false by the way things stand with respect to some given object domain, whether abstract (as in the case of mathematics and logic) or empirical (as with history and the natural sciences). Any theory, like Dummett's, which denies that precept or professes to find it 'intolerable' is one whose undoubted sophistication in conceptual or logico-semantic terms should not too readily dissuade us from enquiring into its other possible motivating aims and interests.

To be sure, such enquiry also needs to take due stock of the justificatory arguments advanced in support of that position. Otherwise, as with Nye's animadversions on Fregean logic, it will clearly invite the charge of adopting a psychologistic or, worse still, a crudely *ad hominem* approach to issues which, in the final analysis, can only be resolved through philosophical treatment rather than by off-the-point polemical remarks about 'the life' as distinct from 'the work'. All the same, as I have said, there is good reason not only to question the motivating impulse of Dummett's anti-realist programme but also to count it philosophically a striking instance of sceptical conclusions arrived at on the basis of dubious or downright false premises. For his argument works only on condition that its major claim goes through, i.e., the claim that it *cannot make sense* to suppose the existence of recognition-transcendent truths since we could never be epistemically placed to assert (or to deny) the truth of any statement which by very definition transcended our utmost powers of verification or falsification. However this claim can be seen to equivocate between 'knowledge' = 'knowing whether statement x is demonstrably true or false' and 'knowledge' = 'knowing that there must be some truth of the matter that could resolve the issue had we but the method of formal proof (in mathematics and logic) or the empirical grounds (in history or the natural sciences) to decide one way or the other'. Thus the principle of bivalence holds, *contra* Dummett, even for those well-formed or truth-apt statements of the disputed class which at present (and maybe forever or in principle) lack any means of decisive adjudication. In which case Dummettian anti-realism comes down to a particularly flagrant instance of the epistemic fallacy that confuses the limits of assertoric warrant according to our best knowledge with those constraints which apply – as the realist would have it – in matters of objective (verification-transcendent) truth or falsehood. This distinction is crucial for any understanding of our knowledge of the growth of knowledge, that is to say, any theory that could possibly explain why we are justified in speaking of *progress* in various disciplines (mathematics, the natural sciences, history, and so on) rather than successive, rationally under-motivated shifts from one to another Kuhnian paradigm or Quinean conceptual scheme. For if truth is reduced to assertoric warrant and this in turn to a function of (formal or empirical) verifiability then there is simply no stopping the further slide from 'knowledge' to whatever counts as such with regard to some given item of accredited belief.

The only means of preventing this slide – and thereby heading off the more extreme varieties of paradigm-relativist thinking – is to acknowledge that truth may always come apart from those various substitute notions (such as assertoric warrant or 'truth' as epistemically constrained) that have figured in the anti-realist literature. The same applies to certain notionally strengthened versions of the case like Crispin Wright's ideas of 'superassertibility' and 'cognitive command', both specified in such a way as to stop just short of objectivist (recognition-transcendent) truth while appearing to answer the kinds of objection raised above.[49] Wright offers his proposals in the wider context of a response-dependent (or response-dispositional) approach to issues of knowledge, validity and truth.[50] Thus he thinks that we can have all that is needed on each of these counts without adopting a full-fledged realist position and thus inviting the standard sceptical riposte, i.e., that this position is plainly self-defeating since it places truth by very definition beyond our utmost cognitive or epistemic reach. However it can readily be shown that such efforts to split the difference between realism and anti-realism by tuning the latter up to more stringent conditions of assertoric warrant cannot offer anything like an adequate response to the realist's challenge.[51] For here again there is an ultimate refusal to concede that certain statements which pass muster even by our best, most widely or expertly agreed-upon epistemic lights might nonetheless fall short of truth, now as so often in the past.

Of course it is always possible for the anti-realist to push yet further along this concessionary path and build in a range of counterfactual clauses which equate 'best opinion' (or optimal response) with the verdict of those maximally qualified to judge when all the evidence is in and subject to rational assessment under ideal epistemic conditions.[52] But at this point the argument becomes merely trivial since 'best opinion' is thereby rendered synonymous with truth and the response-dependence thesis deprived of any genuine epistemic or philosophical content. Thus there seems little hope that an approach along these lines could achieve what Wright and others require of it, i.e., a somewhat scaled-down version of the anti-realist case that would avoid any head-on collision with realism by strengthening its epistemic credentials and adjusting its criteria (whether communal warrant, 'superassertibility', or 'cognitive command') as applied to different areas of discourse with differing standards of evaluation. For no amount of such strengthening or scope for adjustment can obviate the realist's persistent charge that this is just another, more qualified or hedged-about version of the old epistemic fallacy which confuses issues of objective truth with issues of knowledge, best judgement, or rational acceptability. Either that or it identifies these latter with some limit-point conception of idealized epistemic warrant 'at the end of enquiry' which amounts to just a version of objectivist realism that dare not quite speak its name.

It seems to me that Nye's charge against Fregean logic, although off the point in that particular context, nevertheless has some force when applied to such debates as have lately grown up around the topics of rule-following and Dummettian anti-realism. That is to say, those debates are marked by a curious, even pathological fixation on problems which cannot but strike most people – including, I would venture, a fair cross-section of the philosophic community – as pseudo-problems with their likeliest source in some hypercultivated habit of doubt with respect to certain plain truths of knowledge and experience. Thus if anything calls for treatment in such terms it is not so much Frege's project of establishing the objectivity of truth in mathematics, logic and the formal sciences but rather, ironically enough, the sceptical (anti-realist) programme that has emerged very largely in reaction to that same project and its perceived failure. For whatever their psycho-diagnostic pertinence – and however revealing any light they may shed on his misogyny, private frustrations, odious political views, racist attitudes, and so forth – still Nye's remarks can at most be regarded as telling us something of anecdotal interest about the mind-set of a thinker whose (maybe obsessional) dedication to establishing certain philosophic theses went along with a range of other, altogether less rational fears and desires.

Of course this may be held to beg the question against Nye since (as we have seen) it is her central claim not only that Fregean logic was a direct expression of those same psychological flaws but also that it marked the 'insane perfection' of a narrowly rationalist, exclusively male-dominated mode of thought going right back to Parmenides and Plato. Only if one subscribes to that same 'phallocentric' set of values, so Nye maintains, will one view her argument as committing every fallacy in the logical book, among them the cardinal Fregean sin of 'psychologism', or of failing to distinguish 'ideas' in the mind of this or that individual with objective 'thoughts' which altogether transcend any such private dimension of belief or experience.[53] Yet this distinction – though widely contested and (according to thinkers like Dummett) couched in terms of a realist ontology that creates insuperable epistemic problems – is one that has strongly commended itself to a great many well-qualified thinkers.[54] In so far as it comports with the broader realist principle concerning the existence of objective (recognition-transcendent) truth-values for statements in other, for example, natural-scientific or historical areas of discourse it is also a distinction deeply involved with our most basic ideas of rational, truth-seeking enquiry. Moreover, as we have seen, its rejection in favour of an anti-realist approach comes up against some powerful counter-arguments whose philosophic force is further underlined by those curious passages in Dummett's writing where he talks about 'unknowability in principle' as a notion that the anti-realist simply cannot tolerate. Indeed he even goes so far as to suggest, disarmingly enough, that the attempt to hold such discomforting notions at bay by treating truth as epistemically constrained or by restricting it to the scope and limits of warranted assertibility is the chief motivation for adopting that approach.

All of which gives reason to think that, here as elsewhere in recent analytic debate, psychological or temperamental factors play a far greater role than is commonly acknowledged by those who take the Fregean line on such matters. Where Nye gets it wrong (I would suggest) is in pushing too far with this argument to the point of totally annulling the distinction between issues of truth, validity and logical warrant on the one hand and motivational or psycho-explanatory factors on the other. Where her emphasis also falls wide of the mark is in assuming that the latter approach works best – i.e., finds its most rewarding diagnostic material – when applied to the Fregean concern with establishing a realm of objective truth-values quite apart from any merely 'psychologistic' vagaries. To dismiss that concern as nothing more than the product of some private-pathological fixation or socio-political *parti pris* is in effect to discount pretty much the entire history of scientific and philosophical advances achieved through the progressive setting-aside of naïve, 'commonsense', or intuitively self-evident modes of understanding. More in need of a judicious psychological treatment, so it seems to me, is the quantity of high-grade intellectual labour expended on the effort to render anti-realism a halfway plausible philosophic doctrine or to offer some solution to the Kripkensteinian problem about 'following a rule'.[55] For it is this kind of far gone scepticism, rather than the Fregean attempt to vindicate objective standards of truth and falsehood, that opponents can most plausibly adduce as symptomatic of the deep-laid pathology that affects a great deal of current work in the mainstream analytic tradition.

V

This has been a long and rather complicated sequence of argument so let me now summarize the main points and draw some pertinent conclusions. Philosophers are right to reject the sort of takeover bid advanced by psychologizing types – along with sociologists and cultural theorists – who themselves reject any version of the claim that there exist standards of truth, logic, or rational warrant quite aside from explanations in the psycho-diagnostic or socio-political modes. Still they (the philosophers) should at least acknowledge that some topics that have lately come in for more than their share of intensive debate are such as to suggest a high degree of obsessional, even neurotic fixation on basically trivial or non-existent problems. One reason for this is the gap that opened up in the wake of logical empiricism – though with its ultimate source in Kantian epistemology – between sensuous (phenomenal) intuitions and concepts of understanding. Hence Frege's abstract-objectivist conception of truth in logic and mathematics, and hence also those reactive developments (such as Dummettian anti-realism) which pursued that programme to its ultimate conclusion and, in the process, ended up by espousing a sceptical outlook whereby 'truth' could amount to no more than epistemic justification or assertoric warrant.

I have argued that this is a false dilemma though one that has taken hold so deeply as to constitute something like the ruling agenda of analytic philosophy over the past half-century and more. My constructive proposals have been somewhat at risk of getting squeezed out by my focus on the various failures and dead-ends of that particular enterprise. What those proposals have involved, in brief, is a naturalized epistemology which avoids the dilemma-inducing split between empirical and formal or logic-based conceptions of truth but which also (crucially) conserves an adequate normative dimension and thereby resists the disabling slide into Quinean radical empiricism. Indeed one might suggest that it is partly on account of the normative deficit in approaches of this type – their lack of rational-evaluative criteria for assessing episodes of theory-change or conflicts of scientific viewpoint – that naturalized epistemology can so easily be pushed in a different, more radically psychologistic direction. In Quine's case the path is laid open through his coupling of a crudely behaviourist account of belief-formation with the doctrine that logic might always be revised under pressure of recalcitrant empirical data and hence his idea that any 'rational' choice between rival theories or conceptual schemes must finally come down to 'conservatism', the 'quest for simplicity', and 'pragmatic inclination'.[56] For it is no great distance from this Quinean way of putting logic in its place *vis-à-vis* the claims of empirical warrant or 'experience', broadly construed, to Nye's attack on the presumptions of logic as a master-discourse of truth and rationality.

To be sure, Quine's outlook on issues in formal logic is one that seems flatly at odds with all this, adopting as it does an objectivist view of truth-values and an austerely canonical approach that admits no more than the standard apparatus of the first-order quantified predicate calculus.[57] Thus it is hardly surprising that Quine should cut a prominent figure among the thinkers lined up for oppro-brium in Nye's treatment of the topic. Indeed he fills this role to perfection on account of his strict exclusionist policy with regard to modal, epistemic, and other such (in his view) misconceived pseudo-logics whose fault is to muddy the clear waters of a purely extensionalist approach by introducing talk of *de re* necessity, beliefs, states of knowledge, and so forth. Thus modal logic runs into problems with the basic principle of substitutabilty *salva veritate*, that is to say, with the fact that one cannot deduce from the truth of the statement 'the number 9 is necessarily greater than the number 3' the truth of the statement 'the number of planets in the solar system is necessarily greater than three'. (There might have been three or fewer.)[58] And problems arise in epistemic (as likewise in intensional or meaning-related) contexts since one cannot logically conclude from the truth of the sentence 'Alison believes that Quine is a Harvard philosopher' to the truth of the sentence 'Alison believes that the author of "Two Dogmas of Empiricism" is a Harvard philosopher'. (She might not have known that Quine was the author.)

This latter sort of case is especially grist to Nye's mill in so far as it requires a rigorous distinction between statements that can be brought under the regime of an extensionally specified truth-functional logic and statements that fail that test in so far as they involve some ascription of beliefs or propositional attitudes. That is to say, she can treat it as yet another variant on the prototypically Fregean desire to cure logical thought of its bad temptation to fall back on merely subjective, personal, or psychologistic modes of understanding. I have argued that this charge miscarries – that it involves a very basic form of category-mistake – in so far as there do exist objective standards of truth, validity, and logical warrant which cannot be reduced (as Nye would have it) to an expression of the epistemic will-to-power vested in a discourse of patriarchal values and authority. One way of making the point is through a kind of 'transcendental *tu quoque*', that is, by remarking that if Nye's case is to have any rational or argumentative (as distinct from rhetorical) force then it must necessarily involve some appeal to criteria of valid reasoning from agreed-upon premises to properly derived or logically sound conclusions. Yet of course the same argument could just as well apply to the tension that arises between Quine's 'Two Dogmas' revisionist thesis with regard to the ground-rules of classical logic – such as bivalence or excluded middle – and his adherence to those ground-rules not only in his textbook writings on the subject but also in the very process of making that revisionist case.

What I would hope to have shown in the course of this chapter is that such problems are sure to arise when the formal or abstract dimension of logical enquiry becomes so detached from empirical considerations as to lose any purchase on those various kinds of applied (scientific or everyday-practical) reasoning wherein logic has its ultimate basis and justification. Here we may recall Kitcher's point about the growth of mathematical knowledge: that although '[a]t first glance the remoteness of contemporary mathematics from perceptual experience . . . appears to doom any empiricist account', this still leaves it open for the advocate of such an account to 'respond by explaining how "higher" mathematics could emerge from those rudimentary parts of the subject that can be perceptually warranted' (Kitcher, p. 271). This argument applies just as much to debates in philosophy of logic where even the most abstract, highly formalized, or speculative branches of the subject must involve some implicit reference back to the context of real-world, empirically constrained cognitive investigation. That is to say, they will have to make adequate room for the ubiquitous deployment of logical procedures – among them *modus ponens* and *modus tollens* – in our ways of straightforwardly learning from experience and forming various rational (i.e., logically sound *and* empirically testable) beliefs, theories, predictions, and so on.

Thus the kernel of truth in Nye's otherwise over-the-top indictment has to do with the outright Fregean refusal, on Platonist grounds, to acknowledge that issues of logical validity could have *anything whatever* to do with issues of empirical, perceptual, or experiential warrant. Indeed it was Frege's quarrel with Mill in precisely this regard that set the pattern for just about every major debate in twentieth-century philosophy of logic. Hence, as I have argued, its constant proneness – along with other closely allied disciplines such as philosophy of mathematics – to swing back and forth between the twin poles of an abstract-objectivist ontology devoid of any adequate empirical grounding and a radical empiricism devoid of adequate rational or normative criteria. That these two extremes are so oddly yoked together in Quine's case – *vide* his 'Two Dogmas' outlook of full-fledged ontological relativism and (elsewhere) his professed attitude of Platonist realism with respect to numbers, sets, classes and other such abstract entities – is not so much a sign of their having been successfully reconciled as of Quine's still inheriting much of the logical-empiricist baggage that he claims to have shed. If there is any way forward from the lengthy chapter of failed attempts to break with that unfortunate legacy then it

lies (I would suggest) along the path marked out by Kitcher and other proponents of a naturalized epistemology with normative resources sufficient to meet
the Fregean objectivist challenge.

NOTES

1 See, for instance, A. Phillips Griffiths (ed.), *Philosophy, Psychology and Psychiatry*
   (Cambridge: Cambridge University Press, 1995); Morris Lazerowitz, *The Language of
   Philosophy: Freud and Wittgenstein* (Dordrecht: D. Reidel, 1977); Michael P. Levine (ed.),
   The Analytic Freud: Philosophy and Psychoanalysis (London: Routledge, 2000); Jean Piaget,
   Genetic Epistemology, trans. Eleanor Duckworth (New York: Columbia University Press,
   1970) and *Psychology and Epistemology: Towards a Theory of Knowledge*, trans. P. A. Wells
   (Harmondsworth: Penguin, 1970); Richard Wollheim and James Hopkins (eds), *Philo-
   sophical Essays on Freud* (Cambridge University Press, 1982).

2 Richard Rorty, *Consequences of Pragmatism* (Brighton: Harvester, 1982) and *Objectivity,
   Relativism, and Truth* (Cambridge: Cambridge University Press, 1989).

3 See especially Gottlob Frege, 'On Sense and Reference', in Peter Geach and Max Black
   (eds), *Translations from the Philosophical Writings of Gottlob Frege* (Oxford: Blackwell,
   1952), pp. 56–78.

4 Gottlob Frege, review of Edmund Husserl's *Philosophie der Arithmetik*, translated by E.-H.
   W. Kluge, *Mind*, Vol. LXXXI (1972), pp. 321–37; Gilbert Ryle, 'Phenomenology',
   'Review of Martin Farber, *The Foundations of Phenomenology*', and 'Phenomenology versus
   The Concept of Mind', in Ryle, *Collected Papers*, Vol. 1 (London: Hutchinson, 1971),
   pp. 167–78, 215–24, 179–96. See also Michael Dummett, *Origins of Analytical Philosophy*
   (Cambridge, MA: Harvard University Press, 1994); Dagfinn Follesdal, 'Husserl and
   Frege: A Contribution to Elucidating the Origins of Phenomenological Philosophy', in
   Leila Haaparanta (ed.), *Mind, Meaning and Mathematics: Essays on the Philosophical Views of
   Husserl and Frege* (Dordrecht and Boston: Kluwer, 1994), pp. 3–47 and Johanna Maria
   Tito, *Logic in the Husserlian Context* (Evanston, IL: Northwestern University Press, 1990).

5 Edmund Husserl, *Formal and Transcendental Logic*, trans. Dorion Cairns (The Hague:
   Martinus Nijhoff, 1969); also *Experience and Judgement: Investigations in a Genealogy of
   Logic*, trans. James S. Churchill and Karl Ameriks (Northwestern University Press, 1973).

6 See especially W. V. Quine, 'Two Dogmas of Empiricism', in *From a Logical Point of View*,
   2nd edn (Cambridge, MA: Harvard University Press, 1961), pp. 20–46; also *Word and
   Object* (Cambridge, MA: MIT Press, 1960) and *Ontological Relativity and Other Essays* (New
   York: Columbia University Press, 1969).

7 For further discussion see Jaegwon Kim, *Supervenience and Mind* (Cambridge: Cambridge
   University Press, 1993); also L. W. Hahn and P. A. Schilpp (eds), *The Philosophy of W. V.
   Quine*, 2nd edn (Chicago: Open Court, 1998).

8 Quine, 'Two Dogmas of Empiricism' (op. cit.).

9 See entries under Note 1, above.

10 See Note 1, above; also Ludwig Wittgenstein, *Lectures and Conversations on Aesthetics,
   Psychology and Religious Belief*, ed. Cyril Barrett (Oxford: Blackwell, 1966); *Wittgenstein's
   Lectures on Philosophical Psychology*, ed. P. T. Geach (Brighton: Harvester, 1988); *Last
   Writings on the Philosophy of Psychology*, Vols 1 and 2, ed. G. H. von Wright and Heikki
   Nyman (Oxford: Blackwell, 1990 and 1993).

11 Quine, 'Epistemology Naturalized', in *Ontological Relativity and Other Essays* (op. cit.),
   pp. 69–90.

12 Quine, 'Two Dogmas of Empiricism' (op. cit.).

13 See Notes 6 and 11, above.

14 For a range of representative views, see William Bechtel and George Graham (eds),

A Companion to Cognitive Science (Oxford: Blackwell, 1999); Alvin A. Goldman (ed.), *Readings in Philosophy and Cognitive Science* (Cambridge, MA: MIT Press, 1993); Michael I. Posner (ed.), *Foundations of Cognitive Science* (Cambridge, MA: MIT Press, 1989).

15 See Note 3, above; also Frege, 'The Thought: A Logical Enquiry', in Robert M. Harnish (ed.), *Basic Topics in the Philosophy of Language* (Hemel Hempstead: Harvester-Wheatsheaf, 1994), pp. 517–35.

16 J. S. Mill, *A System of Logic Ratiocinative and Inductive*, 2 vols, ed. J. M. Robson (London: Routledge & Kegan Paul, 1973–74).

17 See especially Michael Dummett, *Truth and Other Enigmas* (London: Duckworth, 1978), *The Logical Basis of Metaphysics* (Duckworth, 1991), and *The Seas of Language* (Oxford: Clarendon Press, 1993); Michael Luntley, *Language, Logic and Experience: The Case for Anti-realism* (Duckworth, 1988); Neil Tennant, *Anti-Realism and Logic* (Oxford: Clarendon Press, 1987) and *The Taming of the True* (Oxford: Oxford University Press, 1997); also Paul Benacerraf and Hilary Putnam (eds), *The Philosophy of Mathematics: Selected Essays*, 2nd edn (Cambridge: Cambridge University Press, 1983).

18 See Christopher Norris, *Truth Matters: Realism, Anti-realism, and Response-dependence* (Edinburgh: Edinburgh University Press, 2002).

19 Philip Kitcher, *The Nature of Mathematical Knowledge* (Cambridge: Cambridge University Press, 1984), p. 5. All further references given by 'Kitcher' and page number in the text.

20 Andrea Nye, *Words of Power: A Feminist Reading of the History of Logic* (London: Routledge, 1990).

21 'Diary: Written by Professor Dr. Gottlob Frege in the Time from 10 March to 9 April 1924', *Inquiry*, Vol. 39 (1996), pp. 303–42; also Michael Dummett, *Frege: Philosophy of Language* (London: Duckworth, 1981).

22 See Note 15, above.

23 J. J. Gibson, *The Ecological Approach to Visual Perception* (Boston: Houghton Mifflin, 1979).

24 See Hartry H. Field, *Science Without Numbers: A Defence of Nominalism* (Oxford: Blackwell, 1980); Saul Kripke, *Wittgenstein on Rules and Private Language* (Oxford: Blackwell, 1982).

25 For a good introductory account, see Simon Singh, *Fermat's Last Theorem* (London: Fourth Estate, 1997).

26 For further discussion of these developments, see Norris, *Resources of Realism: Prospects for 'Post-Analytic' Philosophy* (London: Macmillan, 1997); *New Idols of the Cave: On the Limits of Anti-Realism* (Manchester: Manchester University Press, 1997); *Philosophy of Language and the Challenge to Scientific Realism* (London: Routledge, 2004).

27 Norris, *Quantum Theory and the Flight from Realism: Philosophical Responses to Quantum Mechanics* (London: Routledge, 2000).

28 Quine, 'Two Dogmas of Empiricism' (op. cit.); Hilary Putnam, 'Philosophy of Physics', 'A Philosopher Looks at Quantum Mechanics', and 'The Logic of Quantum Mechanics', in *Mathematics, Matter and Method* (Cambridge: Cambridge University Press, 1979), pp. 79–92, 130–58, 174–97.

29 See, for instance, J. L. Aronson, 'Testing for Convergent Realism', *British Journal for the Philosophy of Science*, Vol. 40 (1989), pp. 255–60; Richard Boyd, 'The Current Status of Scientific Realism', in Jarrett Leplin (ed.), *Scientific Realism* (Berkeley and Los Angeles: University of California Press, 1984), pp. 41–82; Gilbert Harman, 'Inference to the Best Explanation', *Philosophical Review*, Vol. 74 (1965), pp. 88–95; Peter Lipton, *Inference to the Best Explanation* (London: Routledge, 1993).

30 See Notes 6 and 28, above.

31 Among the chief proponents of anti-realism are Dummett and Tennant (Note 17, above). For further discussion – including defences of a realist approach to mathematics, logic, and the formal sciences – see Bob Hale, *Abstract Objects* (Oxford: Blackwell, 1987) and 'Is Platonism Epistemologically Bankrupt?', *Philosophical Review*, Vol. 103 (1994), pp. 299–

325; Jerrold J. Katz, *Realistic Rationalism* (Cambridge, MA: MIT Press, 1998); Scott Soames, *Understanding Truth* (Oxford: Oxford University Press, 1999).

32 See Notes 17 and 24, above.

33 Andrea Nye, *Words of Power* (op. cit.). All further references given by 'Nye' and page number in the text.

34 See also Nye, *Feminism and Modern Philosophy* (London: Routledge, 2004); Miranda Fricker and Jennifer Hornsby (eds), *The Cambridge Companion to Feminism in Philosophy* (Cambridge: Cambridge University Press, 2000); Morwena Griffiths and Margaret Whitford (eds), *Feminist Perspectives in Philosophy* (London: Macmillan, 1988).

35 See Note 15, above.

36 For some informative historical and socio-political background, see Otto Neurath, *Modern Man in the Making* (London: Secker & Warburg, 1939); also Nancy Cartwright, Jordi Cat, Lola Fleck and Thomas E. Uebel, *Otto Neurath: Between Science and Politics* (Cambridge: Cambridge University Press, 1996); Michael Friedman, *Reconsidering Logical Positivism* (Cambridge University Press, 1999) and *A Parting of the Ways: Carnap, Cassirer, and Heidegger* (Chicago: Open Court, 2000).

37 See especially Dummett, 'Truth' and 'The Reality of the Past', in *Truth and Other Enigmas* (op. cit.), pp. 1–24, 358–74.

38 See also Dummett, 'Can an Effect Precede its Cause?' and 'Bringing About the Past', in *Truth and Other Enigmas* (op. cit.), pp. 319–32, 333–50.

39 For further discussion, see Norris, *Realism, Anti-Realism, and Response-Dependence* (op. cit.); also Bernhard Weiss, *Dummett* (Chesham: Acumen Press, 2002).

40 I take the remote solar-system example from Scott Soames, *Understanding Truth* (op. cit.). See this and other entries under Note 31, above.

41 See, for instance, J. Aronson, R. Harré and E. Way, *Realism Rescued* (op. cit.); Roy Bhaskar, *A Realist Theory of Science* (Leeds: Leeds Books, 1975); Michael Devitt, *Realism and Truth*, 2nd edn (Princeton, NJ: Princeton University Press, 1991); Jarrett Leplin (ed.), *Scientific Realism* (op. cit.); Stathis Psillos, *Scientific Realism: How Science Tracks Truth* (London: Routledge, 1999).

42 See especially Dummett, *Elements of Intuitionism* (Oxford: Oxford University Press, 1977) and *Frege: Philosophy of Mathematics*, 2nd edn. (London: Duckworth, 1991).

43 Quine, 'Two Dogmas of Empiricism' (op. cit.).

44 Dummett, *Elements of Intuitionism* (op. cit.).

45 See Kripke, *Wittgenstein on Rules and Private Language* (op. cit.); also Alexander Miller and Crispin Wright (eds), *Rule-Following and Meaning* (Chesham: Acumen, 2002).

46 Dummett, *The Logical Basis of Metaphysics* (London: Duckworth, 1991), p. 7.

47 Ibid.

48 Donald Davidson, 'On the Very Idea of a Conceptual Scheme', in *Inquiries into Truth and Interpretation* (Oxford: Oxford University Press, 1984), pp. 183–98; p. 183.

49 Crispin Wright, *Truth and Objectivity* (Cambridge, MA: Harvard University Press, 1992).

50 See, for instance, J. Haldane and C. Wright (eds), *Realism, Representation and Projection* (Oxford: Oxford University Press, 1993); Philip Pettit, *The Common Mind: An Essay on Psychology, Society, and Politics* (Oxford: Oxford University Press, 1992); Crispin Wright, 'Moral Values, Projection, and Secondary Qualities', *Proceedings of the Aristotelian Society*, Supplementary Vol. 62 (1988), pp. 1–26, 'Realism, Antirealism, Irrealism, Quasi-Realism', *Midwest Studies in Philosophy*, Vol. 12 (1988), pp. 25–49; also various essays on response-dependence in *European Review of Philosophy*, Vol. 3 (1998).

51 Norris, *Realism, Anti-Realism, and Response-Dependence* (op. cit.).

52 See especially Mark Johnston, 'Dispositional Theories of Value', *Proceedings of the Aristotelian Society*, Vol. 63 (1989), pp. 139–74, 'How to Speak of the Colours', *Philosophical Studies*, Vol. 68 (1992), pp. 221–63, and 'Objectivity Refigured', in Haldane and Wright (eds), *Realism, Representation and Projection* (op. cit.), pp. 85–130.

53 Nye, *Words of Power* (op. cit.).

54 See Notes 29 and 31, above.
55 See Notes 24 and 45, above; also Norris, 'The Limits of Whose Language? Wittgenstein on Logic, Mathematics, and Science', in *Language, Logic and Epistemology: A Modal-Realist Approach* (London: Macmillan, 2004), pp. 66–110.
56 Quine, 'Two Dogmas of Empiricism' (op. cit.).
57 See Quine, *From a Logical Point of View* (op. cit.); also *Methods of Logic* (New York: Henry Holt, 1950); *Philosophy of Logic* (Englewood Cliffs, NJ: Prentice-Hall, 1970); *Selected Logic Papers* (Cambridge, MA: Harvard University Press, 1995).
58 Quine, 'Reference and Modality', in Linsky (ed.), *Reference and Modality* (Oxford: Oxford University Press, 1971), pp. 17–34.

2

Meaning, Truth, and Causal Explanation:
The 'Humean Condition' Revisited

I

The belief expressed by Quine's famous quip that 'the Humean condition is also the human condition' is one that as yet shows little sign of relaxing its grip on mainstream analytic epistemology and philosophy of science, despite various recent developments which would seem to point in a radically different direction.[1] That is to say, the agenda of current debate with regard to issues of causal explanation still tends to be set by those familiar kinds of sceptical (e.g., positivist or empiricist) argument that take a lead from Hume in denying the existence – or at any rate the knowability – of real-world operative causal forces, powers, or dispositions in nature. Of course there is a crucial distinction to be drawn between full-strength ontological and scaled-down epistemological versions of the sceptic's claim. On the one hand are ranged those old-guard 'orthodox' Humeans (by now perhaps rather few) who would reject any realist or objectivist notion of causality, while on the other can be found subscribers to the lately ascendant, more moderate or revisionist view.[2] According to this we can have no demonstrative proof or knowledge of physical causes even though, by the same token, we have no good reason to deny that they exist and exert their various capacities or powers quite apart from our knowledge (or lack of it) concerning them. Thus scepticism is held within decent, scientifically reputable bounds and can also be made out to comply with the single most basic tenet of philosophic realism, that is, the objectivist claim that truth might always exceed the scope and limits of humanly attainable proof or verification.

Hence perhaps the emergence of this 'new' reading of Hume at just the time when old-style logical empiricism (along with its sceptical upshot) had lost credibility owing to various widely influential attacks from the causal-realist quarter.[3] No doubt its demise was also much hastened by Quine's famous demolition-job which purported to show that the whole programme was based on a pair of residual 'dogmas' – the analytic/synthetic distinction and the idea of scientific statements or predictions as testable one by one against likewise discrete items of empirical evidence – which failed to hold up under critical scrutiny.[4] In its place, Quine proposed, we should adopt a naturalized epistemology that takes its lead from the physical sciences, along with a thoroughly holistic approach to issues of truth, meaning and interpretation which responds to recalcitrant empirical data by allowing truth-values to be redistributed across the entire 'fabric' or 'web' of received scientific belief. At the limit, conceivably, this might entail giving up certain axioms of classical logic – even bivalence or excluded middle – in the interests of conserving well-attested empirical data, such as quantum superposition or wave/particle dualism.[5] Or again, if we want to conserve some especially powerful or well-entrenched physical theory in the face of anomalous empirical findings, then this might require that we reject the presumed self-evidence of perceptual warrant, as for instance by putting the anomalies down to defects in our measuring instruments or limits on our powers of technologically enhanced observation. All this Quine takes as nothing more than a straightforward consequence of the twin principles comprising the so-called 'Duhem-Quine thesis', namely the under-determination of theory by evidence and the theory-laden character of observation statements.[6] Thus any decision about which items of belief to retain and which to revise or give up is primarily a matter of 'pragmatic convenience' – of simplicity, conservatism, maximal coherence with the current range of beliefs-held-true – rather than (as the logical empiricists supposed) a matter of applying certain well-defined methods and protocols for valid, i.e., truth-conducive reasoning on the evidence.

In which case, according to Quine, we have no choice but to push right through with this holistic conception and acknowledge that a naturalized epistemology along the lines that he proposes must also entail an outlook of full-fledged ontological relativity. Such questions as the realist might wish to phrase in objective-sounding terms – 'Do x's exist?', 'Is y a natural kind?', 'What exactly are x's properties, attributes, microstructural features, causal dispositions?', and so on – should rather be treated as questions that arise (and that receive some definite answer) only relative to this or that conceptual framework or ontological scheme. Hence Quine's famously provocative claim that the issue of 'existence' as regards such a diverse range of candidate objects as mathematical sets or classes, centaurs, Homer's gods, or brick houses on Elm Street is one that cannot be settled except by reference to the various systems of belief within which they play or once played a role. Such items are selectively 'imported' into some given scheme as more or less convenient working posits whose reality – along with the truth-value of any statements concerning them – is decided solely on pragmatic grounds, or as a matter of what works best for this or that scheme-relative purpose. Quine is perfectly willing to acknowledge that his own strong preference, 'qua lay physicist', is for the kinds of entity that figure in the discourse of our current best theories in natural science, and not for such objects as centaurs or Homer's gods. He is also – surprising as it might seem – a realist about mathematical entities, and indeed expresses strong Platonist leanings in that regard.[7] However any charge of inconsistency here is briskly set aside by Quine's pragmatist avowal that science (physics especially) provides the most convenient way yet discovered of 'working some structure' into the otherwise inchoate flux of sensory experience. Moreover hypotheses concerning the existence of mathematical objects – right up to the highest-level abstractions of set-theory – are so deeply entrenched within present-day scientific theory and practice as to justify our counting them among the range of well-attested putative realia. All the same, whatever his own inclinations, Quine is adamant that any ontological privilege granted to atoms, numbers, or sets as distinct (say) from centaurs or Homer's gods is something they enjoy only in virtue of belonging to a favoured conceptual scheme.

Thus the question arises as to whether Quine's physicalist outlook – his subscription to a naturalized epistemology that favours such baseline behaviourist posits as our reflex responses to the 'constant bombardment' of incoming sensory stimuli – should itself be taken as just one scheme among the many currently on offer. So likewise with those various 'intensional' items like meanings, thoughts, modalities, propositional contents, attitudes, and so forth, that Quine seeks to purge from philosophical discourse so as to maintain a strictly extensionalist remit and avoid all the well-known problems about quantifying into opaque (i.e., modal or belief-related) contexts.[8] This follows directly from his frontal attack on the two last 'dogmas' of logical empiricism, since – as Quine makes clear – that argument has to be pushed right through to the point of embracing on the one hand a thoroughgoing naturalized, science-led approach which treats the process of belief-formation in purely behaviourist terms, and on the other a wholesale contextualist doctrine of truth, meaning and interpretation which places no limits – no ultimate logical or empirical constraints – on the revisability of any beliefs thus formed. Only thus, he argues, can epistemology assume its rightful place as a sub-branch of the natural sciences whose job it is to explain how the 'meagre input' of sensory promptings to which various subjects are exposed somehow gives rise to their 'torrential output' of hypotheses, predictions, observation statements, scientific theories, and so forth.[9] What drops out completely on Quine's account is the idea of knowledge and progress in the sciences as coming about through a process of increasing conceptual grasp and causal-explanatory depth. That is to say, he pushes the consequences of Humean scepticism to their furthest (and, one may think, their rationally insupportable) extreme even though his argument in 'Two Dogmas' starts out from the rejection of Hume's dichotomy between empirically warranted 'matters of fact' and analytic or a priori 'truths of reason'.

No doubt Quine's essay latched on to some deep-laid problems with that whole way of thinking about issues in epistemology and philosophy of science that had begun with Hume, received a more elaborate (yet scarcely less problematical) treatment in Kant, and thereafter remained as a source of unresolved tensions and aporias in the project of logical empiricism.[10] From a causal-realist standpoint these can be seen to have resulted from a failure (or refusal) to recognize scientific progress as providing adequate warrant for the claim that science must in general be on the right track with regard to those various objects, properties, structures, causal dispositions, and so forth which alone make it possible to explain the manifest achievements of science as anything other than a downright miracle. Such is the case for convergent realism – along with inference to the best, most rational explanation – advanced by those philosophers who have worked their way through and beyond the antinomies bequeathed by that whole previous chapter of developments.[11] Thus we have

Quine to thank for bringing this situation about, that is to say, for showing how downright impossible was the Kantian attempt to overcome Hume's sceptical impasse by embracing a hybrid outlook of 'transcendental idealism' on the one hand and 'empirical realism' on the other.[12] Certainly 'Two Dogmas' did more than any other work to emphasize the kinds of dead-end predicament that thinking was sure to encounter if it started out from any version, no matter how elaborately qualified, of the basic Humean dichotomy.

Nor does there seem much hope of success for latter-day revisionist Kantians, like John McDowell, who propose that we reclaim what is valid in Kant's arguments by simply dumping all that otiose 'transcendental' apparatus (as well as all the talk of a noumenal reality beyond phenomenal appearances) and hanging on to his cardinal insight concerning the strictly inseparable roles of 'spontaneity' and 'receptivity' in every act of conceptually informed and empirically warranted knowledge.[13] For, as I have argued elsewhere, this switch of preferential idioms does nothing to prevent the old dichotomy from cropping up yet again, despite and against McDowell's regular cautions – taking a lead from Wilfrid Sellars – that we should not think of those roles as 'even notionally' separate.[14] Indeed its residual grip on his thinking – as likewise on that of the logical empiricists before him, whatever their determination to expunge all traces of Kantian 'metaphysics' from the discourse of epistemology – is evident in numerous passages where McDowell strives to repress or circumvent such dualist modes of thought. 'If we restrict ourselves to the standpoint of experience itself', he urges, then

> what we find in Kant is precisely the picture I have been recommending: a picture in which reality is not located outside a boundary that encloses the conceptual sphere . . . The fact that experience involves receptivity ensures the required constraint from outside thinking and judging. But since the deliverances of receptivity already draw on capacities that belong to spontaneity, we can coherently suppose that the constraint is rational; that is how the picture avoids the pitfall of the Given.[15]

What emerges most strikingly here is the fact that any claim to move beyond the Humean-Kantian dilemma will need to do more than repeat Kant's arguments against Hume in a scaled-down, naturalized, or 'detranscendentalized' form which nonetheless conserves their basic commitment to a notion of the real as in some sense epistemically constrained or subject to the scope and limits of human cognition. Thus the above passage, like many in McDowell, makes a tortuous, quasi-Hegelian attempt to transcend the subject/object dualism ('reality is not located outside a boundary that encloses the conceptual sphere'), while also following Sellars in its claim that such problems can best be got over by renouncing the empiricist 'Myth of the Given' and accepting that every item of perceptual experience is *always already* conceptually informed.[16]

Of course this idea falls square with Quine's twin theses – taken up from Duhem and embraced by Thomas Kuhn along with many others – concerning the under-determination of theory by evidence and the theory-laden character of observation statements.[17] Where they differ is in Quine's hard-headed physicalist conclusion that this spells the end of any attempt, like McDowell's after him, to reclaim the epistemological ground – the normative or justificatory 'space of reasons' – which Kant laid down as the *sine qua non* of any adequate theory of knowledge. The logical empiricists roundly rejected such claims in keeping with their programmatic drive to wean philosophy off its addiction to bad old Kantian-idealist habits of thought, and thus restore it to a properly serviceable adjutant role *vis-à-vis* the methods and procedures of the natural sciences. Yet, as Quine made clear, that programme still preserved just those elements of Kant's philosophy (chief among them the distinction between analytic truths and matters of empirical warrant) which continued to exert a grip on their thinking despite their claim to have cut epistemology down to size by excluding all notions of a priori knowledge or appeals to the supposed self-evidence of certain apodictic truths. Indeed it is on just this point, so the story goes, that the 'two traditions' split off during the early twentieth century. That is to say, the majority of analytic (chiefly Anglophone) philosophers set out along a logico-linguistic path that steered well clear of such swampy metaphysical ground while 'continental' (i.e., post-Kantian mainland-European) thinkers pursued the alternative path that led from Husserlian phenomenology to various later – and, as the analytic types would have it, equally misguided since 'subjectivist' or 'psychologistic' – movements of thought. That this story is a massive simplification amounting to downright travesty is a case that I have argued at length elsewhere, along with other recent revisionist commentators.[18] What it signally fails to grasp, in brief, is first the extent of that residual Kantian influence which runs right through the analytic tradition from the logical empiricists to a thinker like McDowell, and second the fact that continental thought has itself produced a range of approaches (among them Husserl's writings on logic and mathematics and the French critical-rationalist school in philosophy of the natural sciences) which must themselves be counted 'analytic' on any but a narrowly parochial or partisan usage of that term.[19]

II

Still my point here is not to engage in yet another large-scale redrawing of the intellectual map. Rather it is to comment on the peculiar turn of thought – almost (one is tempted to say) a return of the philosophical repressed – whereby Kantian themes have continued to set the agenda of much analytic debate. With the logical empiricists they are mostly present in a covert or unacknowledged way, while in McDowell they take the form of a selective, quasi-naturalized, or non-'metaphysical' reading of Kant that inherits all the problems outlined above (including those remarked upon by Quine) and moreover yields up any claim to conserve that normative dimension which for Kant could not possibly be redeemed except through the appeal to transcendental modes of reasoning.

Hence, I would suggest, the extraordinary impact of Quine's 'Two Dogmas', managing as it did – perhaps in ways that went beyond his conscious intent – to encapsulate the various dilemmas facing philosophy of language, logic, and language at just that critical stage. What his essay brought out with maximal force was the dead-end predicament of a mode of thought – epitomized in logical empiricism – which failed to break with the most problematical aspects of Kantian epistemology and yet gave up on the hope sustained by other ('continental') thinkers that there might be some alternative way to redeem that project. So there is good reason for the widespread view that 'Two Dogmas' marked the crucial point of transition where analytic philosophy in its first, more assertive and confidently problem-solving mode gave way to those various later developments for which the phrase 'post-analytic' serves as a somewhat vague and catch-all but nonetheless apt description. Thus Quine's is the name most often invoked by thinkers of a broadly ecumenical mind who would advise that the best way forward from these problems with the legacy of old-style analytic philosophy is one that combines his doctrines of theory-ladenness, under-determination, and meaning-holism with a strong-descriptivist or depth-hermeneutic approach that breaks entirely free of that tradition.[20] Only then, so the argument runs, can thinking transcend the deep-laid antinomies of Kant's critical project and their latter-day upshot in the impasse that Quine so shrewdly locates in the discourse of logical empiricism.

However Quine's alternative, more radical (minus-the-dogmas) version of empiricism turned out to harbour problems of its own, among them a marked normativity-deficit – or failure to provide adequate criteria for rational theory-choice – and a consequent inability to explain our knowledge of the growth of scientific knowledge.[21] That is to say, by adopting this science-led (physicalist and behaviourist) approach to epistemological issues it left no room for those normative values of truth, rationality, logical warrant, falsifiability under pressure of conflicting evidence, and so forth, that are basic to the very enterprise of science or any other reputable branch of enquiry. After all, it was just Quine's point that no strongly held belief, theory, or prediction need be thought of as falsified by the empirical evidence just so long as there remained the option of adducing some 'auxiliary hypothesis' or background premise that might instead be revised (or abandoned) so as to save appearances. And again, no empirical observation need be taken as decisive evidence against this or that cherished theory just so long as the appearances might be ascribed to some perceptual distortion, erroneous measurement, or (at the limit) hallucinatory experience on the part of an otherwise well-placed observer. But in that case nothing remains of the idea that knowledge accrues – and can reliably be known to accrue – through certain well-tried procedures of empirical observation, inductive warrant, rational conjecture, hypothesis-testing, and inference to the best (most empirically adequate and theoretically cogent) explanation. To be sure, Quine is perfectly entitled to assert, on his own holistic and framework-relativist terms, that these procedures can all play a variously weighted role in the kinds of pragmatic adjustment between competing methodological claims that define what counts as 'rational' theory-choice once epistemology has managed to break with the two last dogmas of empiricism. However this doctrine – that such choices, 'where rational, are pragmatic' – is one that conspicuously fails to explain why certain rationally motivated choices of one theory over another should have laid claim to something more in the way of justificatory and causal-explanatory warrant than other possible choices. Thus, to take Quine's favoured examples, it would leave us very largely at a loss to account for the sorts of decisive paradigm-shift 'whereby Kepler superseded Ptolemy, or Einstein Newton, or Darwin Aristotle'.[22] That is to say, those classic 'revolutions' in scientific thought would have to be treated – as Kuhn was quick to argue very much in the Quinean spirit – from an ontological-relativist standpoint that allowed no appeal to the kinds of causal or depth-explanatory theory which were ruled out on strict empiricist (ultimately Humean) grounds.[23]

I think the best way to read 'Two Dogmas' is as an exercise in the genre of *reductio ad absurdum*, whatever its original (intended) purport or the question as to whether Quine might himself have been disposed to endorse such a reading. (That he did come around – some four decades on – to moderating certain of its central claims is a different matter though certainly of interest in this regard.)[24] My point is not merely to belabour the problems with old-style logical empiricism and likewise with Quine's radical-empiricist critique of that position. Rather it is to draw the fairly obvious conclusion that Quine so conspicuously failed to draw, i.e., that this entire chapter of developments in mainstream analytic (and 'post-analytic') philosophy amounted to little more than an update on Humean sceptical themes. Thus Quine's version of naturalized epistemology coupled with his doctrine of full-fledged meaning holism ran into a dead-end precisely on account of its refusal to acknowledge the validity of arguments to the best, most adequate (rationally grounded) causal explanation. Of course I am by no means alone in reaching this verdict, one that has been argued with considerable force by Wesley Salmon and other defenders of a causal-realist epistemology against what they see as the stalled enterprise of empiricist and post-empiricist approaches in philosophy of science.[25] Just as telling is the way that thinkers like Hilary Putnam have remained partially in thrall to the strictures of that now presumptively *dépassé* movement of thought even while claiming to have moved beyond it in various decisive respects. Putnam is perhaps the most interesting case, since he started out – in his essays of the late 1960s and early 70s – as a strong advocate of causal realism in epistemology and philosophy of language and then backed away from that position through successive attempts to reformulate his thinking in framework-relativist, 'internal-realist', pragmatist, and other such scaled-down compromise terms.[26] Thus Putnam's progress took just the opposite direction to that other main tendency in the wake of Quine's 'Two Dogmas', namely a widespread recognition that the only way forward from the impasse of old-style logical empiricism was to break with Hume's sceptical legacy and – in Salmon's pithy phrase – to 'put the "cause" back in "because"'.[27]

I have written elsewhere about the various stages by which, as I see it, Putnam was led to give up on his early realist approach through an over-emphasis on problem areas (such as the philosophy of quantum mechanics) which in truth required no such drastic shift in his basic ontological commitments.[28] Without repeating that argument in detail it might be useful to summarize the basic points since they offer so striking a contrast with the case that I am presenting here, i.e., my thesis that causal realism and inference to the best explanation represent the only viable alternative to the kinds of dilemma thrown up by logical empiricism. Thus it is, I would suggest, a curious inversion of priorities that leads Putnam to argue from certain as-yet unresolved anomalies in these relatively specialized branches of enquiry to the conclusion that there must be something wrong – 'metaphysically' over-committed – about any form of sci-entific realism that involves an objectivist ontology and a commitment to the idea of truth-values as potentially transcending our utmost means of proof or verification. All the more so, to repeat, since his own early work provided such a range of strong and resourceful arguments for adopting precisely that position as a counter to various sceptical or anti-realist modes of thought. Indeed it is among his great virtues as a thinker always willing to revisit and revise his previous beliefs that Putnam has responded with an almost seismographic sensitivity to every challenge raised against realism during the past four decades and more. Thus his work has successively registered the impact of (1) logical empiricism with its sceptical (Humean) outlook as regards causal explanation; (2) Quine's radically 'naturalized' approach to epistemological issues, along with his under-determination thesis and doctrines of full-scale meaning-holism and ontological relativity; (3) arguments such as those involving the paradoxes of classical set-theory, Gödel's incompleteness-result, and the Löwenheim-Skolem theorem which he takes to pose enormous problems for an objectivist under-standing of logic, mathematics, and the formal sciences; (4) quantum mechanics on the orthodox (Copenhagen) as well as on various alternative accounts; (5) Dummett-style anti-realism and other such logico-semantic updates on old-style verificationist themes; (6) Wittgenstein's reflections (amplified by Kripke) on the issue as to just what can ultimately count as our standard of correctness in 'following a rule'; and (7) – as a fairly constant refrain – the pragmatist challenge to objective (i.e., non-practice-based) conceptions of truth, knowledge and enquiry.[29] So the chief lesson to be drawn, Putnam thinks, is that henceforth any viable defence of realism will have to make terms with this predicament and acknowledge the extent to which truth is always, inescapably a function of our various interests, priorities, or discipline-specific modes of reasoning. To suppose otherwise – in 'metaphysical'-realist fashion – is to leave the door wide open to scepticism by adopting an objectivist view from nowhere that collapses under the least pressure from arguments of just that sort.

Most recently Putnam has fixed his sights on the fact–value distinction, which he considers just another unfortunate consequence of that old way of thinking – from Hume to the logical empiricists – which sets up a strictly impossible ideal of objectivity and truth, and then proceeds (through a typical pattern of sceptical over-reaction) to deny the rationality of value-judgements or the basis for endorsing a whole vast range of everyday-commonsense beliefs.[30] That is to say, he thinks that the only way to counter such arguments is to accept a sensibly scaled-down 'realist' position which yields no hostages to sceptical fortune in the manner of those other, less cautious realist types who allow – indeed require – that there is always potentially a gap between objectivist truth and knowledge to the best of our epistemic capacities. Putnam now rejects his own middle-period 'internal realist' view, i.e., that one can keep truth in the picture but only when conceived as internal (or relative) to some particular framework of enquiry or motivating programme of research.[31] That approach now strikes him as surrendering too much ground to the kinds of sceptical or 'strong'-constructivist approach that would see nothing more in the notion of truth than a merely honorific or place-filler term that equates, for all practical purposes, with 'true by the lights of this or that community' or 'good in the way of belief'. All the same he is still far from reverting to the argument, so forcefully expressed in the writings of his first decade, that there exist certain objects and natural kinds, along with their intrinsic properties, structures, and causal dispositions which may always quite possibly transcend our best powers of epistemic grasp but which nonetheless determine the truth-value of any well-formed statement, prediction, or hypothesis we may venture concerning them.

On that early-Putnam objectivist and causal-realist account scientific knowledge can be thought of as reliably 'truth-tracking' just to the extent that it manages to pick out such items and to manifest a steadily increasing grasp of their distinctive, defining, or depth-ontological attributes. Thus the fact that our criteria for kind-membership have changed very often beyond recognition – e.g., from surface or phenomenal features of items such as 'acid', 'gold' and 'water' to more precise specification in terms of their subatomic, atomic or molecular structure – is no good reason to suppose (in Quinean-Kuhnian fashion) that these changes involve so drastic a shift of theoretical and ontological commitment as to rule out any prospect of meaningful comparison in point of scientific accuracy or causal-explanatory power. Rather what this shows, according to early Putnam, is that we now possess a better, more adequate knowledge of just those objects (along with their defining or constitutive properties) that were once picked out on the basis of a largely intuitive and in some cases – such as that of iron pyrites or 'fool's gold' – an unreliable or downright fallacious method of identification. Thus one might expect the recent, 'third-period' Putnam who has recoiled from the framework-relativist idea of truth as 'internal' to some given investigative framework or conceptual scheme to accept at least a qualified version of the outlook adopted in his first-period writings. All the more so since he is now even keener to disown any remnant of the old positivist distinction between matters of empirically verifiable fact and issues of an ethical or socio-political nature which supposedly belong to a separate realm – whether one of 'emotive' pseudo-statements or Hare-type categorical prescriptives – that offers no hold for assessment in rational-evaluative terms.[32]

This is just the point of Putnam's attack on the fact/value dichotomy, as argued most forcefully in his recent essays on the work of the economist and moral philosopher Amartya Sen.[33] His admiration for Sen's work is mainly on account of its refusal to accept the kind of orthodox thinking that draws a sharp distinction between means and ends, or questions that can properly be treated in terms of instrumental (e.g., rational-choice) theory and issues that involve some ethical component – some ultimate value – beyond reach of any such method. Putnam sees this as just another bad relic of the same misbegotten habit of thought that Quine so effectively demolished in his attack on the two last dogmas of logical empiricism. Thus he cites with approval the remark of another economist-philosopher, Vivian Walsh, that '[t]o borrow and adapt Quine's vivid image, if a theory may be black with fact and white with convention, it might well (so far as logical empiricism could tell) be red with values. Since for them confirmation *or* falsification had to be a property of a theory *as a whole*, they had no way of unravelling this whole cloth'.[34] That is to say, if their programme came unstuck – as Quine argued – on its failure to make good the distinction between analytic and synthetic statements (or Humean 'truths of reason' and 'matters of fact') then along with it went the likewise untenable and yet more pernicious distinction between factual or verifiable statements on the one hand and ethical or evaluative judgements on the other. In which case 'the moral is clear', Putnam writes: 'when we are dealing with any important value disagreement, we assume that facts are irrelevant at our peril', since '[n]o convincing reason can be given for the *logical* irrelevance of facts to value judgements, even if we accept the positivist conception of what a "fact" is'.[35] Thus Quine serves Putnam as a stalking-horse for his attack on the fact/value dichotomy and – following from that – his case for the rational accountability of judgements that the positivists either consigned to some realm of 'emotive' pseudo-statement or else treated as forms of prescriptive utterance likewise devoid of cognitive, rational, or truth-evaluable content.

However this serviceable aspect of Quine's thought turns out to have sharp limitations when it comes to Putnam's more substantive proposals for the way that philosophy should go once freed from the various dilemmas thrown up in the wake of logical empiricism. After all, Quine's 'solution' swung over so far toward a radical-empiricist (i.e., behaviourist) theory of knowledge-acquisition – a theory devoid of normative or rational-evaluative constraints – as to leave it a mystery how scientific progress could ever have come about, or how we could ever have adequate warrant for claiming to know (on rational, evidential, or causal-explanatory) grounds that genuine progress had occurred.[36] Such was the upshot of a naturalized approach which insisted that philosophy should stick to its role of under-labourer *vis-à-vis* the physical sciences and not fall prey – as had happened so often since Kant – to delusions of epistemological grandeur. Putnam is clear enough that this leaves all the really important questions unanswered, among them (not least) the question as to just what constitutes knowledge as opposed to present-best belief, or truth as opposed to '"truth" by the lights of this or that currently accredited expert community'. Such questions cannot possibly find an answer if one takes it, like Quine, that the only route from 'raw' sensory stimuli to the vast proliferation of theories, hypotheses, covering-law statements, and so forth is one that involves nothing more than a process of ad hoc pragmatic 'adjustment' and a consequent readiness to ditch any item of belief – whether at the logical 'core' or the empirical 'periphery' – that threatens to obstruct that process. What this amounts to is an emptying-out of all those normative criteria of truth, rationality, evidential warrant, and inference to the best (most adequate and powerful) explanation which would otherwise offer a means of avoiding the logical-empiricist impasse. That is to say, it leaves epistemology and philosophy of science with no real work to do save that of remarking how great is the gap between the 'meagre input' of sensory stimuli to which human enquirers are exposed and the 'torrential output' of linguistically articulated theories and beliefs which they somehow manage to generate despite that drastically impoverished database.

Hence Noam Chomsky's well-known critique of Quine, pointing out that no such radical-empiricist approach could begin to explain the human capacity for acquiring and manifesting a whole range of cognitive skills, among them our native competence in language and our ability to frame and test various kinds of rationally formed conjecture, in the natural sciences and elsewhere.[37] Indeed it was largely by way of response to this then-dominant strain of Skinnerian behaviourism in psychology, epistemology and linguistics that Chomsky first developed his theory of transformational-generative grammar, along with his strongly rationalist stance with regard to philosophy of mind.[38] His case against Quine draws much of its force from his 'poverty of the stimulus' argument, i.e., Chomsky's claim that human powers of linguistic expression and rational belief-formation cannot possibly be described or explained by any theory that would treat them in terms of a crudely reductive stimulus-response psychology. Putnam raises similar objections, albeit from a different philosophical angle, when he remarks on the lack of normative criteria for rational, progressive, or knowledge-conducive theory-choice in Quine's approach to these matters. Thus:

> [h]is answer to those who want a more realistic epistemology, an epistemology that concerns how real scientists manage to select real theories on real data, is the famous, 'Why not settle for psychology?' What many of his readers have missed is that when Quine said this he *meant* it. 'Naturalized epistemology' in Quine's sense means the *abandonment* of epistemology. 'Psychology' (which for Quine always means Skinnerian psychology) is all the epistemology we want or need. This is evasion of the epistemological question with a vengeance![39]

One can readily assent to these criticisms of Quine – as also to Chomsky's kindred range of objections – while nonetheless doubting whether Putnam's later stance on the realism issue leaves him strongly placed to sustain them. That is to say, it is not clear that the case for some plausible (i.e., scientifically and philosophically adequate) version of realism can be made to convincing effect while backing off as far as Putnam does – in his post-1980 writings – from the basic realist principles of objectivity, truth as verification-transcendent, and inference to the best causal and rational explanation.

Indeed Putnam's early approach to these matters was in many ways better equipped, from a realist viewpoint, than Chomsky's resolutely internalist (or rationalist) outlook with regard to epistemological issues. Thus Chomsky has come out very firmly against any notion of external reference-fixing – such as that proposed by Kripke or early Putnam – that would (as he sees it) amount to just a slightly more sophisticated version of old-style Skinnerian behaviourism.[40] Hence Chomsky's stress on the native (internal) capacity of the human mind to acquire and manifest modes of rational thought – just as it constructs well-formed grammatical sentences – through a faculty (or 'competence') whose workings can be specified in formal or structural terms, and which depends not at all on 'external' stimuli as supposed by theorists from Skinner to Putnam. His objections to externalism range all the way from 'poverty of the stimulus' (that is, *contra* Skinner, the claim that human infants exhibit a power of acquiring complex grammatical structures far beyond anything available in their formative linguistic environment) to the moral or ethico-political case that behaviourism drastically underrates the capacity and entitlement of human beings to think for themselves and not be subject to Skinnerian techniques of operant conditioning or social control.[41] This is why Chomsky argues strongly against the Kripke-Putnam causal theory of reference-fixing, a theory, in his view, that threatens the interests of human autonomy, rationality and freedom of conscience by placing sharp limits on the scope for exercise of our innate rational and moral-evaluative powers.[42] Thus, on his account, issues of reference or real-world context dependence had best be shunted off into the realm of pragmatics, rather than brought within the stricter remit of theoretical linguistics or cognitive psychology.

However, as I have argued at length elsewhere, this requirement is itself such as to impose a fairly drastic restriction on the scope of those disciplines and, above all, their ability to address the kinds of philosophical question that arise with regard to language in its wider (everyday, scientific, informational, and social-communicative) functions.[43] If these are regarded as merely 'pragmatic' concerns that exert no significant claim on the interest of linguists or cognitive psychologists then there is a problem about Chomsky's larger project. Thus it becomes hard to see how Chomsky can justify his case for the alignment of a rationalist, i.e., anti-behaviourist and non-empiricist theory of mind with an ethics and politics premised on the ability of human subjects to arrive at truth – and to resist the pressures of conformist ideology – through the exercise of factually well-informed critical judgement. Moreover, one may doubt that Chomsky's aims are well served by his adopting so extreme a version of the innatist (Cartesian) hypothesis that explains human knowledge and communicative grasp in terms of a priori concepts, ideas, or powers of rational understanding. For this leads him not only to postulate (in my view) an implausibly large and multifarious range of such ideas but also to cut away some crucial load-bearing structures that are needed in order to make good his claims

for the inherently rational and truth-oriented character of human thought, at
least when not deflected from its aim by the effects of mass-indoctrination or
'manufactured consensus'.[44] Quite simply, without an adequate theory of
reference that establishes the link between word and world – or well-formed,
truth-apt statements and that which renders them objectively truth or false – we
are lacking a basic component in linguistics, epistemology, and philosophy of
mind, as well as a crucial enabling premise of ethics, politics and the social
sciences.

III

Thus Chomsky's powerful arguments against Skinnerian behaviourism and
Quinean radical empiricism are far less convincing when extended to his case
against the causal-realist or externalist theory of reference developed by Kripke,
early Putnam, and others. That is, it signally fails to acknowledge the crucial
difference between a behaviourist account of operant conditioning which leaves
no room for normative criteria of rational theory-choice and an account of
reference-fixing which, on the contrary, rebuts any such charge since it explains
how rival theories can pick out the same kinds of object – and describe or
explain them more or less adequately – despite large divergences of paradigm,
theory, or 'conceptual scheme'. Putnam is very good at making this point
through a range of shrewdly chosen examples where acceptance of Quine's ideas
about 'ontological relativity' or Kuhn's doctrine of 'incommensurable' paradigms must lead to an outlook of extreme scepticism with regard to the very
possibility of scientific knowledge, progress, or truth. Such is indeed the
inevitable upshot if we don't take it that scientists were basically talking about
'the same thing' when they advanced from describing *gold* as a 'yellow, malleable
metal that dissolves in weak nitric acid' to defining it as 'metallic element with
atomic number 79'; or from thinking of *water* as 'liquid stuff that falls as rain,
fills up lakes, boils and freezes at certain temperatures, quenches thirst, has
useful cleansing properties', and so forth, to assigning it the molecular structure
H_2O; or again, from identifying *acids* by their sour taste in dilute form to
picking them out by their property of turning litmus paper red, and then –
through a further advance in knowledge – defining 'acid' as 'proton-donor'.[45]
The crucial point here is that reference is fixed by just that property or structure
that intrinsically distinguishes, say, genuine *gold* from a look-alike substance
such as 'fool's gold' (iron pyrites), or genuine *water* from its Twin-Earth substitute with molecular constitution XYZ. For if we take the alternative,
descriptivist view that 'sense determines reference' – i.e., that whatever we refer
to *just is* anything that satisfies our present-best range of identifying features or
attributes – then it is hard to place limits on the scope for Quinean ontological
relativity or to draw the line short of wholesale Kuhnian paradigm-relativism.

There is no room here for a full-scale account of the various detailed arguments that early Putnam brings up in support of his causal-realist approach.

Sufficient to say that it explains (1) how reference may be at least partially conserved across episodes of even quite radical theory-change; (2) how early usages of terms such as 'gold', 'water', or 'acid' can be thought of as truth-tracking or 'sensitive to future discovery'; (3) why scientific knowledge therefore manifests a pattern of intelligible progress despite what thinkers like Kuhn would see as its sharply discontinuous, paradigm-relative, and hence non-cumulative history to date; and (4) why the causal-externalist account of reference fixing – Putnam's claim that meanings 'just ain't in the head' – is the only one that makes adequate sense in scientific as well as in logico-semantic or modal terms.[46] The point about modality has to do with the Kripke/Putnam case that assertions such as 'water = H$_2$0' or 'gold = metallic element with atomic number 79' are examples of *a posteriori* necessary truth, that is to say, statements whose truth-value holds necessarily in our own and in all worlds compatible with ours in the relevant (physical) respect while clearly in no sense a priori since they must have been found out by some empirical means. However the fact that reference is 'fixed' in this way – sometimes by a range of kind-specific microstructural (e.g., subatomic, molecular, or chromosomal) features that may as yet be unknown – entails absolutely no restriction either on the everyday usage of 'gold' or 'water' as genuine referring expressions or (still less) on our cognitive powers of discovering such features through a process of further investigation. On the contrary: it is a chief virtue of the causal theory of reference that it allows for relative stability of sense across episodes of theory change – even in the case of such contested terms as 'mass', 'element', 'atom', 'electron', or 'gene' – while making full room for those normative values (of rationality, empirical warrant, falsifiability, theoretical scope, explanatory power, and so forth) that are conspicuously lacking in Quine's radical-empiricist or Kuhn's paradigm-relativist accounts.

Thus, *pace* Chomsky, there is nothing in the causal theory that would lay it open to the charge of ignoring, discounting, or drastically under-rating the capacity of human enquirers to exercise their powers of jointly creative and critical-reflective thought in forming and testing rational conjectures with regard to the nature and structure of physical reality. Rather (I would suggest) it is the one approach that does justice to our best intuitions concerning the objective (verification-transcendent) status of scientific truths, the possibility of progress (but also of error or uneven development) in our knowledge of them, and also the fact that we can offer a rational, i.e., non-miraculist account of how such knowledge accrues.[47] Nothing could be further from the kind of reductively physicalist theory of belief-acquisition that does service for 'epistemology' in Quine's treatment of these issues. Indeed it is just this lack of adequately specified normative or justificatory criteria that impels Quine to adopt what might seem the very opposite kind of position, that is, the holistic (scheme-relativist) approach according to which physical objects are merely so many 'posits' imported into this or that ontological scheme so as to make some provisional sense of incoming stimuli or sensory data. What links these two otherwise disparate theses – radical empiricism and radical holism – is, ironically enough, just the same problem that Quine so acutely diagnosed in the discourse of Carnap and other thinkers who inherited the old Humean/Kantian dichotomy between 'truths of reason' and 'matters of fact'.[48] To be sure, Quine is sceptical – famously so – as concerns the possibility of fixing that distinction on valid, substantive, or non-circular grounds. However there is still a conspicuous gap, in normative terms, between Quine's starkly behaviourist account of belief-acquisition and his holistic view of theory-change as a process whose sole criterion of 'rational' warrant is the appeal to what best fits (i.e., what involves least conflict) with our existing framework of belief. This shows the extent to which post-empiricist – more precisely: post-logical-empiricist – approaches have inherited the same kinds of dilemma that characterized previous attempts to cut epistemology down to size, or to treat it as a sub-branch of the natural sciences with no proper warrant to adjudicate in such matters. Or again: it brings out the strange ambivalence that typifies claims (whether by Quine or the logical positivists) to espouse a Lockean 'under-labourer' role *vis-à-vis* physical science while nonetheless staking their own authority on just this special kinship with a method conceived as having no need of such merely 'philosophical' support.

Hence, as I have said, the peculiar Quinean mixture of extreme modesty as regards the normative or rational-evaluative content of his project with an attitude of high 'scientific' disdain for any approach to epistemological issues that would claim something more in the way of adjudicative warrant. For it is precisely this double manoeuvre – putting philosophy very much in its place as compared with the natural sciences but also, by the same token, asserting its own scientific credentials – that creates all the problems with Quinean naturalized epistemology. Chief among them, to repeat, is the normativity deficit which cannot but result from an outlook of radical empiricism coupled with an equally radical conception of meaning-holism. Hence his idea of empirical statements (along with 'laws of nature' and the axioms of classical logic) as always potentially revisable should this seem the best, most conservative, or least disruptive way of maintaining coherence across the entire fabric of beliefs currently held true. In which case it can hardly be said that Quine's arguments have been misunderstood or put to wrong use by those – such as Kuhn, Rorty, and a whole assortment of cultural relativists, linguistic constructivists, and 'strong' sociologists of knowledge – who take him to have shown beyond doubt that realism is simply not a live option in epistemology and philosophy of language.[49] Rather they are drawing the valid implication from a set of claims which, if jointly true, would indeed put an end to the prospect of explaining how we could ever acquire knowledge of an objective, mind-independent reality that wasn't just a construct of our various languages, conceptual schemes, Kuhnian paradigms, and so on. Still one can legitimately turn the question around and ask – as the realist surely will – whether a theory that goes so clean against the evidence of scientific progress to date (thus effectively denying our knowledge of the growth of knowledge) must have left the rails at some point. All the more so when, as in Quine's case, that theory also raises large problems for the idea of translatability between natural languages, or – as with Kuhn – for the claim that we can mostly compare and contrast rival scientific hypotheses in point of their empirical adequacy, predictive power, or rational and causal-explanatory warrant. For there is good reason (scientific as well as philosophical) to conclude that such a theory is demonstrably on the wrong track and is thus better treated as a salutary instance of *reductio ad absurdum* rather than a genuine, credible challenge to our well-tried methods of scientific discovery or knowledge-acquisition.

That is to say, Quine's problem is just that – a problem induced by his own, highly distinctive (not to say idiosyncratic) approach to these issues – and not one that should be seen as posing such a strictly unavoidable challenge. Nor is the problem convincingly resolved by those, like Donald Davidson, who detect a residual third 'dogma' of empiricism in Quine's embrace of the scheme/content dualism, and who therefore urge that we abandon such talk along with its unwelcome consequences, such as ontological relativity and the problem about translating between different schemes, languages, or conceptual frameworks.[50] The trouble with any attempted solution along Davidsonian lines is that it comes down to yet another version, albeit more carefully disguised, of the same old dualism that afflicted in Quine's (on the face of it) radically monistic approach. Thus Davidson's attack on the idea of 'conceptual schemes' again yokes an outlook of downright 'commonsense' empiricism – whence his talk of 're-establish[ing] unmediated touch with the familiar objects whose antics make our sentences and opinions true or false' – to a generalized (Tarskian) theory of truth, meaning and interpretation coupled with a wholesale 'principle of charity' that imputes rationality and truth pretty much across the board.[51] From this point of view, '[i]f we can produce a theory that reconciles charity and the formal conditions for a theory, we have done all that could be done to ensure communication'.[52] And again, '[g]iven the underlying methodology of interpretation, we could not be in a position to judge that others had concepts or beliefs radically different from our own'.[53]

Thus it follows, according to Davidson, not only that we can (*contra* Quine, Kuhn, Whorf and company) have reasonable confidence in our ability to translate across different languages, paradigms, or 'conceptual schemes' but also that other people (like ourselves) must be 'right in most matters' since we and they could otherwise have no such background of shared understanding. For given that truth (or the attitude of holding-true) is basic to all interpretation of meanings and beliefs, and given moreover that we cannot make a start in that process without presupposing a large measure of convergence on truth across various cultures, languages, and individual speakers, therefore it is nonsensical to think that different 'conceptual schemes' might carve things up in such drastically different ways as to render translation or comparison between them strictly impossible. However it is a big and very questionable jump from Davidson's strong point about the conditions of possibility for linguistic understanding to his notion that this leaves us no choice – if we want to understand others – but to count them 'right in most matters'. For this is to conflate the two distinct claims, (1) that getting a handle on their meanings and beliefs requires that we possess and also assume them to possess the basic attitude of holding-true, and (2) that their various holdings-true, like ours, must moreover be largely justified, warranted, or borne out by the way things stand with the world since we should otherwise be pretty much back to square one as regards mutual comprehension. The first claim is highly persuasive and is further backed up by Davidson's point that conceptual-scheme relativists often go wrong by over-stressing the semantic aspects of language – i.e., the fact that different speech-communities have different vocabulary ranges or lexical resources – and under-stressing those logico-syntactic components (quantifiers, connectives, devices for conjunction, disjunction, negation, and so forth) which any language must possess in order to function as an adequate means of communication. But the second claim is apt to look a lot less convincing if one reflects that many people – including entire cultural and indeed scientific communities – have very often been wrong about various deeply held convictions in the past and no doubt still are with regard to some likewise well-entrenched items of belief.

This is where Davidson's theory falls down, that is, in its claim that we should *always* seek to maximize the imputed truth-content of utterances, statements, observations, theories, hypotheses, and so forth on the assumption that we couldn't even start to make sense of what their advocates had in mind except by thus enlarging the range of communal beliefs-held-true. For this is to reverse the natural order of epistemological and linguistic priorities, or – in a typically Davidsonian phrase – to 'get the matter backwards'. It is also where the Kripke/ early Putnam theory of truth, meaning and reference can be seen to provide a more adequate account *both* of how knowledge is conserved and advanced across episodes of even 'revolutionary' theory-change *and* of how successive theories can be truth-tracking – along with their constituent referring terms – despite such periodic upheavals. There is now quite a sizeable literature in history and philosophy of science, as well as philosophical semantics, that has set out to describe particular, well-documented cases of this process at work.[54] Among them are some striking instances – such as the atomist hypothesis or conceptions of mass from Newton to Einstein – where a certain range of theoretical beliefs and associated object-terms can be shown to have undergone decisive transformations of content and yet to have maintained a certain continuity of reference throughout their history to date. Thus Hartry Field makes a strong case that if one takes the three nowadays well-defined operative senses of 'mass' – rest-mass, inertial mass, and relativistic mass – then one can specify the stages through which that concept has evolved without any need for Kuhnian talk of radical incommensurability.[55] So likewise with 'atom' from its ancient Greek speculative origins to the latest theories of subatomic structure, and even with a term like 'electron' that was first introduced in order to denominate whatever it was that produced a certain remote luminescent effect, and thereafter underwent a whole series of often quite drastic redefinitions. In such cases, so the causal theory goes, there is an initial act of reference-fixing (an 'inaugural baptism', in

Kripke's colourful phrase) which ensures a sufficient degree of continuity over subsequent applications of the term, no matter how remote from what its first users had in mind.

Putnam, as we have seen, fills out the picture through a range of examples, ingenious thought-experiments, and counterfactual scenarios designed to support his claim that semantic externalism of this kind – as opposed to the erstwhile dominant descriptivist-internalist account – is the only approach that can resolve those problems thrown up by the doctrines of Quinean ontological relativity and Kuhnian paradigm-relativism. His argument is strengthened – rendered more plausible – by Putnam's idea of the 'linguistic division of labour', that is, his allowance that non-experts can successfully refer to *gold* or *water* without the least knowledge of their subatomic structure or molecular constitution just so long as there are experts around who could, if required, pick out genuine from look-alike samples of the kind.[56] Or again, in his own case, the professed inability to distinguish beeches from elms doesn't mean that any allusion to either sort of tree on Putnam's part must be either mistaken, hopelessly vague, or referentially void.[57] What saves the situation for these non-expert types is the communal sharing of knowledge whereby cognoscenti of various ilk – physicists, chemists, biologists, or arborologists – stand more directly in the causal line of epistemo-linguistic transmission and are always on hand to deliver a verdict in borderline or disputed cases. These latter may range all the way from straightforward instances of classificatory correction (as when children or ill-informed adults discover that whales are mammals, not fish) to more specialist disputes where the expert is called in to decide, say, whether a piece of the semi-precious stone jade – adequately so described for most purposes – belongs to one or other of the two distinct natural kinds *nephrite* or *jadeite*. Thus the Kripke/Putnam causal theory of reference has the signal advantage (as against its descriptivist rival) of explaining both how knowledge accrues through progressively more adequate, e.g., microstructural or depth-explanatory theories and why such advances can be thought of as a matter of communal know-how even if relatively few people have access to the relevant special expertise. Also, as I have said, it gets over the problem – one that lies in wait for descriptivist theories when pushed to their ultimate conclusion – of just what should *count* as an advance in knowledge if scientific theories and their object-terms are construed as radically paradigm-relative and hence as strictly incommensurable one with another.

No doubt there are issues to be raised concerning various aspects and possible shortcomings of the causal theory. Thus some would argue that it fails to account for the manifold ways in which the reference of terms can be modified, extended, refined, or – on occasion – radically transformed through the impact of contingent historical or socio-cultural factors which provide little purchase for that theory (at least in its pure-bred form) since they create so large and disruptive a kink in the postulated 'chain' of transmission. In such cases there looks to be a crucial role for some alternative approach that takes due stock of the extent to which the reference of object-terms is indeed dependent on the range of descriptive criteria or identifying attributes that enable us to pick out this or that candidate item according to our best current knowledge.[58] What seems fairly clear – after much discussion – is the need to devise a hybrid theory which combines the best features of the 'old' descriptivist account with those elements of the Kripke-Putnam approach that offer a solution to the chief problems with that account. Chief among them are its inability to explain our knowledge of the growth of scientific knowledge and the ease with which it slides into a wholesale paradigm-relativist view devoid of substantive rational or causal-explanatory content. However the desired outcome is not to be had from any theory (such as Davidson's) that goes some way toward exposing the aporias and self-refuting arguments of Quinean-Kuhnian talk about 'conceptual schemes' but which stops well short of embracing a causal-realist position.

IV

Davidson famously makes this point on grounds of the performative self-contradiction that scheme-relativists run into when attempting (impossibly, on their own terms) to describe how far and in just what respects the various schemes must be thought to differ. Thus:

> Whorf, wanting to demonstrate that Hopi incorporates a metaphysics so alien to ours that Hopi and English cannot, as he puts it, 'be calibrated', uses English to convey the contents of sample Hopi sentences. Kuhn is brilliant at saying what things were like before the revolution using – what else? – our post-revolutionary idiom. Quine gives us a feel for the 'pre-individuative phase in the evolution of our conceptual scheme', while Bergson tells us where to go to get a view of a mountain undistorted by one or another provincial perspective.[59]

So far as it goes – that is to say, within the limits of an argument based on logico-linguistic and broadly pragmatic considerations – this makes a strong case against the 'very idea' of a conceptual scheme, along with its kindred cultural-relativist or linguistic-constructivist claims. On the other hand it doesn't go anything like far enough if one wants to adopt a realist stance according to which the truth-condition for any given conjecture, prediction, hypothesis, or well-formed (truth-apt) statement is that it satisfy the basic requirement of corresponding precisely to the way things stand with regard to this or that objective, real-world state of affairs. Anti-realism in its currently most influential form works on just the opposite set of premises. These are (1) that 'objectivity' in this sense is by very definition beyond our utmost powers of cognitive or epistemic grasp; (2) that truth therefore cannot exceed our best capacities of proof, ascertainment, or verification; and (3) that we had thus better leave off talking of truth, objectively or realistically conceived, and plump for the more workable conception of assertoric warrant or 'truth' as epistemically constrained, i.e., as coterminous with the scope and limits of human investigative thought.

This argument has been pushed furthest by those, like Michael Dummett, who make out a case on logico-semantic and ultimately metaphysical grounds that statements of the so-called 'disputed class' (those whose truth-value we cannot decide by any means at our disposal) must be thought of as simply not belonging to the class of candidates for truth or falsehood.[60] Thus unproven (maybe unprovable) mathematical statements such as 'Goldbach's Conjecture is true' or empirically unverifiable claims such as 'there exists a duplicate solar system in some remote, radio-telescopically invisible region of the expanding universe' must be treated as neither true nor false, rather than as having some objective truth-value that pertains to them despite our inability to find it out.[61] However it is also close kin to the idea espoused by 'constructive empiricists' like Bas van Fraassen that empirical adequacy, rather than truth, is what science should properly aim at since to assert anything more – such as the truth, realistically construed, of statements concerning recondite items like atoms, electrons, or remote astrophysical bodies – is to stray beyond the bounds of plain observational warrant and hence yield unnecessary hostages to sceptical fortune.[62] That is to say, we are better off rejecting realism with respect to such putative objects and treating them rather as useful, instrumentally convenient posits which earn their keep simply by virtue of figuring importantly in our present-best (so far unfalsified) scientific theories.

Van Fraassen sometimes pushes this doctrine pretty hard, as for instance by arguing that whatever we can see through some fairly basic piece of observational technology (e.g., an optical microscope or telescope) counts as sufficiently 'real' for constructive-empiricist purposes, whereas whatever requires the use of advanced equipment such as an electron-microscope or radio telescope must be counted an artefact of technologically enhanced observation and hence inadmissible on just those stipulative terms. However this involves him in some wiredrawn (not to say absurd) passages of argument. Thus, for instance, it follows that a claim to have truly perceived the moons of some remote planet by an astronaut close up enough to see them through a low-resolution optical telescope is epistemically more reliable than the finding of earthbound astronomers equipped with the latest, most highly sophisticated observational technology. Or again, we are better placed as regards any issue concerning the existence (or reality) of objects on whatever physical scale by deploying optical devices, no matter how primitive, that involve only a stepwise increment to our basic, unaided perceptual powers rather than high-tech devices which interpose all manner of complex instrumentation between us human observers and the various entities concerned. So in the case of objects too tiny, remote, fast-moving, short-lived, or otherwise elusive to show up without the use of advanced electronic equipment we had best take the sensible constructive-empiricist line and remain studiously non-committal as regards their objective reality. Moreover, this means that such talk of relatively 'primitive' or 'advanced' prosthetic devices is talk that must be thought to beg the whole question as to just what we see – whether an object or an artefact of observation – when we look through an electron microscope or radio-telescope.

Thus it follows that we are metaphysically out on a limb if we assume that things have moved on since the time of Galileo or Robert Hooke and that we are now on firm epistemological ground in asserting the objective truth (as opposed to the merely instrumental utility) of statements concerning such items as electrons, atoms, molecules, chromosomes, or remote astrophysical bodies. Much wiser to avoid these excess ontological commitments and not go in for what van Fraassen scornfully describes as the realist's false display of courage in such matters. For if reality *just is* the sum-total of our evidence for it when construed in terms of empirical adequacy, rather than objective truth, then the realist stands neither to gain nor to lose anything worth having by taking this merely notional extra risk. After all, 'it is not an epistemological principle that one might as well hang for a sheep as for a lamb'. And again:

> [i]f I believe a theory to be true and not just empirically adequate, my risk of being shown wrong is exactly the risk that the weaker, entailed belief will conflict with actual experience. Meanwhile, by avowing the stronger belief, I place myself in the position of being able to answer more questions, of having a richer, fuller picture of the world ... But, since the extra opinion is not additionally vulnerable, the risk is – in human terms – illusory, and *therefore so is the wealth*. It is but empty strutting and posturing, this display of courage not under fire and avowal of additional resources that cannot feel the pinch of misfortune any earlier.[63]

This is why constructive empiricism requires 'a resolute rejection of the demand for an explanation of the regularities in the observable course of nature, by means of truths concerning a reality beyond what is actual and observable, as a demand which plays no role in the scientific enterprise'.[64] Causal realism might look good by comparison with empiricism or instrumentalism in so far as one endorses this deluded idea that there is something over and above the warrant of straightforward empirical evidence that decides the truth-value of our statements, predictions, or explanatory hypotheses quite apart from that evidence itself. Yet if one takes a sceptical view of such claims then it will look much more like a faith position with little to commend it bar a vague and wholly unjustified sense of taking additional risks for greater rewards.

Van Fraassen's is basically a refined update on the Mach-inspired positivist doctrine that we are entitled to carry on talking about atoms and suchlike invisible entities in so far as they play a useful role in our various scientific theories and just so long as we don't take the further (ontologically extravagant) step of assuming their existence as a matter of objective, knowledge-independent truth. What this rules out – in the name of parsimony, commonsense, and philosophic hygiene – is any version of the argument from inference to the best causal and rational explanation that would justify realism with respect to those entities precisely on the grounds of their playing that not merely useful but *strictly indispensable* role. Besides, there is something odd about a theory that reduces truth to the limits of perceptual or empirical verifiability, and this in turn to the scope of unaided (or minimally enhanced) human observation. Hence the objection of some critics – Paul Churchland among them – that van Fraassen's is a protagorean doctrine which, if consistently applied, would indeed make 'man the measure' and thus turn its back on all those advances in scientific knowledge that have come about precisely by discounting or rejecting the plain self-evidence of the senses.[65] (Churchland makes the point rather nicely by imagining an 'arboreally rooted' philosopher, one Douglas van Firssen, whose notion of reality encompasses nothing beyond his drastically limited purview.) Besides, there is a strong case to be made that we understand enough about the working principles, design, and construction of various present-day advanced observational technologies to more than offset what van Fraassen regards as their inherently complex and hence perceptually unreliable character. For there seems little virtue in an argument that would attach more weight to the result of observations conducted through Galileo's telescope and interpreted according to the then current state of optical theory than to results achieved with modern instruments, however complex, whose design incorporates just the sorts of knowledge that enable us the better to allow for any possible distortions, artefacts, interference-effects, and so forth.

Moreover it is hard to maintain any version of empiricism, 'constructive' or otherwise, which ignores the sheer amount of cognitive processing involved in even the simplest, most basic forms of perceptual experience. Such, after all, is the chief lesson of just every research-programme in cognitive psychology and neuro-science over the past two decades and more.[66] On the one hand these findings might be taken to support the Quinean-Kuhnian idea that observations are always, inextricably theory-laden and theories always under-determined by the best empirical evidence. On the other – and I think more plausibly – they may be taken to support just the opposite conclusion. Such is the realist and causal-explanatory claim that scientific progress most often comes about through a complex interplay of empirical observation and theory which can itself be tracked through a careful application of historico-philosophical analysis and which therefore involves no such premature (scepticism-inducing) conflation of realms. That is to say, it still leaves ample room for explaining the advancement of knowledge in terms that allow for the theory-laden character of even the most basic observation-statements but which nonetheless account for that advance-ment precisely by adducing the cumulative nature of the various changes thus brought about in our state of theoretical-informed observation. Thus, for instance, it is wrong to conclude – like Kuhn on the basis of Quinean radical empiricism plus wholesale ontological relativity – that there is ultimately no distinguishing in point of rational warrant between Galileo versus Aristotle on swinging stones, or Lavoisier versus Priestley on the process of combustion, or Darwin versus the advocates of preformationism on the nature and development of species.[67] What counts most decisively in favour of the latter and against the former hypothesis in each case is its greater extent of empirical warrant and also its far superior degree of theoretical and causal-explanatory power. Theory-ladenness is no more a threat to our knowledge of the growth of scientific knowledge than the fact of our dependence, when advancing such claims, on ever more complex and sophisticated forms of technologically enhanced observation. In both cases we have good warrant for supposing such knowledge to be adequately grounded, whether by appeal to our existing stock of empirical evidence and developed theoretical understanding or – closely allied to that – through the range of accumulated scientific know-how embodied in those various technologies.

At any rate there is no need to go along with the Quine-Kuhn thesis in its full-fledged version, i.e., the radically holistic and paradigm-relativist claim that observations are always theory-laden and theories always underdetermined by the best empirical evidence. For this is to ignore the fairly obvious point that *some* very basic observations – those that are not subject to dispute between rival hypotheses or paradigms – can be counted theory-neutral for all practical scientific purposes, while *some* basic theoretical commitments hold firm across a range of otherwise divergent or conflicting claims with regard to that evidence. Of course there is no reverting to the old Baconian-inductivist idea of the quest for scientific knowledge as a patient but largely random accumulation of raw, theoretically untainted empirical data which somehow produce a whole range of valid hypotheses, laws and predictions. On the other hand it is just as wrong – and equally at odds with the record of scientific progress to date – if philosophers swing to the opposite reactive extreme and take for granted (after Quine) the absolute impossibility of distinguishing the empirical from the theoretical content of any given hypothesis. For this argument quickly leads, via Kuhn, to those varieties of thoroughgoing cultural-relativist or social-constructivist approach that likewise trade on the under-determination and theory-ladenness doctrines in order to controvert the very notions of scientific reason, objectivity, or truth. Hence the frequent setting up of a straw-man 'positivist' opponent who is supposed to believe, like Bacon, that the advancement of knowledge requires nothing more than a passive gathering of facts or empirical data which can simply be relied upon to speak for themselves once laid out in perspicuous fashion. Actually this does nothing like justice to Bacon's account of inductive method, let alone to the work of those logical positivists or empiricists (like Carnap) whose attempt to uphold some version of the observation/theory dualism – along with that between empirical 'matters of fact' and logical 'truths of reason' – was the chief target of Quine's 'Two Dogmas' and a good many subsequent critiques.[68] Still, as I have said, there is a sense in which those thinkers laid themselves open to attack in so far as they followed Hume in adopting a sceptical or studiously nescient attitude with regard to any kind of realist epistemology that went beyond the empirical evidence or purported to account for that evidence in causal or depth-explanatory terms. This left them no adequate line of defence when confronted with the charge – pressed to such powerful effect by Quine – that their programme ran aground on the failure to justify its own most basic premise, namely the existence of a sharp, substantive, and non-circular distinction between the empirical content and the logical structure of scientific theories. For if one thing is clear from the history of debate on this topic from Hume to Quine it is the fact that scepticism will always win out, on its own favoured terms of engagement, so long as the issue is framed in such a way as to exclude or disallow any ultimate appeal to causal explanation as the grounding rationale of a realist ontology and epistemology.

Moreover, I would suggest, the prospects are not much better for responses to Quine, Kuhn, *et al.* which seek to maintain the priority of truth (or the attitude of holding-true) as a counter to paradigm-relativist talk of variant conceptual schemes, but which still go along with the linguistic turn at least to the extent of supposing that such issues can only be resolved in logico-semantic terms. This is Davidson's ruling idea throughout his entire body of work on truth, meaning and interpretation, despite his occasional guarded hints – most often under pressure from critics of a realist bent – that the Tarskian formal theory of truth requires a more substantive specification if it is not to invite charges of redundancy or vacuously circular definition.[69] Like Tarski, he is at times strongly drawn to endorsing some version of the correspondence-theory in order to make up this deficit, yet prone to espouse a safer (less 'metaphysically' committed) position when confronted with the various well-known objections to that theory mounted by Quine, Putnam, Rorty, and others.[70] Thus Davidson opts for a coherence theory of truth but one that supposedly avoids any wholesale scheme-relativist outcome by building in a truth-based theory of meaning, belief, and communicative uptake.[71] This latter provides sufficient guarantee, so he claims, that, as language-users, we just *can't* be subject to 'total failure' or even (more remarkably) to 'partial failure' of mutual comprehension between different languages, cultures, paradigms, conceptual schemes, or whatever. Thus, to repeat: '[g]iven the underlying methodology of interpretation, we could not be in a position to judge that other people had concepts or beliefs radically different from our own' (Davidson, p. 197). However the fact (if such it is) of our being 'in no position to judge' whether we and other people are on different doxastic, linguistic, conceptual, or communicative wavelengths can scarcely be taken as offering support for a truth-based theory of interpretation unless one interprets 'truth' itself – as Davidson would surely be loath to admit – along Rortian-pragmatist lines, i.e., as what is currently and contingently 'good in the way of belief'.

This is how Rorty takes Davidson's point that if we can't make sense of their utterances in a way that that brings them out 'true' (or at any rate rationally motivated) according to those same, i.e., *our* accredited standards then they are just not candidates for interpretation on any (to us) comprehensible or rationally explicable terms.[72] However it ignores a very basic feature of all human communication, namely our ability to interpret what other people mean, intend, or believe *even though* we may sometimes consider their beliefs either false, misguided, or downright irrational. In which case the principle of charity works out as something more complex and nuanced than a matter of always imputing maximal truth-content to whatever they say or whatever we 'charitably' take them to mean. Rather it functions as a general directive to make full allowance for the variety of ways in which beliefs may be either truth-tracking or subject to certain aberrations that we can best understand through an effort to see all around those various predicaments – of partial information, restricted epistemic access, fixed preconceptions, ideological bias, and so forth – whereby such erroneous beliefs become rationally or causally explicable. No doubt this involves sometimes counting them wrong and ourselves in the right with regard to both particular, small-scale, or localized differences of opinion or matters of a more fundamental character involving (say) a clash of scientific worldviews or a deep-laid disagreement over questions of historical fact. Still if one takes a truth-based and to that extent a realist view of these matters – as Davidson most often does – then logically there is no choice but to admit that, in such cases, the condition of one party's having got things right is that the other has got things wrong. Otherwise there is no stopping the slide to some version of the anti-realist argument according to which that condition, i.e. the logical axiom of bivalent truth/falsehood, extends no further than the range of statements for which we possess some means of proof or verification.

Davidson is generally keen to avoid this Dummettian way of posing the issue in metaphysical and logico-semantic terms, that is to say, as a question of whether or not we can conceive the existence of objective truth-values for statements of the disputed (unprovable or unverifiable) class.[73] Though concurring with Dummett that such questions are best framed in a linguistic mode he sees the main benefit of this approach as a matter of its clarifying issues in epistemology – what we can reasonably claim to know concerning (e.g.) the well-foundedness of our own and other people's beliefs – rather than its raising the issue of truth as objectively determined or epistemically constrained. Still the success of Davidson's theory must be seen to rest on its capacity to find room for objective (recognition-transcendent) truth-values and also, crucially, on its managing to combine that standpoint with a due allowance for the various rationally explicable ways in which belief can fall short of epistemically warranted knowledge and present-best knowledge fall short of objective truth. This applies not only in the specialized contexts of epistemology and philosophy of science but also in matters of everyday linguistic understanding or communicative grasp where the truth-maximizing principle of charity needs to go along with a due allowance for the kinds and degrees of intelligibly motivated error. Thus we shall do much better *by them and ourselves* if we recognize the limits on truth-maximization and instead seek to explain what we take as erroneous beliefs on a principle that counts them not so much 'right in most matters' but as rationally justified within the limits of their own knowledge, understanding, or access to the relevant information sources.

This argument often runs up against objections in so far as it invites us to treat other people's beliefs (where they differ from ours) as resulting from certain causal factors – factors external to the 'space of reasons' – and hence deny them any claim to genuine autonomy as thinking and judging agents.[74] It is a similar worry, as we have seen, that motivates Chomsky's outright rejection of externalist theories of reference-fixing such as that advanced by Kripke and early Putnam. However there is an equal and opposite risk of pressing too hard on this distinction between *reasons for* and *causes of* belief. That is, we can end up by holding people directly at fault for imputed failures – whether of reasoning on the evidence or acting on the basis of received moral and social values – which could better (more charitably) be put down to the intervention of just such causal or externally operative factors. Thus proponents of an ethical, social, or legal philosophy based on the belief in absolute freedom of autonomous moral will are as likely to hail from the conservative or right-wing authoritarian quarter (since offenders or misfits can then be held fully to account) as from a 'left' libertarian standpoint, like Chomsky's, devoted to defending the unfettered exercise of individual conscience. On the other hand those who make the case for some more or less qualified determinist outlook can justifiably claim that it accords far better with the principles of justice and enlightened social policy.[75] From their point of view this allows for the manifold ways in which persons qua moral agents may be thought not to enjoy such a measure of free (hence potentially culpable or blameworthy) choice owing to the various causal factors that might be entered as legal pleas under the headings of 'diminished responsibility' or 'mitigating circumstances'.

V

Clearly these are complex issues in moral philosophy as likewise in other current fields of interest – such as virtue-based epistemology – where questions of belief, knowledge and truth are conceived as involving certain ethical standards of well-conducted, responsible enquiry.[76] At any rate there seems good reason to think that a doctrine of unqualified doxastic voluntarism fails to take adequate stock of those causal factors, even though, just as plainly, a doctrine of unqualified determinism fails to explain how we could ever be justified in holding people to account for their morally repugnant actions or beliefs. Also it is worth noting that the distinction between reasons and causes is one that has been applied with particular emphasis by Wittgensteinian philosophers of action who derive from it the lesson that we always go wrong – merely demonstrate our own false claims to superior wisdom – when we presume to explain the beliefs of other (e.g., 'primitive') cultures in terms of their causal aetiology rather than the kinds of justification that the believers would produce if asked.[77] This position no doubt has the face-value appeal of a tolerant, pluralist, liberal-minded attitude which acknowledges the variety of human belief-systems and thus serves as a hedge against dogmatisms of whatever kind, not to mention the more doctrinaire versions of 'enlightened' progressivist thought. However, as critics have pointed out, it also has the marked disadvantage of opening the way to an outlook of extreme cognitive and cultural relativism that leaves us utterly bereft of arguments for rejecting any kind of irrational creed or condemning any instance of (to us) morally repugnant behaviour which nonetheless has its recognized place in some other value-system or cultural life-form.[78] So this principled veto on causal explanation when it comes to assessing the rationality of beliefs or the moral rightness of actions is one that ironically turns out to undermine any standards of rational or ethical accountability. Besides, it can easily be seen to rebound against the intentions of those who propose it, at least in so far as they seek to redress the asymmetrical relation between those whose beliefs are being explained in such reductive terms and those who purport to do the explaining. For if indeed one takes the view (following Wittgenstein) that what counts as 'rational or 'right' is a matter of conformity with this or that language-game or 'form of life' then we can have no choice – from our own cultural vantage-point – but to count other people wrong in so far as their doxastic commitments or principles of action fail to comply with our own. However this argument clearly backfires since it deprives both them and us of the jointly reason-ascribing and causal-explanatory resources that enable human beings to communicate across otherwise large divergences of language, culture and belief.

To be sure, Davidson comes close to acknowledging this point when he says that the 'guiding policy' in such matters is to optimize the truth-content of their utterances on the standard principle of charity, but always 'subject to considerations of simplicity, hunches about the effects of social conditioning, and of course our common-sense or scientific knowledge of explicable error' (Davidson, p. 196). In which case there would be plenty of room, after all, for what otherwise seems to drop out on Davidson's account, that is, for the fact that – in history and philosophy of science as well as in contexts of everyday communication – we are constantly making allowance for such 'explicable error' and doing so, moreover, in ways that involve some large-scale (even 'radical') differences of view on just the matters principally at issue. But we shall then have to reject, downplay, or drastically reinterpret various passages of Davidson's essay that would seem, on the face of it, scarcely to support such a reading. Among them is his central and much-quoted assertion that '[c]harity is forced on us', since 'whether we like it or not, if we want to understand others, we must count them right in most matters' (p. 197). And again (to repeat): '[i]f we can produce a theory that reconciles charity and the formal conditions for a theory, we have done all that could be done to secure communication' (ibid.). Yet the main problems with Davidson's account can be seen to arise from just this combination of across-the-board, truth-maximizing 'charity' with a formal (Tarskian) truth-theoretic approach that lacks any definite, substantive content when applied to issues of natural-language understanding, or indeed to issues in epistemology and philosophy of science.

What is missing here, as likewise in Quine's case and in the case of those logical-empiricist theories that Quine set out to demolish, is any adequate means to explain just how we come by the kinds of improved knowledge or communicative uptake that can and do occur whatever doubts may be raised by sceptically inclined philosophers or even by those, like Davidson, who think them out of place but who argue in terms set by that same sceptical agenda. As I have said this involves a twofold deficit, firstly with regard to those normative values (of truth, rationality, explanatory power, and so forth) which provide an indispensable basis for the interpretation and evaluation of beliefs, and secondly as concerns that causal component that enters the process of belief-formation at every stage. Thus the rational allowance for such causal factors extends all the way from our own history of firsthand dealings with the physical world to our acquired knowledge of scientific laws and – crucially for matters of linguistic understanding – our grasp of how such dealings have affected the beliefs of others. In the latter case we may judge them to operate in ways that are reliably truth-conducive or (on occasion) in ways that are prone to produce certain kinds of erroneous, e.g., perceptually distorted or conceptually mistaken belief. To be sure, Davidson's truth-based, logico-semantic theory represents an improvement on Quine's radical-empiricist approach. That is to say, it offers a degree of rational assurance that we are not, after all, stuck with the notion of wholesale ontological relativity, or condemned to the hopeless situation of a 'radical translator' required to interpret the sentences of native informants with whom she has nothing in common – no linguistic or conceptual resources – bar a certain momentarily occurrent range of incoming sensory stimuli.[79] All the same Davidson's alternative account can be seen to swing back and forth between a formalized (Tarskian) truth-theoretic approach devoid of substantive empirical content and a radical-empiricist doctrine which effectively sides with Quine in treating epistemology as just another sub-branch of natural science or behavioural psychology.

Hence his famous concluding dictum that '[i]n giving up the dualism of scheme and world, we do not give up the world, but re-establish unmediated touch with the familiar objects whose antics make our sentences and opinions true or false' (Davidson, p. 198). Or again, to similar deflationary effect as regards any normative conception of epistemology:

> {t}hat experience takes a certain course, *that* our skin is warm or punc-tured, *that* the universe is finite, these facts, if we like to talk that way, make sentences and theories true. But the point is put better without mention of facts. The sentence 'My skin is warm' is true if and only if my skin is warm. Here there is no reference to a fact, a world, an experience, or a piece of evidence. (p. 194)

Here as so often with Davidson one gets the impression that he has simply lost interest in philosophy, or at least in the sorts of philosophical issue – the 'problem of knowledge' as debated by thinkers from Descartes, Hume and Kant to the logical empiricists, Quine, Sellars and beyond – which after all constitute the chief focus and motivating interest of his own work. What this passage amounts to is effectively a vote of no confidence in the whole epistemological enterprise conceived as offering, potentially at least, a means of deliverance from the toils of sceptical doubt. Of course it is just the point of Davidson's extensive writings on truth, meaning and interpretation to offer such deliverance and do so moreover on terms that would count philosophically as meeting every form of sceptical-relativist challenge. Yet this desirable outcome is beyond reach of any theory – like Davidson's – that starts out from the assumed priority of formal (logico-linguistic) considerations over matters of causal-explanatory warrant conjoined with inference to the best, most rational understanding.

One problem concerns the applicability to natural languages in everyday communicative contexts of a Tarskian truth-theoretic approach – a formal definition of truth-in-L – whose original purpose was to specify terms for the analysis of logically 'perfect' languages, i.e., those that were capable of regimentation according to the first-order quantified predicate calculus.[80] Davidson puts up a case for the validity of just that move since, on his account, it is the logical components of a natural language – its quantifiers and stock of devices for conjunction, disjunction, negation, anaphora, and so forth – which provide the basic means of communicative grasp both for native speakers/interpreters and for translators out of some other (even if culturally remote) tongue. Such is of course the main plank of his argument *contra* Quine for the in-principle possibility of 'radical translation' and the mistake of supposing that it is somehow ruled out – or rendered deeply problematic – by the existence of disparate language-relative 'ontologies' or conceptual schemes. However this remains a highly formal and abstract line of approach that makes little contact with the detailed practicalities of natural-language understanding and which bears all the marks of its direct source in Tarski's more specialized logico-semantic programme. Hence the second problem, most directly addressed in Davidson's series of essays on 'The Structure and Content of Truth': that when it comes to matters of empirical content or 'truth' in a substantive, other than formally specified sense then any theory that banks so heavily on the Tarskian apparatus will not get us very far in that direction.[81] This is I think why Davidson is reduced to pre-empting such likely rejoinders by treating them as merely irrelevant – just products of the old epistemological mind-set – and opting instead for the straightforward belief that our 'sentences and opinions' are made 'true or false' by 'unmediated contact' with real-world objects and events. However his striking insouciance in this regard (as if the claim were wholly unproblematic) cannot disguise the lack of any reasoned or philosophically adequate justification for supposing that issues of truth and falsehood can be settled by appeal to the plain self-evidence of sensory-perceptual warrant. Indeed it offers no more in the way of normative or justificatory grounds than Quine's radical-empiricist notion of 'epistemology naturalized'.

Here we might recall Putnam's remark about the Quinean suggestion that psychology provides all that is needed for that particular purpose. Thus: ' "[n]aturalized epistemology" in Quine's sense means the *abandonment* of epistemology. "Psychology" (which for Quine always means Skinnerian psychology) is all the epistemology we want or need. This is evasion of the epistemological question with a vengeance!'[82] Despite Davidson's claim to have exposed and overcome the residual third dogma of empiricism in Quine's thought – i.e., the dualism of scheme and content – it seems to me that Davidson is himself still hooked on a version of that same dogma. At any rate this helps to explain his veering-about between (on the one hand) a formal or logically regimented theory of truth, meaning and interpretation and (on the other) a radical empiricist notion of direct or 'unmediated' sensory-perceptual content. According to Davidson the third (Quinean-Kuhnian) dogma – that of 'scheme and content' or 'organizing system and something waiting to be organized' – is probably the last which needs exposing, since 'if we give it up it is not clear that there is anything distinctive left to call empiricism' (Davidson, p. 189). At that stage it will make no sense – after centuries of inconclusive debate – to think that there is some genuine (other than merely notional) dispute between rationalist and empiricist philosophies of mind, knowledge and language. Quite simply, we can push right through with Quine's revisionist programme (just as Quine claimed to push right through with the programme of those who had somehow stopped short on the same path) and thereby arrive at a point where these distinctions drop out since truth *just is* whatever counts as such by our best evidential lights.

Thus '[t]he totality of sensory evidence is what we want provided it is all the evidence there is; and all the evidence there is is just what it takes to make our sentences or theories true' (p. 194). However, one then has to ask what becomes of 'truth' when that concept is so directly linked to an empiricist notion of evidential warrant, and the 'evidence' in question is itself subject only to an abstract (Tarskian) conception of truth that offers no guidance in specific contexts of interpretative grasp or correct understanding. Once again, the lesson seems clear: that any adequate approach to such matters will have to incorporate a theory of reference that finds sufficient room for normative criteria beyond those envisaged by Davidson's idea of our somehow regaining 'unmediated touch' with the 'familiar objects' that fix the truth-conditions of our various candidate statements, hypotheses, predictions, and so forth. Also, as I have said, it will need to reconcile the otherwise conflicting claims of a truth-based, rationality-optimizing theory as to how meanings and beliefs can be best, most charitably construed and a causal-explanatory account which anchors them in certain objective features of the world and our own or other people's more or less adequate understanding of it.[83] That this is not to be had from any approach (whether logical-empiricist, Quinean, or Davidsonian) which conserves some remnant of the scheme/content or theory/evidence dichotomy is a case fully borne out by the past half-century of intensive debate on these issues of truth, knowledge and interpretation.

NOTES

1 W. V. Quine, *Ontological Relativity and Other Essays* (New York: Columbia University Press, 1969), p. 72.
2 For further discussion from a range of viewpoints, see Tom L. Beauchamp and Alexander Rosenberg, *Hume and the Problem of Causation* (New York: Oxford University Press, 1981); H. O. Mounce, *Hume's Naturalism* (London: Routledge, 1999); David F. Norton (ed.), *The Cambridge Companion to Hume* (Cambridge: Cambridge University Press, 1993); Rupert Read and Kenneth A. Richman (eds), *The New Hume Debate* (London: Routledge, 2000); Galen Strawson, *The Secret Connexion: Causation, Realism, and David Hume* (Oxford: Clarendon Press, 1989).

3 See, for instance, J. Aronson, R. Harré and E. Way, *Realism Rescued: How Scientific Progress is Possible* (London: Duckworth, 1994); Roy Bhaskar, *A Realist Theory of Science* (Leeds: Leeds Books, 1975); Michael Devitt, *Realism and Truth*, 2nd edn (Oxford: Blackwell, 1986); R. Harré and E. H. Madden, *Causal Powers* (Oxford: Blackwell, 1975); Jarrett Leplin (ed.), *Scientific Realism* (Berkeley: University of California Press, 1984); Stathis Psillos, *Scientific Realism: How Science Tracks Truth* (London: Routledge, 1999); Wesley C. Salmon, *Scientific Realism and the Causal Structure of the World* (Princeton, NJ: Princeton University Press, 1984); M. Tooley, *Causation: A Realist Approach* (Oxford: Blackwell, 1988).

4 W. V. Quine, 'Two Dogmas of Empiricism', in *From a Logical Point of View*, 2nd edn (Cambridge, MA: Harvard University Press, 1961), pp. 20–46; also Quine, 'Epistemology Naturalized', in *Ontological Relativity and Other Essays* (op. cit.), pp. 69–90.

5 See also Peter Gibbins, *Particles and Paradoxes: The Limits of Quantum Logic* (Cambridge: Cambridge University Press, 1987); Susan Haack, *Deviant Logic: Some Philosophical Issues* (Cambridge University Press, 1974); Hilary Putnam, 'How to Think Quantum-Logically', *Synthèse*, Vol. 74 (1974), pp. 55–61.

6 See Sandra G. Harding (ed.), *Can Theories be Refuted? Essays on the Duhem-Quine Thesis* (Dordrecht: D. Reidel, 1976).

7 See especially Quine, *From a Logical Point of View* (op. cit.); also *Ontological Relativity and Other Essays* (New York: Columbia University Press, 1969); *Selected Logic Papers*, 2nd edn (Cambridge, MA: Harvard University Press, 1995); *The Ways of Paradox and Other Essays* (New York: Random House, 1966).

8 Quine, 'Reference and Modality', in Leonard Linsky (ed.), *Reference and Modality* (Oxford: Oxford University Press, 1971), pp. 17–34.

9 Quine, 'Epistemology Naturalized' (op. cit.).

10 See especially Wesley C. Salmon, *Hans Reichenbach: Logical Empiricist* (Dordrecht: D. Reidel, 1979) and *Four Decades of Scientific Explanation* (Minneapolis: University of Minnesota Press, 1989).

11 See Richard Boyd, 'The Current Status of Scientific Realism', in Leplin (ed.), *Scientific Realism* (op. cit.), pp. 41–82; also – for a similar statement of the case – Hilary Putnam, *Mathematics, Matter and Method* (Cambridge: Cambridge University Press, 1975), p. 73. For some sceptical counter-arguments see Larry Laudan, 'A Confutation of Convergent Realism', *Philosophy of Science*, Vol. 48 (1981), pp. 19–49.

12 Quine, 'Two Dogmas of Empiricism' (op. cit.).

13 John McDowell, *Mind and World* (Cambridge, MA: Harvard University Press, 1994).

14 Christopher Norris, 'McDowell on Kant: Redrawing the Bounds of Sense' and 'The Limits of Naturalism: Further Thoughts on McDowell's *Mind and World*', in *Minding the Gap: Epistemology and Philosophy of Science in the Two Traditions* (Amherst, MA: University of Massachusetts Press, 2000), pp. 172–96, 197–230.

15 McDowell, *Mind and World* (op. cit.), p. 41.

16 Wilfrid Sellars, *Empiricism and the Philosophy of Mind* (Cambridge, MA: Harvard University Press, 1997).

17 See Notes 4 and 6 above; also Thomas S. Kuhn, *The Structure of Scientific Revolutions*, 2nd edn (Chicago: University of Chicago Press, 1970).

18 For further discussion see Michael Friedman, *A Parting of the Ways: Carnap, Cassirer, and Heidegger* (Chicago: Open Court, 2000).

19 See various contributions to Simon Glendinning (ed.), *The Edinburgh Encyclopaedia of Continental Philosophy* (Edinburgh: Edinburgh University Press, 1999); also Norris, *Minding the Gap* (op. cit.) and *Resources of Realism: Prospects for 'Post-analytic' Philosophy* (London: Macmillan, 1997).

20 See, for instance, Joseph Rouse, *Knowledge and Power: Toward a Political Philosophy of Science* (Ithaca, NY: Cornell University Press, 1987); Richard Rorty, *Consequences of Pragmatism* (Brighton: Harvester, 1982) and *Objectivity, Relativism, and Truth* (Cambridge

University Press, 1991); also Richard J. Bernstein, *Beyond Objectivism and Relativism: Science, Hermeneutics, and Praxis* (Philadelphia: University of Pennsylvania Press, 1983).

21 See Jaegwon Kim, *Supervenience and Mind: Selected Philosophical Essays* (Cambridge: Cambridge University Press, 1993).

22 Quine, 'Two Dogmas of Empiricism' (op. cit.), p. 43.

23 Kuhn, *The Structure of Scientific Revolutions* (op. cit.).

24 Quine, *Pursuit of Truth* (Cambridge, MA: Harvard University Press, 1990).

25 See Notes 3, 10 and 11 above; also Norris, *New Idols of the Cave: On the Limits of Anti-Realism* (Manchester: Manchester University Press, 1997) and *Philosophy of Language and the Challenge to Scientific Realism* (London: Routledge, 2004).

26 For early (causal-realist) Putnam, see especially the essays collected in his *Mind, Language and Reality* (Cambridge: Cambridge University Press, 1975). By the time of *Reason, Truth and History* (Cambridge University Press, 1981) he had adopted an 'internal' or framework-relative version of (quasi-)realism and has since explored a wide range of alternative pragmatist, naturalist, or 'commonsense' approaches. See *Realism and Reason* (Cambridge University Press, 1983); *Pragmatism: An Open Question* (Oxford: Blackwell, 1995); *The Many Faces of Realism* (La Salle, IL: Open Court, 1987); *Representation and Reality* (Cambridge University Press, 1988); *Realism With a Human Face* (Cambridge, MA: Harvard University Press, 1990); *Renewing Philosophy* (Harvard University Press, 1992).

27 Salmon, *Scientific Realism and the Causal Structure of the World* (op. cit.).

28 Norris, *Hilary Putnam: Reason, Realism, and the Uses of Uncertainty* (Manchester: Manchester University Press, 2002).

29 See Note 26, above; also Putnam, *Mathematics, Matter and Method* (Cambridge: Cambridge University Press, 1975).

30 Putnam, *The Collapse of the Fact/Value Dichotomy and Other Essays* (Cambridge, MA: Harvard University Press, 2002).

31 Putnam, *Reason, Truth and History* (op. cit.).

32 Putnam, *Mind, Language and Reality* (op. cit.); also Gregory McCulloch, *The Mind and Its World* (London: Routledge, 1995).

33 See, for instance, Amartya Sen, *On Ethics and Economics* (Oxford: Blackwell, 1987); *Inequality Reexamined* (Cambridge, MA: Harvard University Press, 1992); and *Development as Freedom* (New York: Anchor Books, 2000).

34 Cited by Putnam, *The Collapse of the Fact/Value Dichotomy* (op. cit.), p. 30.

35 Ibid., p. 31.

36 See Notes 1, 4, 7 and 24, above.

37 Noam Chomsky, 'Quine's Empirical Assumptions', *Synthèse*, Vol. 19 (1968), pp. 53–68.

38 Chomsky, 'A Review of B. F. Skinner's *Verbal Behavior*', *Language*, Vol. 35 (1959), pp. 126–58; also *Cartesian Linguistics* (New York: Harper & Row, 1966) and *Language and Mind* (New York: Harcourt, Brace, Jovanovich, 1972).

39 Putnam, *The Collapse of the Fact/Value Dichotomy* (op. cit.), p. 139.

40 Chomsky, *New Horizons in the Study of Language and Mind* (Cambridge: Cambridge University Press, 2000). See also James McGilvray, *Chomsky: Language, Mind, and Politics* (Cambridge: Polity Press, 1999).

41 See especially Chomsky, *Language and Problems of Knowledge: The Managua Lectures* (Cambridge, MA: MIT Press, 1988).

42 Chomsky, 'Discussion of Putnam's Comments', in B. Beakley and P. Ludlow (eds), *The Philosophy of Mind: Classical Problems/Contemporary Issues* (Cambridge, MA: MIT Press, 1992), pp. 411–22.

43 Norris, 'Modularity, Nativism, and Reference-Fixing: On Chomsky's Internalist Assumptions', in *Language, Logic and Epistemology* (London: Macmillan, 2004), pp. 111–49.

44 See Edward Herman and Noam Chomsky, *Manufacturing Consent* (New York: Pantheon, 1988).

45 See Putnam, *Mind, Language and Reality* (op. cit.).

46 Putnam, ibid.; also Saul Kripke, *Naming and Necessity* (Oxford: Blackwell, 1980); David Lewis, *Counterfactuals* (Blackwell, 1973); M. Loux (ed.), *The Possible and the Actual* (Ithaca, NY: Cornell University Press, 1979); Stephen Schwartz (ed.), *Naming, Necessity, and Natural Kinds* (Ithaca, NY: Cornell University Press, 1977); R. C. Stalnaker, *Inquiry* (Cambridge, MA: MIT Press, 1987); David Wiggins, *Sameness and Substance* (Blackwell, 1980).

47 See Notes 3 and 11, above; also Gilbert Harman, 'Inference to the Best Explanation', *Philosophical Review*, Vol. 74 (1965), pp. 88–95; Peter Lipton, *Inference to the Best Explanation* (London: Routledge, 1993).

48 Quine, 'Two Dogmas of Empiricism' (op. cit.).

49 For further discussion see Norris, *Against Relativism: Philosophy of Science, Deconstruction and Critical Theory* (Oxford: Blackwell, 1997).

50 Donald Davidson, 'On the Very Idea of a Conceptual Scheme', in *Inquiries into Truth and Interpretation* (Oxford: Oxford University Press, 1984), pp. 183–98.

51 Ibid., p. 198; see also Rudolf Carnap, *The Logical Structure of the World* (Berkeley: University of California Press, 1967).

52 Davidson, 'The Very Idea' (op. cit.), p. 197.

53 Ibid., p. 197.

54 See especially Psillos, *Scientific Realism* (op. cit.) and other entries under Notes 3, 11 and 47, above.

55 See Hartry Field, 'Theory Change and the Indeterminacy of Reference', *Journal of Philosophy*, Vol. 70 (1973), pp. 462–81 and 'Quine and the Correspondence Theory', *Philosophical Review*, Vol. 83 (1974), pp. 200–28.

56 Putnam, *Mind, Language and Reality* (op. cit.).

57 For a different view of these matters, see Jerry Fodor, *The Elm and the Expert: Mentalese and Its Semantics* (Cambridge, MA: Bradford Books, 1995).

58 See, for instance, Schwartz (ed.), *Naming, Necessity and Natural Kinds* (op. cit.); also Gareth Evans, *The Varieties of Reference*, ed. J. McDowell (Oxford: Clarendon Press, 1982) and Gregory McCulloch, *The Game of the Name: Introducing Logic, Language and Mind* (Oxford: Clarendon, 1989).

59 Davidson, 'On the Very Idea' (op. cit.), p. 184.

60 See especially Michael Dummett, *Truth and Other Enigmas* (London: Duckworth, 1978), *The Logical Basis of Metaphysics* (Duckworth, 1991), and *The Seas of Language* (Oxford: Clarendon Press, 1993); also Michael Luntley, *Language, Logic and Experience: The Case for Anti-Realism* (Duckworth, 1988); Neil Tennant, *Anti-Realism and Logic* (Oxford: Clarendon Press, 1987) and *The Taming of the True* (Oxford: Oxford University Press, 1997).

61 My source for this particularly apt example is Scott Soames, *Understanding Truth* (Oxford: Oxford University Press, 1999).

62 See Bas van Fraassen, *The Scientific Image* (Oxford: Clarendon Press, 1980) and *Laws and Symmetry* (Clarendon, 1989).

63 van Fraassen, 'Empiricism in the Philosophy of Language', in Paul Churchland and Clifford Hooker (eds), *Images of Science: Essays on Realism and Empiricism, With a Reply from Bas C. van Fraassen* (Chicago: University of Chicago Press, 1985), p. 255.

64 Ibid., p. 255.

65 Paul Churchland, 'The Ontological Status of Observables: In Praise of the Superempirical Virtues', in Churchland and Hooker (eds), *Images of Science* (op. cit.).

66 For a range of representative views, see William Bechtel and George Graham (eds), *A Companion to Cognitive Science* (Oxford: Blackwell, 1999); Alvin A. Goldman (ed.), *Readings in Philosophy and Cognitive Science* (Cambridge, MA: MIT Press, 1993); Michael I. Posner (ed.), *Foundations of Cognitive Science* (MIT Press, 1989).

67 Kuhn, *The Structure of Scientific Revolutions* (op. cit.).

68 See Notes 4, 10 and 51 above.

69 Alfred Tarski 'The Concept of Truth in Formalised Languages', in *Logic, Semantics and Metamathematics*, trans. J. H. Woodger (Oxford: Oxford University Press, 1956), pp. 152–278; also Davidson, 'In Defence of Convention T', in *Inquiries into Truth and Interpretation* (op. cit.), pp. 65–75; Simon Blackburn and Keith Simmons (eds), *Truth* (Oxford: Oxford University Press, 1999); Richard L. Kirkham, *Theories of Truth: A Critical Introduction* (Cambridge, MA: MIT Press, 1992).

70 See especially Davidson, 'The Structure and Content of Truth', *The Journal of Philosophy*, Vol. 87 (1990), pp. 279–328.

71 Davidson, 'A Coherence Theory of Truth and Knowledge', in Ernest LePore (ed.), *Truth and Interpretation: Perspectives on the Philosophy of Donald Davidson* (Oxford: Blackwell, 1986), pp. 307–19.

72 See Rorty, 'Pragmatism, Davidson and Truth', in *Objectivity, Relativism, and Truth* (Cambridge: Cambridge University Press, 1991), pp. 126–50 and 'Is Truth a Goal of Inquiry? Donald Davidson versus Crispin Wright', in *Truth and Progress* (Cambridge University Press, 1998), pp. 19–42; also Davidson, 'Afterthoughts, 1987', in Alan R. Malachowski (ed.), *Reading Rorty: Critical Responses to* Philosophy and the Mirror of Nature, *and Beyond* (Oxford: Blackwell, 1990), pp. 134–8.

73 See Note 60, above; also Norris, *Truth Matters: Realism, Anti-realism and Response-Dependence* (Edinburgh: Edinburgh University Press, 2002).

74 See especially Davidson, *Essays on Actions and Events* (Oxford: Clarendon Press, 1980); also Kim, *Supervenience and Mind* (Note 21, above); G. H. von Wright, *Explanation and Understanding* (Ithaca, NY: Cornell University Press, 1971).

75 See, for instance, Ted Honderich, *Theory of Determinism: The Mind, Neuroscience and Life-Hopes* (Oxford: Clarendon Press, 1988) and *How Free Are You?: The Determinism Problem* (Oxford: Oxford University Press, 1993); also Honderich (ed.), *Essays on Freedom of Action* (London: Routledge & Kegan Paul, 1973).

76 See Lorraine Code, *Epistemic Responsibility* (Hanover, NH: University Press of New England, 1987); M. DePaul and L. Zagzebski (eds), *Intellectual Virtue: Perspectives from Ethics and Epistemology* (Oxford: Oxford University Press, 2002); A. Fairweather and L. Zagzebski (eds), *Virtue Epistemology: Essays on Epistemic Virtue and Responsibility* (Oxford: Oxford University Press, 2001); L. Zagzebski, *Virtues of the Mind: An Inquiry into the Nature of Virtue and the Ethical Foundations of Knowledge* (Cambridge: Cambridge University Press, 1996).

77 For the most widely influential statement of this view, see Peter Winch, *The Idea of a Social Science and Its Relation to Philosophy* (London: Routledge & Kegan Paul, 1958) and *Trying to Make Sense* (Oxford: Blackwell, 1987).

78 See, for instance, Alasdair MacIntyre, *Against the Self-Images of the Age: Essays on Ideology and Philosophy* (London: Duckworth, 1971) and Norris, *Against Relativism* (op. cit.).

79 See Notes 1 and 4 above; also Quine, *Word and Object* (Cambridge, MA: MIT Press, 1960).

80 See Note 69, above.

81 See Note 70, above.

82 Putnam, *The Collapse of the Fact/Value Dichotomy* (op. cit.), p. 139.

83 See, for instance, Alvin Goldman, *Epistemology and Cognition* (Cambridge, MA: Harvard University Press, 1986) and *Knowledge in a Social World* (Oxford: Clarendon Press, 1999); Hilary Kornblith (ed.), *Naturalizing Epistemology* (Cambridge, MA: MIT Press, 1985); David Papineau, *Philosophical Naturalism* (Oxford: Blackwell, 1993); Ernest Sosa, *Knowledge in Perspective: Selected Essays in Epistemology* (Cambridge: Cambridge University Press, 1991).

3

Epistemology, Language, and the Realism Debate

I

Nobody has done more to illuminate the issue about scientific realism than Hilary Putnam in the vast number of books and articles that he has published over the past four decades. That is to say, he has shown it up in a sharply revealing and intensely critical light, even if – as will emerge in the course of this chapter – one may differ just as sharply with some of the lessons he has drawn. For much of that time (since the mid-1970s) Putnam has been engaged in testing various alternatives to his previous outlook of causal realism plus inference to the best, most rational explanation.[1] In the process he has espoused a range of compromise positions – 'internal realist', framework-relativist, naturalist, Peircean or Jamesian pragmatist, and so forth – aimed at producing a conception of truth that would make due allowance for our strong realist intuitions with regard to the growth of scientific knowledge without falling back on what he now regards as a hopelessly outdated 'metaphysical'-realist approach.[2] However one may doubt that it is possible to achieve this aim if the latter charge is taken to apply to any kind of realist epistemology grounded on the three main premises of Putnam's earlier approach. These were, briefly stated, (1) the existence of a real-world physical domain comprising various mind- and language-independent objects, structures, causal dispositions, and properties thereof; (2) the possibility that well-formed statements concerning them might always be rendered objectively true or false by the way things stand in reality, quite apart from our present-best (or even our future-best-possible) state of knowledge; and (3), despite this, the claim that such statements and their various constituent terms can be 'truth-tracking' or 'sensitive to future discovery' in so far as they succeed in referring to items of which, as yet, we may possess only a partial or scientifically inadequate knowledge.[3]

Such claims now strike Putnam as metaphysically over-committed since they imply some kind of essentialist, quasi-Aristotelian doctrine concerning those various objects and properties picked out along the road of scientific progress from commonsense perception to the latest theories of subatomic physics or molecular biology. It is chiefly this idea, together with his growing conviction that the formal sciences (logic and mathematics, in particular classical set-theory) harbour a range of likewise intractable problems, that can be seen to have driven the retreat from his early realist stance.[4] Yet there is something odd about Putnam's desire to retain the strong intuitive appeal of that approach – its answer to the question of how science has achieved such otherwise sheerly miraculous advances in its history to date – while nevertheless abandoning just about every main plank in his erstwhile argument for causal realism and inference to the best explanation on jointly scientific, logico-semantic, and metaphysical grounds. It seems to me that early Putnam got it right in this respect and that any theory which takes the nowadays well-nigh obligatory detour via logico-linguistic considerations *even with a view to defending some version of realism* is sure to run into problems. I have argued this case at length in a recent critical study of Putnam's work which attempts to show how the various objections that he raises to his own, now abandoned causal-realist approach are by no means decisive and very often beg the question by making an appeal to problematical *topoi* – such as those instanced above, along with the unresolved paradoxes of quantum theory – which in truth cannot bear such a probative or evidential weight.[5] However I shall say no more about him here save to register the fact that Putnam more than anyone has set the terms and laid the conceptual ground for debates in this currently high-profile and intensely disputed area. Thus his later (post-1980) work offers a striking example of the way that anti-realist or sceptical-relativist trends have captured the high ground of recent debate in epistemology and philosophy of science. All the more so, indeed, for Putnam's keen and continuing sense of the objections that tend to rise up against such ideas when confronted with the kinds of intuitive or commonsense realism that typify not only our everyday dealings with the world but also the default attitude of most scientists.

Clearly any adequate counter-argument will need to go beyond a straight-forward appeal to what most people think before being got at by sceptically inclined philosophers. What I therefore propose to do in this chapter is revisit some of the central issues and put the case for realism in various fields of enquiry by looking more closely at the alternatives now on offer. Let me say straight off that this issue is 'philosophical' in precisely the sense that it cannot be resolved by some ultimate, knockdown argumentative move that would convince the sceptic – or the anti-realist – that they had simply been mistaken all along and had better convert to a realist persuasion without further ado. If one thing is clear from the long and continuing debate about these matters it is the fact that sceptics can always hold their ground by professing to doubt every kind of evidential, inductive, demonstrative, or causal-explanatory reasoning that could ever be adduced by scientific realists or proponents of inference to the best (most rational or adequate) account of the matter in hand. Nor is it much use to take the line, with followers of late Wittgenstein, that these questions ultimately make no sense in so far as they result from a failure to grasp that the way we talk about a whole range of entities from electrons and DNA molecules to cabbages and kings *just is* what properly counts for us as 'realist' talk within the language-game or cultural life-form of subatomic physics, molecular biology, or everyday-practical discourse.[6] For whatever its realist avowals this idea amounts to just another, less overt version of the language-relativist or framework-internalist thesis according to which there is no conceiving of truth – no intelligible means of cashing that notion out – except in relation to some going range of linguistically expressible and culturally salient beliefs-held-true. That is to say, it is 'realist' only in the sense of counting anti-realism (or scepticism) a kind of pathological disorder brought about through 'the bewitchment of our intelligence by language', and realism therefore as the default outlook that we naturally fall back to once released from the travails of sceptical doubt. Thus Wittgensteinian 'realists' are wont to adduce the master's claim that philosophy 'leaves everything as it is', including our commonplace and scientific habits of referring to a whole range of physical objects on every scale from electrons to galaxies.[7] However this promised means of deliverance turns out to be no such thing but rather a doctrine that in effect renders truth a product of social or cultural consensus, and such consensus in turn a matter of what counts as 'real' by the lights of some particular, whether everyday or relatively specialized language-game. And from this point it is no great distance to a Rortian neo-pragmatist (for which read cultural-relativist) position whereby truth comes out as what's currently and contingently 'good in the way of belief'.[8] Either that, or the Wittgensteinian appeal to communal 'agreement in judgement' as the furthest we can get toward justification gives rise to the kinds of ultra-sceptical take on issues of truth, knowledge, and epistemic warrant that have dominated so much recent debate in these areas since Kripke came up with his communitarian 'solution' to the rule-following paradox.[9]

So it is, to say the least, very far from self-evident that these lessons from Wittgenstein offer a means of allaying our sceptical doubts or resolving them in favour of a properly realist (as distinct from a quasi-realist or downright anti-realist) approach. One line of counter-argument that has considerable force in this context is the above-mentioned variant of inference to the best, most rational explanation which presents us with a flat choice between accounting for the sheer efficacy of science as an outcome of various advances in our knowledge of reality and viewing it as something that cannot be explained in such terms, and hence as nothing short of 'miraculous'.[10] In response other, more sceptically inclined philosophers are apt to point out that the history of science is littered with obsolete, false, or now abandoned theories and that we are therefore on shaky ground if we suppose our present-best theories to constitute a large-scale exception to the rule.[11] However the realist can then come back with a classic *tu quoque* rejoinder to the effect that this argument itself relies on an objectivist conception of truth and falsehood and, what's more, a confident appeal to our knowledge of the growth of knowledge.[12] Of course there is a sense – a distinctively philosophic sense – in which scepticism will always have the last word just so long as the sceptic sticks to his guns and professes to doubt whatever evidence, reasons, or justificatory grounds the realist may produce in the course of their exchange. However this is no reason to conclude that the sceptic has all the best arguments, at least if the relevant criteria are taken to extend beyond the compass of intra-philosophical debate and include the sorts of reasoning that play a large role in everyday-practical as well as more specialized scientific modes of enquiry.

II

Such was famously Hume's view of the matter in his more sanguine, less sceptically driven moments and such also the conclusion of those who may feel the force of sceptical doubt as a spur to philosophical reflection but who nonetheless recognize its ultimate failure to dislodge the deep-laid epistemic, cognitive and historical grounds of their belief in the objectivity of truth and possibility of progress in knowledge. The force comes out in Michael Williams' pithy rendition of the sceptical case: that 'if the world is an objective world, statements about how things appear must be logically unconnected with statements about how they are'. From which it follows that 'to realise our vulnerability to scepticism we need only recognise the simple logical point that our experience could be just what it is *and all our beliefs about the world could be false*'.[13] However the failure also comes out in Williams' observation that there is 'something peculiar about sceptical hypotheses', namely that 'I have a way of telling that they do not obtain only if they do not obtain'. Whence his neat diagnosis of the Humean predicament: '[t]he sceptic's fallacy is that he takes the discovery that, in the study, knowledge of the world is impossible for the discovery, in the study, that knowledge is impossible generally'.[14] Still it is clear from much of what Williams has to say on this topic – not to mention the pointedly relevant title of his book, *Unnatural Doubts: Epistemological Realism and the Basis of Scepticism* – that he inclines less toward a realist (or objectivist) standpoint than to a view of these issues that would treat them (like Wittgenstein) as so many pseudo-dilemmas thrown up by the futile quest for standards of truth and knowledge that would somehow transcend our various language-games, practices, or 'forms of life'.

To be sure, Williams rejects any version of the argument that offers no more than the placid assurance that everything is right with our accustomed modes of talk just so long as we refrain from raising doubts where no such doubts can properly or sensibly be raised. All the same he goes some way in this Wittgensteinian direction by suggesting that scepticism is often the flipside – or the preordained upshot – of a hard-line realist/objectivist approach which makes it strictly inconceivable that knowledge could ever lay claim to truth or truth be brought within the compass of humanly attainable knowledge. However, as we have seen, any answer to the sceptic that involves a retreat to this supposedly safer communitarian ground is one that also runs the risk of being pushed toward a 'Kripkensteinian' denouement where truth – or correctness in formal procedures such as 'following a rule' in elementary arithmetic – becomes just a matter of sticking to the practices that count as warranted or justified by our own communal lights.[15] That is to say, the 'problem of knowledge' won't go away if one simply adopts the therapeutic line (again with its source in late Wittgenstein) that it was always a product of hyper-cultivated sceptical doubt, and that the best, indeed only cure for such typically philosophic ailments is a return to the commonsense wisdom enshrined in our everyday language-games and life-forms. For this is to ignore the self-evident fact – 'self-evident', that is, from any but a far-gone sceptical, anti-realist, strong-sociological, or cultural-relativist viewpoint – that widely held beliefs have often been (and indeed still are) plain wrong, and moreover that their wrongness has much to do with the influence of certain linguistically entrenched or acculturated ways of thinking. It is at this point – to borrow Wittgenstein's phrase, though against its original intent – that 'our spade is turned' and we discover the need for an account of knowledge and scientific progress that goes beyond anything available in terms of conformity with this or that shared discourse or communal practice.

Thus the realist will perhaps do best to point out those many well-documented episodes from the history of scientific progress to date where scepticism has served as a jointly creative and critical impulse, releasing thought from its bondage to fixed habits of belief and opening the way to new and otherwise unthinkable developments.[16] Such, for instance, was Einstein's early adoption of a Machian positivist-instrumentalist outlook during the period when relativity theory was still drastically at odds with the dominant (Newtonian) scientific worldview, and when a full-fledged realist commitment to its claims would have been neither warranted by the evidence nor wise as a matter of strategic choice in confronting the resistance of orthodox beliefs.[17] It is also fairly typical of other, more extended developmental patterns in the history of scientific thought where theories have begun as speculative ventures and then, if successful, turned out to acquire an increasing measure of rational, empirical, and causal-explanatory warrant. Thus the atomist hypothesis started out (with the ancient Greeks) as a product of sheer a priori speculation and only much later, with Dalton's discovery of atomic weights, became the most rational means of explaining certain hitherto unexplained chemical properties.[18] Even so, more than a century on, Ernst Mach could profess to doubt their existence – or at any rate count it unproven – on the strict empiricist grounds that one should never embrace ontological commitments beyond those entailed or borne out by the plain observational data.[19] Not until those data eventually showed up with the development of electron microscopes or yet more powerful and refined technologies would the issue be resolved in favour of realism *vis-à-vis* such erstwhile recondite entities or posits.

All the same there are still those – among them 'constructive empiricists' like Bas van Fraassen – who insist that realism is metaphysically or ontologically *de trop* when it comes to putative 'objects' too small, too remote, or too fast-moving to show up without the aid of technologically enhanced methods of observation.[20] Thus, according to van Fraassen, we can count something 'real' without risk of over-commitment just so long as it is visible through an optical microscope or – as for instance in the case of remote astrophysical bodies – if it were viewed by some astronaut peering with an optical telescope through her spaceship window. However we shall err on the side of ontological extravagance if we extend that predicate to molecules, atoms, electrons, and other such microphysical 'objects' beyond our technologically unaided perceptual range, or again, to far-off and rapidly receding celestial bodies that cannot be viewed except through a radio-telescope. Van Fraassen's doctrine of constructive empiricism is therefore best seen as an update on Machian instrumentalist themes which likewise seeks to save the empirical appearances while yielding as few hostages as possible to the prospect of future disconfirmation should our present-best hypotheses turn out false or metaphysically on the wrong track. However, as I have argued at length elsewhere, this doctrine is itself open to various telling objections.[21] Among them are its blatantly anthropocentric bias, its arbitrary drawing of a stipulative line between supposedly distinct modes of technological enhancement, and its failure to acknowledge the extent to which all perception is theoretically informed. Also, closely related to that, there is its preference for observational results attained through the use of crude and primitive technologies over those achieved through the deployment of sophisticated instruments whose working principles (along with their limits, margins of error, possible defects and so forth) are all the better understood for their having been subject to a process of intensively researched design and development.[22]

In short, van Fraassen's is a curiously retrograde outlook which in effect reverses the usual order of scientific progress from pure speculation to the framing of well-formed hypotheses and thence, via rational theory-construction, to the stage where realism (e.g., concerning the existence of atoms, molecules, or remote supernovae) can be justified as a matter of inference to the best causal-explanatory account.[23] It therefore stands within a line of descent that may be said to have its source in the doctrinal position adopted by Cardinal Bellarmine and the Catholic Church when confronted with the claims of Copernican and Galilean heliocentric astronomy. That is, it counsels an attitude of wise abstention as regards any realist (ontological) commitments and a willingness to treat the empirical data – or plain observational results – as entailing no conclusion either way with respect to the 'two world systems' of Galileo's time or the reality of those various subatomic particles that appear to leave tracks in cloud-chambers or to collide with each other in cyclotrons. Thus the doctrine served, temporarily at least, to head off any direct conflict between the claims of orthodox religion and heterodox science, just as it serves (albeit with somewhat less at stake) to defuse the issue between scientific realists on the one hand and instrumentalists, pragmatists, and van Fraassen-style 'constructive empiricists' on the other. Among its most influential recent advocates was Pierre Duhem, the philosopher-historian of science whose Catholic beliefs were quite explicitly linked to his promotion of the view that science should seek only to 'save the (empirical) appearances', and not concern itself with 'metaphysical' issues that lay beyond its proper remit.[24] In comparison van Fraassen's argument seems curiously under-motivated, since he has no obvious doctrinal or ideological axe to grind and is not – like Duhem – concerned to advance a revisionist account of intellectual history which places far greater value and significance on the work of those late-medieval thinkers who (on his submission) laid the ground for what we normally think of as 'early modern' science. Even stranger is the case of Paul Feyerabend, whose outlook of 'epistemological anarchism' in books like *Against Method* led him to mount a rearguard defence of Bellarmine and the church authorities *contra* Galileo, but who can also be found, in his earlier work, denouncing instrumentalist and empiricist approaches as mere techniques for evading the issue of scientific truth. Thus: 'this sly procedure is only one (the most "modern" one) of the many devices which have been invented for the purpose of saving an incorrect theory in the face of refuting evidence and . . . consistently applied, it must lead to the arrest of scientific progress and to stagnation'.[25]

To be sure, what seems chiefly to motivate Feyerabend's stance is his idea that such progress can come about only through the clash of opposing theories, hypotheses, or scientific worldviews, and hence that, in the interests of more vigorous debate, their protagonists had better be committed to the truth (rather than the mere empirical adequacy) of whatever claims they may advance. It is therefore an argument that has more to do with the psychology of belief and the sociology of knowledge than with the issue of scientific realism in its meta-physical, ontological, or even epistemological aspects. Nor indeed can it fairly be said that van Fraassen's theory of 'constructive empiricism' is in any way ana-logous or close kin to Feyerabend's notion of epistemological anarchism, that is, his proposal that 'anything goes' as a matter of acceptable scientific method or procedure. Still this comparison does throw an interesting light on the way that radical empiricism can be enlisted on the side of certain doctrinal, even dogmatic creeds, despite its seemingly pluralist credentials and – at least in the case of Ernst Mach – its overt opposition to the kinds of top-down, authoritarian approach that stifle scientific creativity at source.[26] That Machian positivism was a socially progressive, democratically inspired conception of science and one designed to promote the widest range of participant activity at every level is a case that has been argued with exemplary scholarship and splendid verve in a recent study by Steve Fuller. Central to that case is the contrast between Mach's emancipatory programme and what he (Fuller) sets about revealing as the altogether opposite, i.e., narrowly orthodox and inertly conformist approach to history and philosophy of science that found its most favoured source-text in Kuhn's *The Structure of Scientific Revolutions*.[27] However this only goes to emphasize the point that empiricism is very much a two-edged sword. Thus in some contexts it offers a powerful resource for resisting doctrinaire conceptions of truth and method, while in others it can work to contrary effect and dissuade scientists (along with philosophers) from raising questions or advancing hypotheses that challenge the doxastic status quo. Hence, as I have argued elsewhere, the clearly marked change of mind that Einstein underwent with regard to Machian positivism when his concern shifted from finding some useful compromise strategy in face of orthodox objections to relativity-theory toward making sense – realist and causal-explanatory sense – of the issues thrown up by quantum mechanics on the orthodox (Copenhagen) interpretation.[28] For there is something distinctly odd, obscurantist and strongly counter-intuitive about a theory which raises the impossibility of passing beyond empirical appearances to a high point of principle that dogmatically rejects any prospect of accounting for those same appearances in more adequate realist and causal-explanatory terms.

What basically distinguishes Mach's kind of radical empiricism from that of van Fraassen and other exponents of its latter-day, more 'sophisticated' variant is the fact that Mach's philosophical reflections took rise from his work as a practising physicist and educator while theirs is most often arrived at through engagement with issues that belong very squarely to the context of intra-philosophical debate. Thus van Fraassen's is clearly an approach that has its source in the verificationist doctrine espoused by the logical positivists, along with the various refinements adopted by subsequent thinkers – Dummett among them – who have sought to recast that doctrine in a form less open to the standard objections and more in line with those criteria of assertoric warrant supplied by the 'linguistic turn' after Frege, Russell and Wittgenstein.[29] However one may reasonably doubt whether first-order issues in ontology, epistemology and philosophy of science can best be resolved or most usefully raised through an analysis of second-order issues about language and repre-sentation. Michael Devitt makes the point to good effect when he asks just why – on what rational grounds – we should suppose certain highly speculative theses in fields such as philosophical semantics to trump the plain evidence of progress in so many scientific fields. Thus, according to Devitt, realism

> is an overarching empirical (scientific) theory or principle. It is initially plausible. It is supported by arguments that make no appeal to theories of language or understanding ... What firmer place could there be to stand than Realism, as we theorize in such undeveloped areas as those of language and understanding? In contrast, the poor state of theories in those areas, whether verificationist or not, makes them a bad place from which to start theorizing, particularly in determining overarching principles about the nature of reality. To think otherwise is to put the cart before the horse.[30]

Devitt's main targets here are the various strains of lately emergent anti-realist, cultural-relativist, or social-constructivist thought which take for granted the idea that language is in some sense the furthest one can get toward the justi-fication of belief or the grounds of rational assent. That this notion derives from a highly disparate range of philosophic sources – among them Frege, late Wittgenstein, Quine, Heidegger, Saussure, and Richard Rorty's synthesis of all these plus a good few others – suggests how the present-day 'linguistic turn' cuts across some otherwise large differences of standpoint and orientation.[31] Thus, for instance, Dummett's anti-realist approach draws on Frege for its compositional theory of sentence-meaning and assertoric warrant, but on Wittgenstein for its most distinctive claim that such warrant cannot possibly transcend the scope and limits of proof or potential verification.[32] This despite the evident conflict between a theory (Frege's) whose central premise is the objective, i.e., the non-epistemic or verification-transcendent character of truth-values whether in the formal or the natural sciences and, on the other hand, a theory (Wittgenstein's) according to which truth must always be conceived to lie within the bounds of attainable knowledge or linguistic expressibility.[33]

That Dummett can nonetheless purport to reconcile these two contradictory positions is a sure sign that some crucial issues have been swept under the carpet by this prevalent idea of language – on no matter what precise understanding – as the ultimate horizon of truth, knowledge and intelligibility. This is why Devitt's charge that such thinking is strictly preposterous – a plain case of 'putting the cart before the horse' – applies not only to anti-realists and relativists but also to those (like Donald Davidson) who rest their case against such arguments on principally logico-semantic grounds.[34] For if one thing has emerged with daylight clarity from the course of debate on these topics since Frege and Wittgenstein it is the fact that any realist conception of truth advanced on such grounds can always be pushed just that further step – as in Dummett's conflation of these two sources – which relativizes truth to the scope and limits of assertoric warrant. That is to say, once you take it (like Dummett) that the linguistic turn is the single most significant advance in modern epistemology and that it marks a decisive, irreversible break with previous approaches then there is a sense in which the whole issue about realism and anti-realism has already gone by default, i.e., in favour of the anti-realist position. Hence the otherwise extraordinary ease with which Dummett can claim Fregean warrant for his theses concerning compositionality and the truth-functional analysis of language at the level of sentence structure while fully endorsing Wittgenstein's idea that sentences possess meaning only in virtue of the role they play within some particular language-game or cultural life-form. For, as Quine remarks in 'Two Dogmas of Empiricism', there is a kind of natural momentum about the context-principle that may begin by taking sentences (rather than individual terms) as the basic units of significance but which can then scarcely be restrained from pressing on to the point where meanings or truth-values become relativized to the entire existing body of beliefs-held-true at any given time.[35]

III

Dummett is understandably keen to resist any such drift toward full-fledged meaning-holism since, on his account, it leaves us at a loss to explain how language-users could ever acquire, recognize, or manifest a grasp of those sentence-specific conditions of 'warranted assertibility' that alone provide the basis for communicative uptake.[36] However it is far from clear that this Fregean element in Dummett's thinking can be reconciled with his Wittgensteinian appeal to the communal nature of all understanding, i.e., the extent to which normative values of truth, rationality, and right interpretation are always dependent on (or relative to) some larger – at the limit, culture-wide – context of shared meanings and beliefs. This in turn suggests that there is not after all such a clearly marked difference between, on the one hand, Quine's radical (minus-the-dogmas) empiricist approach combined with his doctrine of meaning-holism and, on the other, Dummett's preferred way into these issues via a logico-semantic theory that grants priority to sentence-sized items such as propositional contents and attitudes toward them. What they share is the premise that any adequate theory of truth and knowledge must go by way of another, more basic theory which aims to specify the terms and conditions of linguistic-communicative grasp. For Quine this latter is best, most reliably arrived at through a form of behaviourist or stimulus-response psychology that rejects any dubious 'mentalist' appeal to suspect items such as thoughts, meanings, beliefs, intentions, attitudes, and so on, and which finds room for nothing but observable instances of speech-behaviour under certain (likewise observable) ambient conditions. Thus the Quinean project of 'epistemology naturalized' is one that abjures any normative pretensions, treats itself as a sub-branch of physical science, and henceforth conceives its task as a matter of explaining how the 'meagre input' of sensory stimuli to which human beings are subject is somehow transformed into a 'torrential output' of statements, hypotheses, theories, predictions, and so forth.[37] In the process not only are issues of truth and knowledge reduced to issues of linguistic comprehension but these latter are likewise and yet more drastically reduced to a dead level of stimulus-response psychology that permits no recourse to normative criteria of rational interpretation or theory-choice.

That is to say, Quine's approach leaves epistemology devoid of any standards for assessing rival theories or interpretations except those enjoined by a prag-matist concern to save empirical appearances so far as can be managed with least adjustment to the range of existing beliefs-held-true along with a decent measure of coherence among them and a due regard for the precepts of classical logic. Even so, as Quine famously allows, those precepts might conceivably have to be abandoned or revised should the empirical evidence require it. Thus, for instance, it might be more 'rational' to interpret the evidence of quantum superposition or wave/particle dualism as requiring the shift from a logic grounded on the principles of bivalence and excluded middle to a three-valued logic that is able to accommodate these and kindred phenomena without thereby producing any downright contradiction.[38] However there are large philosophical problems with this Quinean idea that theory-change is always 'where rational, pragmatic', that is, aimed to conserve maximum coherence across the overall 'fabric' of beliefs and to minimize any disturbance or threat to existing habits of thought. Among them are its glaring normativity-deficit and its failure to explain why scientists should ever feel compelled to respond to recalcitrant, i.e., anomalous or unlooked-for experimental results by revising their basic theore-tical commitments rather than adopting a pragmatist line of least resistance. Hence the controversial though widely accepted Duhem-Quine thesis according to which observation-statements are always theoretically informed and theories always under-determined by the best empirical evidence.[39] The consequence of this, so the argument goes, is that cherished theories can never be refuted by any such recalcitrant result (or so-called *experimentum crucis*) since the evidence in question can always be discounted by invoking alternative auxiliary hypotheses, or by putting it down to observational error, perceptual bias, or maybe some defect in the measuring apparatus. However it is then hard to see how one theory can count as better than another, 'better' (that is to say) as a matter of improved causal-explanatory grasp or superior capacity to make rational sense of certain well-founded and agreed-upon empirical data.

So it is that Quine can advance his claim with regard to the in-principle revisability of logic under pressure from the anomalies of quantum mechanics as nothing more than an extension of the same process 'whereby Kepler superseded Ptolemy, or Einstein Newton, or Darwin Aristotle'.[40] On this view – which follows 'logically' enough from Quine's combination of radical empiricism and radical meaning-holism – there is ultimately just no distinguishing in point of rationality between giving up empirically based beliefs in the face of 'recalcitrant' empirical evidence and giving up certain axioms of classical logic such as bivalence or excluded middle should they turn out to generate conflicts with the latest findings of subatomic physics. Having written at length on this topic elsewhere I shall not go into more technical aspects of the question whether quantum mechanics – or the orthodox version of it – is indeed so well established and theoretically secure that it can properly be held to justify any such far-reaching revisionist proposal.[41] Suffice it to say (1) that there exists a viable alternative (causal-realist) interpretation which perfectly conserves the existing empirical and predictive data, and (2) that on this account there is simply no need to contemplate changing or suspending the ground rules of classical bivalent logic.[42] My point is that the notion of ultimate revisability with respect to those presumptive 'laws of thought' is one that has arisen in two very different philosophical contexts: as an outcome of Quinean radical empiricism and as the upshot of Dummett's logico-semantic and metaphysical case for denying the objective truth or falsehood of statements in the so-called 'disputed class', i.e., those that lie beyond reach of proof or verification. What they have in common, despite this disparity of motivating interest, is the notion that truth cannot possibly transcend the scope and limits of assertoric warrant, whether these be conceived in empiricist terms (so that logic is revisable under pressure of counter-evidence) or in terms of a Dummettian anti-realist approach that has its chief source in mathematics and the formal sciences.

That is to say, there is a striking convergence on similar claims from these two, as it might seem sharply opposed movements of thought in the wake of logical empiricism. Where Quine, in 'Two Dogmas', presses right through with the idea of logic as simply a means of working some structure into the otherwise inchoate flux of sensory experience Dummett starts out from certain formal or proof-theoretical issues in philosophy of mathematics, then extends the resulting (anti-realist) line of argument to scientific, historical and other empirically based areas of discourse.[43] Indeed the main difference between them as concerns the revisability thesis is that Quine conceives the suspension of bivalence or excluded middle very much as a strategy of last resort under pressure of conflicting evidence whereas, for Dummett, there is a vast (indeed potentially infinite) range of well-formed statements for which we lack any means of proof or verification and that must hence be regarded as lacking any objective (bivalent) truth-value. However both thinkers go far enough in this direction to raise crucial issues concerning the extent to which epistemology, as a normative discipline, must be thought to entail certain basic standards of logical consistency and truth. Hilary Putnam makes the point with regard to Quine in a recent reflection on the problems that arise with any thoroughgoing physicalist or naturalized approach to such issues. Thus:

> [Quine's] answer to those who want a more realistic epistemology, an epistemology that concerns how real scientists manage to select real theories on real data, is the famous, 'Why not settle for psychology?' What many of his readers have missed is that when Quine said this he *meant* it. 'Naturalized epistemology' in Quine's sense means the *abandonment* of epistemology. 'Psychology' (which for Quine always means Skinnerian psychology) is all the epistemology we want or need. This is evasion of the epistemological question with a vengeance![44]

In this respect Quine's is just one, albeit highly prominent expression of that drastic scheme/content dualism that has marked so many episodes of post-1930 Anglophone philosophic thought. That is to say, his critique of logical empiricism for cleaving to the Humean distinction between 'matters of fact' and 'truths of reason', or the Kantian dichotomy between synthetic and analytic judgements, is one that swings so far toward the radical-empiricist pole as to leave itself bereft of any adequate normative resources. This in turn has to do with the question that Putnam very pointedly raises concerning the limits of Quinean 'naturalized epistemology' and whether that approach can come close to explaining 'how real scientists manage to select real theories on real data'. For if 'realism' is to have any genuine, substantive meaning in each of these contexts then it will have to involve more in the way of rational and causal-explanatory warrant than could ever be supplied by a crudely behaviourist account of belief-acquisition and a likewise crude (since normatively vacuous) theory of how knowledge accrues in various fields of scientific enquiry. Hence the failure of Quine's radical empiricism to break with those dualist habits of thought which form the chief target of his essay, a failure that results from his espousing just one side of the dichotomy and leaving the other – the rational-normative – all the more conspicuous for its absence.[45]

Hence also, on a different but related tack, the strange conjunction in Davidson's thought of a direct realism blithely assured of our having direct perceptual access to the world with a truth-theoretic approach devoid of any content save that supplied by the formal (strictly tautologous) structure of a Tarskian semantics.[46] Thus, as Davidson puts it, '[i]n giving up the dualism of scheme and world, we do not give up the world, but re-establish unmediated touch with the familiar objects whose antics make our sentences and opinions true or false'.[47] Such is the dualism that Davidson attributes to Quine and which he sees as primarily responsible for Quine's having saddled epistemology and philosophy of language with such vexing problems as those of ontological relativity and radical translation. Yet if Quine's was indeed, as Davidson argues, the third dogma of empiricism then the fourth might be said to make its appearance in Davidson's proposal for releasing the grip of this otherwise end-lessly self-replicating pattern of errors. That proposal is that we should hence-forth drop all the otiose talk of Kuhnian paradigms, Whorfian languages, Quinean 'conceptual schemes', and so forth, and acknowledge the jointly sufficient character, for all practical purposes, of a Tarskian truth-based formal semantics along with an assurance that things just are (cannot be other than) the way they strike us as a matter of direct, 'unmediated' sensory-perceptual warrant. However it will look less promising and more like yet another covert dualism if one asks how the truth-theoretic approach, devised as it was for application to formal rather than natural languages, can play any valid or effective role in the latter (i.e., everyday-communicative) kinds of linguistic context. Of course it is a main plank in Davidson's argument – and a claim more guardedly expressed on occasion by Tarski himself – that the theory can indeed be so applied with suitable adjustments or modifications.[48] Yet this still leaves the problem very squarely in place as to how it can help if we approach these issues equipped, on the one hand, with a formalized semantic conception of truth whose tautological nature renders it devoid of empirical or other such substantive content and, on the other, with a notion of direct realism that allows no role for such 'mediating' factors as judgement, rationality, or inference to the best causal explanation. In short there is a sense in which Davidson may be seen to have thrown out the baby with the bathwater, or attempted to resolve the dead-end dilemmas of conceptual-scheme relativism by adopting a sharply dichotomous approach that finds no room for the exercise of just those knowledge-conducive conceptual powers.

IV

It seems to me that Devitt is right and that there is simply no escaping such problems once epistemology takes the turn toward language (on whatever construal) as the baseline of all enquiry into matters of knowledge and truth. For the way is then open from Fregean logico-semantic objectivism to Wittgen-steinian ideas about truth as 'internal' to some given cultural life-form, or from logical empiricism of the Tarski/Carnap variety to Quinean scheme-dependence and ontological relativity, or again, from Davidson's sturdy defence of truth – or the attitude of holding-true – as the precondition for all understanding to his various changes of philosophic tack in response to Richard Rorty's claim that 'truth' is just the compliment we pay to our currently most favoured items of belief.[49] Above all it is this nowadays widely assumed priority of linguistic and logico-semantic issues over issues of substantive epistemological import that has allowed Dummettian anti-realism to set the agenda for so much recent debate. Thus, in Dummett's words, '[t]he whole point of my approach ... has been to show that the theory of meaning underlies metaphysics. If I have made any worthwhile contribution to philosophy, I think it must lie in having raised the issue in these terms.' All the same, he insists,

> [t]he opinion is sometimes expressed that I succeeded in opening up a genuine philosophical problem, or range of problems, but that the resulting topic has little to do with traditional disputes concerning realism. That was certainly not my intention: I meant to apply a new technique to such wholly traditional questions as realism about the external world and about the mental, questions which I continue to believe I characterised correctly.[50]

This no doubt with an eye to critics like Devitt who maintain that, so far from having set philosophy to rights by adopting his anti-realist version of the linguistic turn, Dummett has instead produced a kind of unintended *reductio ad absurdum*, a demonstration of the fact that any language-first approach to issues of knowledge and truth will end up by endorsing some such strictly untenable position. 'Untenable', that is, on the basic premise that where two theories or metaphysical commitments are so completely at odds as those of realism and anti-realism then the issue between them can only be decided by asking which accords best with the evidence to hand and the most rational (or least credibility-stretching) explanation of that evidence.

Here again Devitt has a strong case when he remarks that this principle is regularly flouted by anti-realists, paradigm-relativists, and sundry proponents of the linguistic turn who attach more weight to conclusions based on highly dubious or speculative theories in philosophy of language than to the cumulative record of scientific knowledge and progress to date. Thus he asks quite simply 'What has truth to do with Realism?', and answers: 'On the face of it, nothing at all', since '{r}ealism says nothing semantic at all beyond, in its use of "objective", making the negative point that our semantic capacities do *not* constitute the world'.[51] Hence what he takes to be the basic strategy of all arguments in the language-first or logico-semantic mode, whether aimed (like Dummett's) to prepare the ground for an anti-realist approach or aimed – misguidedly, so Devitt thinks – to controvert that case but on terms which its proponents have effectively decreed in advance. Such arguments typically start out, he remarks,

> with a properly metaphysical statement of the issue. This is immediately replaced by a formulation in terms of truth, which is then taken ... as part of a theory of meaning. Whatever the merits of the various theories of meaning then proposed, the theories are (almost) irrelevant ... to the metaphysical issue which they are alleged to settle. For the metaphysical issue is not one about meaning.[52]

This seems to me spot-on as a diagnostic statement of how the whole debate between realists and anti-realists has been skewed away from substantive issues of truth, rationality and knowledge and refocused on topics in philosophy of language that at most have only a tangential bearing on the question in hand. That question is 'metaphysical' just in the sense that it concerns the existence of objects, properties, structures, events, causal dispositions, formal or abstract (e.g., mathematical) entities, and so forth, whose ontological status – their reality or otherwise – is an issue wholly distinct from that raised by Dummett with regard to our grasp of the validity-conditions, or conditions of assertoric warrant, for statements concerning them. Thus Dummett's three criteria for admission to the class of assertible statements – that, in any given instance, we should be epistemically so placed as to *acquire, recognize,* and *manifest* the fact of our possessing such grasp – are quite beside the point when it comes to matters of objective, i.e., verification-transcendent truth and falsehood. What begins with the slide (so evident in Quine) from ontological to epistemological issues is carried yet further by the turn toward language – on whatever precise conception – as the reference-point by which to define or specify those criteria.

This is why, as I have said, there is not much hope for any truth-based theory of interpretation (like Davidson's) which sets out expressly to controvert the claims of Quinean and kindred relativist doctrines, but does so from a standpoint deeply in hock to some other, presumptively more adequate version of the logico-semantic approach. Hence Davidson's odd habit of making what would seem very large and – from his own professed standpoint – highly damaging concessions to the adversary camp while appearing not to recognize that they constitute any such thing. Thus: '[o]f course truth of sentences is relative to language, but that is as objective as can be'.[53] And again, in typically laid-back style: '[w]hat sounded at first like a thrilling discovery – that truth is relative to a conceptual scheme – has not so far been shown to be anything more than the pedestrian and familiar fact that the truth of a sentence is relative to (among other things) the language to which it belongs'.[54] Davidson clearly thinks that he can well afford to take this line since by now he has established (1) that such relativity-to-language can always be trumped – or rendered innocuous – by appealing to a shared conception of truth which must underlie any surface differences of logico-semantic structure, and (2) that this is sufficient to ensure the possibility of straightforward communicative uptake or even of Quinean 'radical translation' across widely divergent conceptual schemes. After all, it is just his point that such scheme-relativist (or radical-divergence) talk can simply drop out – or be made to look wholly irrelevant – if one adopts the more sensible, since problem-dissolving 'truth first' order of priorities. On this account the attitude of holding-true is one that must necessarily find expression in any language that is up to the basic task of communicating ideas, meanings, beliefs, inferential commitments, and so forth.

Such is Davidson's chief argument against Quinean, Kuhnian, or Whorfian versions of scheme-relativism. These thinkers typically rest their case on the idea of language as primarily a field of *semantic* resources varying from one culture to another in accordance with local expressive needs and priorities, rather than looking to those deeper structural (i.e., logico-syntactic) features that manifest

no such wide variation since they play a strictly indispensable role in all
linguistic understanding. Thus:

> what forms the skeleton of what we call a language is the pattern of
> inference and structure created by the logical constants: the sentential
> connectives, quantifiers, and devices for cross-reference. If we can apply our
> general method of interpretation to a speaker at all – if we can make even a
> start on understanding him on the assumption that his language is like
> ours, it will be because we can treat his structure-forming devices as we
> treat ours.[55]

In which case philosophers are getting things backwards when they claim that
cultural-linguistic 'conventions' are prerequisite to such understanding, and
hence that truth – or our various holdings-true – must be thought of as
dependent on those same language-relative or culture-specific conventions.
Rather it is the case that our conception of truth as expressed in the 'pattern of
inference and structure created by the logical constants' is itself the precondition
for our having a language, and this in turn – the fact of our competence as
language speakers and interpreters – the precondition for our grasp of what is
involved in the practice of grasping or following conventions. Thus the 'problems' of conceptual-scheme relativism and radical translation begin to look more
like pseudo-problems brought about by a false, systematically inverted sense of
priorities. Moreover, any difficulties created by divergences of natural-language
meaning or structure can register as such only on condition that they show up
against this wider background of shared logical or syntactic resources. Whence
our ability to spot them in the first place, perceive how they disrupt the process
of communicative uptake, and then cast around for the best explanation of just
why they have occurred, whether through some deep-laid disparity of worldviews, or more likely, some localized case of semantic or lexical mismatch.

According to Davidson, this is what saves us from the pyrrhic upshot of
conceptual-scheme relativism in its various forms. In short, it is our knowledge
– when confronting the speaker of a culturally remote language or the adherent
to a belief-system markedly at odds with our own – that communication can at
least make a start since 'we can treat his structure-forming devices as we treat
ours'. We can then bring in the Principle of Charity so as to adopt the best, most
generous or truth-optimizing method for treating him (the interlocutor) as
probably 'right in most matters'. That is to say, we ourselves will have a much
better chance of getting him right – of correctly interpreting his intended gist –
if we impute the maximum degree of rationality to his various assertions and,
where these seem to entail the holding of false or irrational beliefs, if we always
make allowance for the standing possibility of our having been mistaken on this
or that detailed point of translation or interpretative grasp. Such, to repeat, is
Davidson's chief claim for the 'method of truth in metaphysics': that 'whether
we like it or not, if we want to understand others, we must count them right in
most matters', and hence that '[i]f we can produce a theory that reconciles

charity and the formal conditions for a theory, we have done all that could be done to ensure communication'.[56]

However, once again, there are sentences and passages in Davidson's essay which seem to take away with one hand what he so confidently holds out in the other. One such passage occurs in the penultimate paragraph and gives the strange but typical impression of his somehow losing interest in the topic, or being suddenly seized by the conviction that it just wasn't worth all that philosophic labour. 'It would', he concludes,

> be wrong to summarize by saying we have shown how communication is possible between people who have different schemes, a way that works without need of what there cannot be, namely a neutral ground, or a common co-ordinate system. For we have found no intelligible basis on which it can be said that schemes are different. It would be equally wrong to announce the glorious news that all mankind – all speakers of language, at least – share a common scheme or ontology. For if we cannot intelligibly say that schemes are different, neither can we intelligibly say that they are one.[57]

This suggests an attitude of outright disdain for all such merely abstract concepts or categories, here transferred to a context (analytic philosophy of language) where it works out as a desire to have done with the whole tedious business. For it is hard to see what can possibly be left of Davidson's argument if *each and every version* of its purpose or intent as summarized in the above passage should be counted plain 'wrong', or as missing the point, or as just another lapse into bad old dualist habits of thought. After all, that argument *does* indeed depend on the idea of a 'common co-ordinate system', namely (as we have seen) the system that Davidson invokes when he criticizes Quine, Kuhn and company for drawing far-gone relativist conclusions on the basis of a chiefly semantic, rather than logico-syntactic approach to issues of interlingual translation or intralinguistic communicative grasp. Maybe it is the case – from this hard-won perspective beyond all the vexing dilemmas of post-Kantian epistemology or post-Fregean philosophy of language – that one shouldn't espouse either side of the delusory choice on offer, whether the Quine/Kuhn relativist notion that 'schemes are different' or the equally 'unintelligible' notion that 'all schemes are one'. More to the point: any viable theory of how we actually do, for the most part, succeed in making sense of each other's meanings, intentions and beliefs despite large differences of cultural background will have to take both possibilities into account, rather than treating both as mere products of a false, artificially contrived dilemma. For there are certain distinctly puzzling aspects of human communication across distances of time, culture, language, or 'conceptual scheme' which cannot be wished away by any argument that would either collapse those distances to zero or accept their existence (since 'of course truth of sentences is relative to language') but nonetheless deny that this poses any obstacle to our powers of communicative grasp. What tends to drop out on

Davidson's truth-based, logico-semantic account is the need to preserve a lively sense of the problems and resistances that sometimes crop up in the business of interlingual translation or intralinguistic grasp and yet, despite that, to make due allowance for the surely self-evident fact that we *can and do* most often manage to achieve a good measure of communicative uptake.

Thus when Davidson says that we shall get him wrong if we suppose him to have shown how 'communication is possible between people who have different schemes', and shall also get him wrong if we take him to have shown the opposite (i.e., that such communication is impossible just because 'schemes are different'), then we have to assume – with ample warrant from the text – that, for Davidson, scheme-talk of whatever kind is misconceived and a source of manifold errors and confusions. But in that case we are back with a radical empiricist (or direct realist) doctrine according to which, quite simply, once we give up the 'dualism of scheme and world' all those needless perplexities fall away and we can henceforth enjoy 'unmediated touch' with the whole range of 'familiar items whose antics make our sentences and opinions true or false'. No doubt, as the realist will fervently agree, there is a strong case for seeking some alternative to those various tenacious dualisms that have plagued epistemology and philosophy of mind from Kant to the logical empiricists and beyond. Nor will the realist wish to take issue with Davidson's proposal that we can best make a start by rejecting that particular dualism which creates so many intractable problems by driving a merely notional wedge between empirical 'content' and formal or logico-semantic 'scheme'. Where they *will* beg to differ is with regard to Davidson's claim that those problems can be overcome by adopting the twin expedients of a Tarskian, truth-based semantics devoid of substantive empirical content and a qualified version of Quinean radical empiricism which departs from that doctrine only in so far as it incorporates the Tarskian truth-theoretical apparatus. Thus the realist may very well agree with Davidson when he says, *à propos* Quine and Kuhn, that 'this dualism of scheme and content, of organizing system and something waiting to be organized, cannot be made intelligible and defensible'.[58] Moreover they will most likely endorse his claim that this scheme/content dichotomy 'is itself a dogma of empiricism . . . [t]he third, and perhaps the last, for if we give it up it is not clear that there is anything distinctive left to call empiricism'.[59] Yet if the notion of our having epistemic contact with objects of perceptual experience which thereby confer truth or falsehood on our statements, theories, or predictions concerning them doesn't count as a version of 'empiricism' then it is hard to conceive what might qualify for that description.

To be sure, it is not so much empiricism *per se* that Davidson is out to confute but rather that particular 'dogma' of logical empiricism – the scheme/content dichotomy – which he regards as a wholly unfortunate excrescence and a chief cause of all the problems that afflict present-day epistemology and philosophy of language. Still there is something odd about a theory that claims to get over those problems by promoting two such disparate approaches as a Tarskian (i.e., formalized and meta-linguistic) method of truth-functional analysis and a direct appeal to perceptual self-evidence as the ultimate, indubitable basis of knowledge and truth. What this amounts to is a kind of amnesiac regression to the predicament that Kant confronted when he sought some alternative path beyond the opposite (and equally dead-end) extremes of Leibnizian rationalism on the one hand and Humean empiricism on the other. That is to say, it is a further example of the dilemma that always results when epistemologists fail to heed Kant's famous dictum in the First *Critique* that 'concepts without intuitions are empty', while 'intuitions without concepts are blind'.[60] Not that Kant can really be credited – despite his high claims and extraordinary labours to make them good – with having set philosophy on that alternative path or produced an argument that would finally lay those dilemmas to rest. For it is clear from some of the murkier passages in the First *Critique*, as well as from the exegetical travails of his well-disposed commentators, that Kant was in the end unable to deliver on his promise of reconciling 'transcendental idealism' with 'empirical realism'. Thus they are supposed to be united via the same faculty that accomplishes the bringing of sensuous intuitions under concepts of understanding. This faculty is that of 'judgement' which in turn depends on the mediating power of certain innate 'schematisms', these latter conceived as resulting from the agency of 'productive imagination', which Kant then defines – in far from perspicuous terms – as 'a blind but indispensable function of the soul, without which we should have no knowledge whatsoever, but of which we are scarcely ever conscious'.[61]

Nor have these obscurities been much clarified by recent rediscoverers of Kant in the broadly 'analytic' camp – such as John McDowell – who suggest that we should switch focus from his problem-creating dualist talk of 'sensuous intuitions' *vis-à-vis* 'concepts of understanding'.[62] Instead we should look to his twin ideas of 'receptivity' and 'spontaneity' as aspects of our cognitive dealing with the world that are only 'notionally separable' and should rather be thought of as indissolubly bound up together in our every act of knowledge or judgement. However, as I have argued at length elsewhere, MacDowell's various attempts to achieve an acceptable (non-dualist) formulation of this wished-for alternative path end up by reproducing the same dilemmas in a different but closely related key.[63] Nor is this at all surprising, given that McDowell – like Quine, Davidson, and a good many others with similar ends in view – still subscribes to what might (somewhat wearily) be called the 'fourth dogma' of empiricism, namely the Hume-derived sceptical belief that while 'causation is not under a description, explanation is'.[64] One can see why this particular, typically offhand phrase of Davidson's has been cited by Rorty as evidence enough that he (Davidson) is a pragmatist at heart, one who has no use for talk of 'truth' except as a purely honorific term, that is, as the compliment we normally pay to just those sentences that best fit with our range of currently favoured beliefs.[65] For if one takes it, after Hume, that there can be no rational justification or probative warrant for any causal explanation that presumes to go beyond the (supposed) self-evidence of empirical data then the way is clearly open for Rorty to conclude – in accordance with Davidson's dictum – that the raw sense-data may be 'real' enough but that otherwise interpretation goes 'all the way down', whether as regards the most basic observation-sentences or the highest-level theories of the natural sciences.

Thus, according to Rorty: '[w]hen Galileo saw the moons of Jupiter through his telescope, it might be said, the impact on his retina was "hard" in the relevant sense, even though its consequences were, to be sure, different for different communities'. And again: 'the astronomers of Padua took it [the telescopic evidence] as merely one more anomaly which had somehow to be worked into a more or less Aristotelian cosmology, whereas Galileo's admirers took it as shattering the crystalline spheres once and for all. But the datum *itself*, it might be argued, is utterly real quite apart from the interpretation it receives'.[66] Rorty in turn takes the whole episode as bearing out his case that scientific realism with respect to (say) atoms, molecules, genes, or the moons of Jupiter is again just a complimentary mode of talk, in which case the truth of sentences concerning them is 'truth' only relative to this or that language-game, Kuhnian paradigm, or presently favoured descriptive scheme. To be sure, '[t]he pragmatist agrees that there is such a thing as brute physical resistance – the pressure of light waves on Galileo's eyeball, or of the stone on Dr. Johnson's boot. But he sees no way of transferring this nonlinguistic brutality to *facts*, to the truth of sentences'.[67] Thus what Rorty in effect manages to do with Davidson's (on the face of it) fairly minor and carefully phrased concession to the Humean position is use it – like so many anti-realists before him – as the thin end of a finely honed and rapidly expanding sceptical wedge. For the argument can then be driven home so as to maintain a wholesale version of the 'strong'-descriptivist claim, i.e., that whatever the brute reality of those incoming sensory data they are neither here nor there when it comes to assessing our various observation-sentences, theories, causal-explanatory hypotheses, and so forth. Quite simply, these latter are products of interpretation which may (in some rock-bottom, notional sense) be constrained by the empirical evidence, but which are borne out by that evidence only when viewed under one or another such description, and are hence incapable of ranking or comparison in terms of their truth-content or their depth of causal-explanatory grasp.

V

So Rorty is right to this extent at least: that his own strong-descriptivist and cultural-constructivist outlook is the end of the road that philosophy has been travelling at least since Quine's 'Two Dogmas', and indeed – as he would claim – since thinkers like Frege, Russell, Austin and late Wittgenstein first proposed their different versions of the 'linguistic turn'.[68] That is to say, it is an upshot that Rorty can plausibly regard as lying in wait for both main branches of the post-1920 analytic tradition, despite their otherwise basic disagreement on the issue of priority concerning the claims of logico-semantic analysis *vis-à-vis* those of logically unregimented natural or 'ordinary' language as our last, best source of philosophic guidance. Where his argument is less convincing – but (for present purposes) diagnostically spot-on – is in simply accepting Quine's pyrrhic verdict that so far as causality is concerned the human condition is the Humean condition.[69] For then it follows that, since explanations are always under some description or other, there is just no escaping the predicament of those – Davidson among them – who seek to reinstate some viable realist conception of truth while nonetheless avoiding any commitment to a more substantive, i.e., depth-ontological or causal-explanatory account. Hence the odd sequence of shifting positions that has characterized Davidson's dealing with Rorty over the years. At times his response has tended strongly in a realist direction whereby the requirements for an adequate theory of truth are taken to exceed any purely formal mode of specification, while at other times he has veered more toward Rorty's notion that truth-values can be cashed out for all practical (or pragmatist) purposes in terms of the Tarskian formal schema plus a straightforward appeal to the presumptive self-evidence of empirical warrant.[70] There is a similar vacillation in Tarski's writings between a studiously non-committal attitude in this regard and a suggestion that the formalized (logico-semantic) approach requires not only a correspondence theory of truth but also a more developed filling-out in substantive realist terms.[71] It is a dilemma that finds perhaps inadvertent expression in the title of Davidson's series of essays on 'The Structure and Content of Truth', and which emerges very clearly in the course of those essays as he attempts to negotiate a path between the claims of a moderately robust realist position and those of a more pragmatic (though short of wholesale Rortian) approach.[72] However, as I have argued, that third-way solution is simply not to be had since if the concept of truth is restricted to 'the formal conditions for a theory' plus 'unmediated touch' with the objects of empirical acquaintance then this leads straight back to the same intractable dilemma that has afflicted philosophy from Kant, via logical empiricism, to Quine, Davidson, McDowell and others.

Hence the otherwise extraordinary ease with which Davidson can pass from statements in a meta-linguistic (Tarskian) mode where the paradigm instance is a pure tautology such as ' "snow is white" is true if and only if snow is white' to statements in a radical-empiricist mode where the prime exemplars are sensory events such as 'losing a button or stubbing a toe, having a sensation of warmth or hearing an oboe'.[73] That is to say, there is no problem about making the shift from a material to a formal register just so long as it is accomplished by a double move which leaves the formal effectively devoid of empirical content and the material confined to a notion of direct, 'unmediated' sensory contact. To this extent Davidson is merely restating in a new and – despite his own claims to the contrary – a starkly polarized or dualist way those same antinomies of scheme and content or 'sensuous intuitions' and 'concepts of understanding' that have been such a constant feature of epistemological debate from Kant to the present. What drops out completely – as it did for Hume and as it has for Hume's large and otherwise diverse latter-day progeny – is the idea that epistemology can be naturalized and yet retain sufficient in the way of normative and causal-explanatory resources to prevent that gap from opening up once again.[74] From this perspective it would seem that the 'linguistic turn' in its various manifestations has not so much achieved its professed aim of resolving (or therapeutically treating) those problems bequeathed by the old, Descartes-to-Kant epistemological enterprise but has rather transposed them to a different key without any change of tune. Least of all can it be hoped that they will find resolution through the kind of linguistically oriented approach that reverses the rational order of things by staking its most confident (even when confidently sceptical) claims on arguments whose degree of rational warrant or probative force cannot come anywhere close to that attained by our knowledge of developments in the natural sciences.

That so many basic issues concerning our knowledge of objects and events in the world have been thus recast as second-order issues concerning their modes of linguistic representation is a development that may strike exponents like Dummett as marking an epochal advance beyond anything that came before. And indeed one can agree that it has clarified those issues by presenting them in a guise – i.e., the more refined, logico-semantically reformulated version of verificationism developed by Dummett as a challenge to realist precepts and principles – that has usefully sharpened the terms of debate. On the other hand it is apt to look more like an obstacle to progress when it dictates those terms to the extent of constituting not so much (as Dummett is sometimes wont to claim) a research programme with no preconceptions either way but a definite anti-realist agenda pursued by treating all such matters as a sub-branch of logico-semantic enquiry or philosophy of language. Hence (to repeat) Devitt's surely justified complaint that '[w]hatever the merits of the various theories of meaning then proposed, the theories are (almost) irrelevant ... to the metaphysical issue which they are alleged to settle'.[75] The parenthetical 'almost' should not be taken as a bet-hedging strategy on Devitt's part nor indeed as a large, potentially disabling, concession to the Dummettian claim that our capacity to acquire, recognize, and manifest the conditions of warranted assertibility for this or that utterance is prerequisite to its counting among the class of bivalent (true or false) statements. Rather it is simply to acknowledge the point that we had better try to work out a viable theory of just how our various truth-claims and assertions find adequate linguistic expression even though, on any rational weighing of the evidence, such issues must surely be ranked below the primary concern of epistemology with questions of justificatory warrant and inference to the best explanation. For otherwise, on the language-first conception, we shall risk losing sight of that primary concern and becoming fixated on matters of a strictly second-order, ancillary interest. Of course the anti-realist will then come back and ask how these questions can possibly be raised except by way of a prior address to the issue concerning their intelligibility as questions that fall within the scope and limits of our probative grasp. Or again, like Neil Tennant in his recent, splendidly titled book *The Taming of the True*, he may give this argument a Popperian twist and ask instead what it could possibly mean to maintain the bivalent (either-true-or-false) status of assertions that lie beyond our utmost powers of decisive falsification.[76] However the realist will again respond that these questions exemplify that strictly preposterous, cart-before-the horse way of thinking which attaches more weight to certain highly contentious doctrines in philosophy of language than to the kinds of rational inference to be drawn from our knowledge of the growth of scientific knowledge.

To be sure, there are others, Davidson among them, who have espoused a truth-based and at any rate a more realism-friendly standpoint despite endorsing the presently widespread view that language is in some sense the necessary starting-point for philosophical reflection on issues of knowledge and truth. Thus it would clearly be wrong to treat all subscribers to the 'linguistic turn' as anti-realists under the skin, or as thereby committed to some version – however qualified or hedged about – of Dummettian logico-semantic anti-realism. Still less should that description be allowed to conceal the crucial differences of standpoint and priority that distinguish work in the mainstream analytic tradition descending from Frege and Russell – a tradition for the most part strongly marked by its commitment to values of objectivity and truth – from the sorts of unqualified 'language-first' approach adopted by followers of late Wittgenstein.[77] Still there is a sense in which these two, seemingly opposed strains of thought nevertheless have sufficient in common (i.e., the basic fact of their primarily linguistic orientation) to leave the former constantly exposed to anti-realist raids and incursions. Hence Dummett's odd conjunction of, on the one hand, a Fregean compositional and truth-based theory of meaning which takes the sentence as its basic unit of intelligibility and firmly rejects any wider, more holistic (e.g., Quinean) approach with, on the other hand, a Wittgensteinian idea of assertoric warrant according to which it is the role of sentences in whole 'language-games' or cultural 'forms of life' that decides their meaning from one context to another.[78] Whatever the specific problems with Dummett's position it can stand as representative of much that has transpired during the past half-century of philosophical debate and that has resulted mainly from the language-dominated treatment of fundamental issues in metaphysics, ontology, epistemology, and philosophy of science.

Where Dummett sees this as a great advance and also as his own most important contribution – that of having set new terms for the debate between realism and anti-realism – one might very well argue to contrary effect: that the linguistic turn in whichever variant has been chiefly a distraction from the most important business of those disciplines.[79] All the more so, I would suggest, since that approach has very often worked out – not least through the nowadays pervasive influence of Wittgenstein's later writings – as a means of promoting anti-realist arguments in the guise of a purely investigative programme with no such foregone doctrinal commitment. Thus it is often presented as seeking nothing more than to specify truth in relation to this or that area of discourse, and to do so in such a way as to bring it back within the scope of assertoric warrant, that is to say, of linguistically recognizable and manifestable knowledge.[80] Yet of course this is just what the realist will reject, i.e., the claim that truth is epistemically constrained, or that the truth-value of well-formed and meaningful even if unproven or unverified propositions is in any way affected by our present-best or future-best-possible state of knowledge concerning them. In which case she will very likely conclude that the linguistic turn, so far from representing the single most important advance in recent analytic philosophy, has in fact served mainly to obfuscate the issues and to sidetrack debate from such first-order questions as those concerning the grounds of knowledge, the nature of causal explanation, and the conditions for valid (truth-preserving or truth-conducive) inference in the sciences and elsewhere. To the extent that it has helped to clarify such matters through more scrupulous attention to linguistic detail this movement of thought may be counted a genuine contribution to better understanding. To the extent that it has become a main focus of attention and thereby a means of deflecting enquiry from substantive to subsidiary issues it must be counted among the most unfortunate (since large-scale and persistent) aberrations of recent philosophical thought.

NOTES

1   See especially Hilary Putnam, *Mind, Language and Reality* (Cambridge: Cambridge University Press, 1975); *Reason, Truth and History* (Cambridge University Press, 1981); *Realism and Reason* (Cambridge University Press, 1983); *Representation and Reality* (Cambridge University Press, 1988); *Realism With a Human Face* (Cambridge, MA: Harvard University Press, 1990); *Renewing Philosophy* (Harvard University Press, 1992).

2   For further discussion see Christopher Norris, *Hilary Putnam: Realism, Reason, and the Uses of Uncertainty* (Manchester: Manchester University Press, 2002).

3   Putnam, *Mind, Language and Reality* (op. cit.); also J. Aronson, R. Harré and E. Way, *Realism Rescued: How Scientific Progress is Possible* (London: Duckworth, 1994); Michael Devitt, *Realism and Truth*, 2nd edn (Oxford: Blackwell, 1986); Jarrett Leplin (ed.), *Scientific Realism* (Berkeley: University of California Press, 1984); Stathis Psillos, *Scientific Realism: How Science Tracks Truth* (London: Routledge, 1999); Wesley C. Salmon, *Scientific Explanation and the Causal Structure of the World* (Princeton, NJ: Princeton University Press, 1984).

4   See especially Putnam, *Mathematics, Matter and Method* (Cambridge: Cambridge University Press, 1975).

5   Norris, *Hilary Putnam* (op. cit.).

6   Ludwig Wittgenstein, *Philosophical Investigations*, trans. G. E. M. Anscombe (Oxford: Blackwell, 1958) and *On Certainty*, ed. and trans. Anscombe and G. H. von Wright (Blackwell, 1969); also Cora Diamond, *The Realistic Spirit: Wittgenstein, Philosophy, and the Mind* (Cambridge, MA: MIT Press, 1991).

7   See, for instance, Diamond, *The Realistic Spirit* (op. cit.); also – from a different but not unrelated perspective – Derek L. Phillips, *Wittgenstein and Scientific Knowledge: A Sociological Perspective* (London: Macmillan, 1977).

8   See Richard Rorty, *Consequences of Pragmatism* (Brighton: Harvester, 1982) and *Objectivity, Relativism, and Truth* (Cambridge: Cambridge University Press, 1991).

9   Saul Kripke, *Wittgenstein on Rules and Private Language* (Oxford: Blackwell, 1982); also Alexander Miller and Crispin Wright (eds), *Rule-following and Meaning* (Chesham: Acumen, 2002).

10   See, for instance, J. L. Aronson, 'Testing for Convergent Realism', *British Journal for the Philosophy of Science*, Vol. 40 (1989), pp. 255–60; Richard Boyd, 'The Current Status of

Scientific Realism', in Leplin (ed.), *Scientific Realism* (op. cit.), pp. 41–82; Putnam, *Mind, Language and Reality* (op. cit.).

11 Cf. Larry Laudan, 'A Confutation of Convergent Realism', *Philosophy of Science*, Vol. 48 (1981), 19–49.

12 See Notes 3 and 10, above; also Gilbert Harman, 'Inference to the Best Explanation', *Philosophical Review*, Vol. 74 (1965), pp. 88–95 and Peter Lipton, *Inference to the Best Explanation* (London: Routledge, 1993).

13 Michael Williams, *Unnatural Doubts: Epistemological Scepticism and the Basis of Realism* (Princeton, NJ: Princeton University Press, 1996), pp. 56, 74.

14 Ibid., pp. 327, 359.

15 See Note 9, above.

16 See, for instance, Alan Musgrave, *Common Sense, Science, and Scepticism: A Historical Introduction to the Theory of Knowledge* (Cambridge: Cambridge University Press, 1993) and John Watkins, *Science and Scepticism* (London: Hutchinson, 1984).

17 Albert Einstein, 'Autobiographical Notes' and 'Reply to Criticisms', in P. A. Schilpp (ed.), *Albert Einstein: Philosopher-Scientist* (La Salle, IL: Open Court, 1969), pp. 3–94, 665–88; Arthur Fine, *The Shaky Game: Einstein, Realism, and Quantum Theory* (Chicago: University of Chicago Press, 1986).

18 M. Gardner, 'Realism and Instrumentalism in Nineteenth-Century Atomism', *Philosophy of Science*, Vol. 46 (1979), pp. 1–34; J. Perrin, *Atoms*, trans. D. L. Hammick (New York: Van Nostrand, 1923); Mary Jo Nye, *Molecular Reality* (London: MacDonald, 1972).

19 See Ernst Mach, *The Analysis of Sensations* (London: Thoemmes Press, 1996); also Robert S. Cohen and Raymond J. Seeger (eds), *Ernst Mach: Physicist and Philosopher* (Dordrecht: D. Reidel, 1970) and C. J. Misak, *Verificationism: Its History and Prospects* (London: Routledge, 1995).

20 Bas C. van Fraassen, *The Scientific Image* (Oxford: Clarendon Press, 1980).

21 Christopher Norris, 'Anti-Realism and Constructive Empiricism: Is There a (Real) Difference?' and 'Ontology According to van Fraassen: Some Problems with Constructive Empiricism', in *Against Relativism: Philosophy of Science, Deconstruction and Critical Theory* (Oxford: Blackwell, 1997), pp. 167–95, 196–217.

22 See especially Ian Hacking, *Representing and Intervening: Introductory Topics in the Philosophy of Natural Science* (Cambridge: Cambridge University Press, 1983) and 'Do We See Through a Microscope?', *Pacific Philosophical Quarterly*, Vol. 62 (1981), pp. 305–22.

23 See Notes 3, 10, 12 and 18 above.

24 Pierre Duhem, *The Aims and Structure of Physical Theory*, trans. P. Wiener (Princeton, NJ: Princeton University Press, 1958) and *To Save the Appearances: An Essay on the Idea of Physical Theory from Plato to Galileo*, trans. E. Dolan and C. Maschler (Chicago: University of Chicago Press, 1969).

25 Paul K. Feyerabend, 'Reichenbach's Interpretation of Quantum Mechanics', *Philosophical Studies*, Vol. XX (1958), p. 50. See also Feyerabend, *Against Method: Outline of an Anarchist Theory of Knowledge* (London: Verso, 1978) and *Science in a Free Society* (Verso, 1982).

26 See Note 19, above.

27 Steve Fuller, *Thomas Kuhn: A Philosophical History for Our Times* (Chicago: University of Chicago Press, 2000); Thomas S. Kuhn, *The Structure of Scientific Revolutions*, 2nd edn. (Chicago University Press, 1970).

28 See Note 17, above; also Don Howard, 'Was Einstein Really a Realist?', *Perspectives on Science*, Vol. 1 (1993), pp. 204–51; Max Jammer, *Philosophy of Quantum Mechanics* (New York: Wiley, 1974); M. Klein, 'The First Phase of the Bohr-Einstein Dialogue', *Historical Studies in the Physical Sciences*, Vol. 2 (1970), pp. 1–39; Christopher Norris, *Quantum Theory and the Flight from Realism: Philosophical Responses to Quantum Mechanics* (London: Routledge, 2000).

29 See especially Michael Dummett, *Truth and Other Enigmas* (London: Duckworth, 1978) and *The Logical Basis of Metaphysics* (London: Duckworth, 1991); also Michael Luntley, *Language, Logic and Experience: The Case for Anti-Realism* (London: Duckworth, 1988); Christopher Norris, *Truth Matters: Realism, Anti-Realism and Response-dependence* (Edinburgh: Edinburgh University Press, 2002); Neil Tennant, *Anti-Realism and Logic* (Oxford: Clarendon Press, 1987) and *The Taming of the True* (Clarendon Press, 2002).

30 Devitt, *Realism and Truth* (op. cit.), p. 284.

31 See Richard Rorty (ed.), *The Linguistic Turn: Recent Essays in Philosophical Method* (Chicago: University of Chicago Press, 1967) and *Consequences of Pragmatism* (Brighton: Harvester, 1978); also Norris, *Resources of Realism: Prospects for 'Post-Analytic' Philosophy* (London: Macmillan, 1997) and *Philosophy of Language and the Challenge to Scientific Realism* (London: Routledge, 2004).

32 See Note 29, above.

33 See Note 29, above; also Gottlob Frege, 'The Thought: A Logical Enquiry', in Robert M. Harnish (ed.), *Basic Topics in the Philosophy of Language* (Hemel Hempstead: Harvester-Wheatsheaf, 1994), pp. 517–35 and 'On Sense and Reference', in Peter Geach and Max Black (eds), *Translations from the Philosophical Writings of Gottlob Frege* (Oxford: Blackwell, 1952), pp. 56–78; Wittgenstein, *Philosophical Investigations* (op. cit.).

34 Donald Davidson, *Inquiries into Truth and Interpretation* (Oxford: Oxford University Press, 1984).

35 W. V. Quine, 'Two Dogmas of Empiricism', in *From a Logical Point of View*, 2nd edn (Cambridge, MA: Harvard University Press, 1961), pp. 20–46.

36 See Note 29, above; also Dummett, *Frege: Philosophy of Language* (London: Duckworth, 1973) and *Frege and Other Philosophers* (Oxford: Clarendon Press, 1991).

37 Quine, 'Epistemology Naturalized', in *Ontological Relativity and Other Essays* (New York: Columbia University Press, 1969), pp. 69–90.

38 See Quine, 'Two Dogmas of Empiricism' (op. cit.); also Peter Gibbins, *Particles and Paradoxes: The Limits of Quantum Logic* (Cambridge: Cambridge University Press, 1987); Susan Haack, *Deviant Logic: Some Philosophical Issues* (Cambridge University Press, 1974); Christopher Norris, 'Quantum Theory and Three-Valued Logic: Is it (Realistically) an Option?', *Journal of Critical Realism*, Vol. 5, No. 1 (May 2002), pp. 39–50; Hilary Putnam, 'How to Think Quantum-Logically', *Synthèse*, Vol. 74 (1974), pp. 55–61.

39 Sandra Harding (ed.), *Can Theories be Refuted? Essays on the Duhem-Quine Thesis* (Dordrecht: Reidel, 1976).

40 Quine, 'Two Dogmas of Empiricism' (op. cit.), p. 43.

41 Norris, *Quantum Theory and the Flight from Realism* (op. cit.).

42 See Note 38, above; also David Bohm, *Causality and Chance in Modern Physics* (London: Routledge & Kegan Paul, 1957); David Bohm and B. J. Hiley, *The Undivided Universe: An Ontological Interpretation of Quantum Theory* (London: Routledge, 1993); Peter Holland, *The Quantum Theory of Motion: An Account of the de Broglie-Bohm Causal Interpretation of Quantum Mechanics* (Cambridge: Cambridge University Press, 1993); Peter Mittelstaedt, *Quantum Logic* (Princeton, NJ: Princeton University Press, 1994).

43 See Note 29, above; also Dummett, *Elements of Intuitionism*, 2nd edn. (Oxford: Clarendon Press, 2000).

44 Putnam, *The Collapse of the Fact/Value Dichotomy* (Cambridge, MA: Harvard University Press, 2002), p. 139.

45 For further discussion see Jaegwon Kim, *Supervenience and Mind: Selected Philosophical Essays* (Cambridge: Cambridge University Press, 1993).

46 Davidson, *Inquiries into Truth and Interpretation* (op. cit.).

47 Davidson, 'On the Very Idea of a Conceptual Scheme' (op. cit.), p. 198.

48 Alfred Tarski 'The Concept of Truth in Formalised Languages', in *Logic, Semantics and Metamathematics*, trans. J. H. Woodger (Oxford: Oxford University Press, 1956), pp. 152–278; also Davidson, 'In Defence of Convention T', in *Inquiries into Truth and*

Interpretation (op. cit.), pp. 65–75; Simon Blackburn and Keith Simmons (eds), *Truth* (Oxford: Oxford University Press, 1999); Richard L. Kirkham, *Theories of Truth: A Critical Introduction* (Cambridge, MA: MIT Press, 1992).

49 See Note 31, above.

50 Dummett, *The Seas of Language* (Oxford: Clarendon Press, 1993), p. 468.

51 Devitt, *Realism and Truth* (op. cit.), p. 39.

52 Devitt, 'Aberrations of the Realism Debate', *Philosophical Studies*, Vol. 61 (1991), pp. 43–63; p. 51.

53 Davidson, 'On the Very Idea of a Conceptual Scheme' (op. cit.), p. 198.

54 Ibid., p. 189.

55 Davidson, *Inquiries into Truth and Interpretation* (op. cit.), p. 225.

56 Ibid., p. 197.

57 Ibid., p. 198.

58 Ibid., p. 189.

59 Ibid.

60 Immanuel Kant, *Critique of Pure Reason*, trans. N. Kemp Smith (London: Macmillan, 1964).

61 Ibid., p. 112.

62 John McDowell, *Mind and World* (Cambridge, MA: Harvard University Press, 1994).

63 Christopher Norris, 'McDowell on Kant: Redrawing the Bounds of Sense' and 'The Limits of Naturalism: Further Thoughts on McDowell's *Mind and World*', in *Minding the Gap: Epistemology and Philosophy of Science in the Two Traditions* (Amherst, MA: University of Massachusetts Press, 2000), pp. 172–96, 197–230.

64 See, for instance, Rorty, 'Texts and Lumps', in *Objectivity, Relativism, and Truth* (op. cit.), pp. 78–92; p. 81.

65 See Rorty, 'Pragmatism, Davidson and Truth', in *Objectivity, Relativism, and Truth* (op. cit.), pp. 126–50 and 'Is Truth a Goal of Inquiry? Donald Davidson versus Crispin Wright', in *Truth and Progress* (Cambridge University Press, 1998), pp. 19–42; also Davidson, 'Afterthoughts, 1987', in Alan R. Malachowski (ed.), *Reading Rorty: Critical Responses to* Philosophy and the Mirror of Nature, *and Beyond* (Oxford: Blackwell, 1990), pp. 134–8.

66 Rorty, 'Texts and Lumps' (op. cit.), p. 81.

67 Ibid.

68 See Note 31, above.

69 W. V. Quine, *Ontological Relativity and Other Essays* (New York: Columbia University Press, 1969), p. 72.

70 See Note 65, above; also Davidson, 'The Structure and Content of Truth', *The Journal of Philosophy*, Vol. 87 (1990), pp. 279–328.

71 See Note 48, above.

72 Davidson, 'The Structure and Content of Truth' (op. cit.).

73 Davidson, 'On the Very Idea of a Conceptual Scheme' (op. cit.), p. 192.

74 For further discussion, see Tom L. Beauchamp and Alexander Rosenberg, *Hume and the Problem of Causation* (New York: Oxford University Press, 1981); Galen Strawson, *The Secret Connexion: Causation, Realism, and David Hume* (Oxford: Clarendon Press, 1989); Rupert Read and Kenneth A. Richman (eds), *The New Hume Debate* (Routledge, 2000).

75 Devitt, 'Aberrations of the Realism Debate' (op. cit.), p. 51.

76 See Note 29, above.

77 See also Norris, *Language, Logic and Epistemology: A Modal-realist Approach* (London: Macmillan, 2004).

78 See Note 33, above.

79 For further argument to this effect, see Norris, *Philosophy of Language and the Challenge to Scientific Realism* (op. cit.).

80 See especially Dummett, *Truth and Other Enigmas* (op. cit.).

4

The Blank and the Die: More Dilemmas of Post-Empiricism

I

It will be my contention here, following on from topics broached in the previous chapter, that present-day analytic philosophy of language and logic is still hung up on certain problems bequeathed by W. V. Quine's landmark 1951 essay 'Two Dogmas of Empiricism'.[1] In particular I shall seek to show how they resurface in various later attempts – most notably, that of Donald Davidson – to steer a path through and beyond this post-Quinean predicament.[2] Those problems include: (1) the issue as to whether, as Quine maintains, the axioms of classical logic (like bivalence or excluded middle) might conceivably be revised under pressure of conflicting empirical evidence; (2) his scheme-relativist idea that objects and their properties can be taken to 'exist' only in relation to some given conceptual framework or ontological scheme; and (3) his cognate theses concerning the 'under-determination' of theory by evidence and the 'theory-laden' character of even the most basic observation-statements. In addition there is (4) his strict veto on talk of 'intensional' items such as meanings, attitudes, or beliefs, and (5) his rejection of modal logic – the logic of necessity and possibility – as likewise muddying the clear waters of a purely extensionalist/physicalist approach.[3] Most controversial of all is Quine's claim (6) that epistemology should henceforth be thoroughly 'naturalized', i.e., take a lead from the physical sciences, shed its old delusions of philosophic grandeur, and adopt a behaviourist approach that seeks to understand how the 'meagre input' of physical stimuli gives rise to the 'torrential output' of our various sentences, theories, hypotheses, covering-law statements, and so forth.[4]

There have been a great many critiques of Quine on each of these points, that is, with regard to his doctrines of logical revisionism and ontological relativity, his failure to offer sufficient grounds for distinguishing rationally from irrationally motivated episodes of scientific theory-change, and – by the same token – the absence of any normative dimension that would account for our knowledge of the growth of scientific knowledge.[5] Also there is the case that epistemology must involve some appeal to modal and intensional (meaning-related) aspects of language and thought if it is to find room for that missing normative dimension.[6] Otherwise it will lack any means of describing how science typically advances through certain well-tried procedures – such as that of inference to the best, most adequate causal explanation – which necessarily partake of both. That is to say, a naturalized epistemology in the full-fledged Quinean (physicalist) sense of that term will be wholly at a loss to account for the difference between beliefs arrived at through passive exposure to the incoming barrage of ambient sensory stimuli and knowledge arrived at by a due process of rational-evaluative thought. Thus our access to modal truths such as those concerning matters of this-world physical necessity or laws of nature – not to mention the transworld necessary truths of logic or mathematics – is itself dependent on forms of reasoning that find no place in Quine's austerely reductionist account.

Moreover, that account can scarcely explain how human beings manage to communicate for everyday, practical purposes quite apart from such relatively specialized issues in epistemology and philosophy of science. This follows from the famous problem of 'radical translation', namely – as Quine conceives it – the predicament of anyone attempting to translate utterances in a language so culturally remote from her own that it might, for all she knows, embody a wholly different conceptual scheme. Thus if the native informant regularly utters the phonetic sequence 'gavagai' whilst pointing at a rabbit then 'gavagai = rabbit' would seem a strong candidate for entry in her translation-manual. Yet it might just be that the informant's language gave expression to an alternative worldview which recognized no such natural kinds or (more exotically) which found no room for such spatially discrete and temporally enduring objects. That is to say, it might embody the kind of 'process metaphysic' developed in a broadly scientific context by Quine's Harvard colleague A. N. Whitehead, and attributed to the Hopi Indian language by the ethnolinguist B. L. Whorf. In which case 'gavagai' could equally well be translated as 'rabbiteth', or 'undetached rabbit-part', or 'spatio-temporal slice of rabbithood', each of them – again for all that she can know – on a par with the rendering 'Lo, a rabbit!' as regards their claim to determine just what sort of object (or aspect thereof) the native informant has in mind. Moreover, as Quine makes clear, this problem is not confined to such far-fetched imaginary scenarios but can be held to apply – in principle at least – to every context of human linguistic interaction or communicative exchange. For if one joins the three main theses summarized above – ontological relativity, the under-determination of theory by evidence, and the opacity of reference from one conceptual scheme to another – then their combined effect is to make it a mystery how language-users could possibly overcome even those localized impediments to mutual comprehension that result from differences of referential purport within (as well as between) various natural languages. Indeed, the very notion of a shared language then becomes highly problematic since each and every utterance in every such language will itself give room for radically divergent translations according to the kinds of conceptual scheme (or standing ontological commitment) brought to bear by this or that interpreter.

The situation becomes yet more baffling when Quine presses his case against the two last 'dogmas' of logical empiricism, that is, the analytic/synthetic distinction bequeathed by Kant to his latter-day progeny and the idea of scientific statements, hypotheses, or predictions as capable of somehow being checked off one-for-one against likewise discrete items of empirical evidence. For the result of Quine's radically contextualist approach – his claim (via the under-determination thesis) that the totality of our scientific knowledge at any given time must meet the 'tribunal of experience' as a whole – is to undercut the grounds for a rational assessment of theory-change in response to specific observational anomalies or items of recalcitrant evidence. Here again this doctrine has wider implications, i.e., reaches out from the relatively specialized case of 'incommensurability' between rival scientific paradigms or ontological schemes to the question of what could possibly serve to distinguish cases of successful from cases of failed or blocked translation between (or within) natural languages. Nor is it very much help when Quine allows – in accord with his naturalizing bent – that sentences may yet be treated as 'stimulus-analytic' or 'stimulus-synthetic' in so far as their utterance by this or that speaker when subject to some given (empirically observable) range of sensory stimuli offers grounds for ascription of the relevant sentence-type on strictly behaviourist terms. For just as Quinean philosophy of science excludes all normative criteria for rational theory-choice save those of conservatism, simplicity, and pragmatic convenience – thus failing to explain how science achieves progress through stages of conceptual rectification and critique – so Quinean philosophy of language excludes any adequate account of how speakers and interpreters manage (or sometimes fail) to achieve mutual understanding through a kindred process of rational-evaluative thought.

That is to say, his strictly extensionalist semantics goes along with his rejection of 'mentalist' talk in whatever guise, including – as Quine would have it – any appeal to modal, intensional, or other such 'referentially opaque' contexts of utterance. On his view these departures from the straight and narrow of an austerely canonical first-order quantified predicate logic plus a likewise pared-down physicalist ontology and naturalized epistemology are such as to create all manner of confusion and sidetrack philosophy from its proper, i.e., ancillary role *vis-à-vis* the physical sciences. To which his critics typically respond that this approach leaves science (or philosophy of science) devoid of any normative, rational, or adequate causal-explanatory grounds and language – or philosophy of language – likewise unfortunately placed. What is lacking, in each case, is an account of how advances in knowledge come about or how linguistic-commu-nicative uptake transpires to an extent beyond anything remotely explainable on Quine's hard-line behaviourist understanding of the matter.

II

For Quine, such objections are wholly beside the point since they involve pseudo-entities (meanings, beliefs, intentions, propositional contents and atti-tudes, and so forth) which cannot be cashed out in physicalist terms and should therefore find no place in any ontological scheme that takes a lead from the current best theories of the natural sciences. Thus mathematical items like numbers, sets and classes have a fair claim to admission since they figure indispensably in any account of scientific knowledge, while talk of 'meanings' and 'beliefs' – along with modal concepts like those of necessity or possibility – has no such claim since it exceeds the Quinean (strict empiricist) remit and, besides, causes all sorts of unwelcome problem with the business of quantifying into opaque contexts.[7] That is to say, given the two sentences 'Alison believes that the author of "Two Dogmas of Empiricism" was a Harvard philosopher' and 'Alison believes that Quine was a Harvard philosopher' we cannot substitute the variant expressions *salva veritate* (i.e., preserving their truth-values) since Alison might not know that Quine was in fact the author of 'Two Dogmas of Empiricism'. Or again – with respect to modality – although we take it that there are nine planets in the solar system nevertheless we should be wrong to assert a logical equivalence between the statements 'necessarily nine is greater than three' and 'necessarily the number of planets in the solar system is greater then three'. For the latter, if true, is contingently so – a question of the way things happen to stand in our particular region of the universe – while the former holds (necessarily so) irrespective of any such this-world pertinent yet might-have-been-otherwise conditions. At which point modal logicians are apt to remark that Quine is availing himself of notions (such as that of necessity across all logically possible rather than physically compatible worlds) which derive their argumentative force from just the kinds of modal distinction that Quine wishes to exclude.[8] Moreover, they will beg to point out that the commonly assumed order of priority between truth-functional and modal logic is one that demonstrably gets things backward since deductive validity has always been conceived – from Aristotle down – in terms of the *necessary* truth-preserving form of certain (e.g., syllogistic) arguments.

To be sure, one of Quine's chief aims (as a radical empiricist) is to cast doubt on the very idea that there exists such a well-defined class of analytic truths whose hallmark would be their unrevisable status or their immunity to any kind of empirical disconfirmation. In which case – or so one might think – he has no need to take sides on the above issue of priority, committed as he is to a sceptical or strong-revisionist view regarding the axioms of classical logic and an approach that purports to have no truck with modal or intensional concepts. Still it is clear from Quine's other, more 'text-book' writings on the topic that, so far from consistently maintaining that view, he is keen to assert that any suspension of the basic classical axioms (such as bivalence and excluded middle) must be thought of very much as a strategy of last resort, and one which – if adopted – is sure to create all manner of philosophical as well as communicative problems.[9] Besides, as I have said, it can readily be shown that Quine argues his case with the strictest regard for those axioms even when, as in 'Two Dogmas', the argument is intended as a root-and-branch attack on the very distinction (i.e., that between synthetic and analytic statements) which they would seem to presuppose as a condition of their own validity.

My point is that epistemology *cannot but* acknowledge certain normative standards – standards (moreover) which set it apart from any 'naturalized',

behaviourist, or wholesale empiricist approach – if it is to carry the least degree
of philosophic force. For it will otherwise reduce – no doubt in accordance with
Quine's overt prescription but surely against his argumentative purpose – to a
branch of applied behavioural psychology rather than epistemology or philosophy of language and logic.[10] That is to say, such a project if carried through
to its self-avowed goal would end up devoid of adequate criteria for distinguishing truth from falsehood, valid from invalid arguments, or rational-pro-
gressive from irrational or retrograde modes of scientific thinking. These are
problems that emerge even more sharply from Thomas Kuhn's notion of paradigm-relativism, one source of which was the Quinean thesis that epistemology
should be naturalized to the point where it involved nothing more than a
behaviourist (stimulus-response) psychology and, beyond that, a recognition of
the manifold, perhaps radically divergent conceptual schemes that might always
lead different observers to perceive different things.[11] Thus ontological relativity
– that 'heady and exotic' idea, as Donald Davidson describes it – is a doctrine
that most readily gets a hold through the kind of normative deficit engendered
by hard-line physicalist theories. One should also note his qualifying judgement
that 'as so often in philosophy, it is hard to improve intelligibility while
retaining the excitement'.[12] That is, the doctrine turns out – like others of its
kind, among them Kuhnian paradigm-relativism – to be self-refuting in its
strong version, problematic on a somewhat weaker construal, and otherwise (if
sensibly interpreted) not in the least 'heady' or 'exotic'. All that is left of it, on
Davidson's account, is the prosaic idea that what makes our sentences true or
false is just the way things happen to stand with the world. More precisely: it is
the way things stand according to just that range of truth-apt statements for
which one can construct a T-sentence in the formal Tarskian mode – i.e., a
biconditional of the form ' "Snow is white" if and only if snow is white' – so as to
obviate such troublesome relativist talk of 'conceptual schemes'.[13] Thus by
taking truth (or the attitude of holding-true) as logically primitive one can
block the idea of ontological relativity and at the same time prevent the Quinean
problem of 'radical translation' from ever getting a hold.

However there are well-known difficulties with Davidson's answer to Quine,
not least its espousal of a truth-theoretic position devoid of substantive content
(since devised by Tarski for purely formal rather than natural languages) and –
closely related to that – its lack of adequate rational-normative criteria.[14] Hence
Davidson's concluding paragraph in 'The Very Idea of a Conceptual Scheme'
where these problems emerge with particular force.

> In giving up dependence on the concept of an uninterpreted reality,
> something outside of all schemes and science, we do not relinquish the
> idea of objective truth – quite the contrary. Given the dogma of a dualism
> of scheme and reality, we get conceptual relativity, and truth relative to a
> scheme. Without the dogma, this kind of relativity goes by the board. Of
> course truth of sentences remains relative to language, but that is as
> objective as can be. In giving up the dualism of scheme and world, we do

not give up the world, but re-establish unmediated touch with the familiar objects whose antics make our sentences and opinions true or false.[15]

What comes across here is the odd conjunction, in Davidson's thought, of a direct realism (or maybe a radical empiricism) which cuts out talk of 'conceptual schemes' along with any kind of rational, epistemological, or normative warrant and a Tarskian theory which preserves truth-values and the possibility of radical translation but only at the cost of reducing 'truth' to a product of purely formal or circular definition. Hence his claim that we can have all the 'objectivity' we want just by giving up the 'dualism of scheme and reality', ceasing to think of 'truth [as] relative to a scheme', and treating it rather – in Tarskian style – as a notion which effectively cancels out so as to render just those sentences true which possess that claim as a matter of straightforward empirical or evidential warrant. This idea has the obvious appeal of seeming to resolve at a stroke all the problems that have vexed the discourse of epistemology from Kant to logical empiricism and which still leave their mark – as Davidson argues – on the residual 'third dogma' of Quinean radical empiricism, i.e., the scheme/content distinction and its upshot in the doctrine of conceptual relativity.[16] However it also gives rise to some other, equally intractable problems, among them the fact that Davidson's theory can just as well be taken – by thinkers like Richard Rorty – as a licence for arguing that 'truth' is nothing more than the compliment we pay to those various sentences which happen to jibe with our range of currently favoured or accepted beliefs.[17] For if the biconditional cancels straight through (as required by Tarski's disquotational account) and if this leaves the theory of truth with no work to do save that of satisfying a purely formal condition then one is left with just the kind of inertly empiricist outlook that Davidson suggests with his insouciant talk of those 'familiar objects whose antics make our sentences and opinions true or false'.

Thus it is no great distance from here to Rorty's wholesale pragmatist claim that Davidsonian truth-talk is otiose since really it amounts to just a sensible (if somewhat evasive) acknowledgement that truth cannot possibly transcend the limits of communal warrant or what is currently and contingently 'good in the way of belief'.[18] Of course Davidson appears to reject any such idea in passages like that cited above where (on the face of it) he takes a robustly realist view of the relation between knowledge and objects of knowledge, or truth-apt sentences and whatever it is about the nature or structure of reality that fixes their truth-value.[19] Nevertheless, Rorty argues, this impression is deceptive since Davidsonian 'realism' extends only to those notional items that we suppose to exist quite apart from our knowledge of them or our present-best powers of descriptive, theoretical, or causal-explanatory grasp.[20] That is to say, we can perfectly well entertain such a notion – like Kant's idea of a noumenal reality beyond phenomenal appearances – just so long as we don't vainly suppose that it might be cashed out in epistemological terms, i.e., as a matter of humanly attainable knowledge. Hence Rorty's fondness for Davidson's pithy remark that

'causation is not under a description, but explanation is'.[21] No doubt this is true
– uncontroversially so – in the sense that explanations are to some extent
interest-relative, or that different explanatory factors will acquire salience
according to one's reasons (scientific, historical, socio-cultural or whatever) for
adopting some particular line of enquiry. However, Rorty's argument pushes
much further in an anti-realist or paradigm-relativist direction. On his account
there is no passage – no possible reasoning in normative or causal-explanatory
terms – from such 'brute' occurrences as the impact of photons on Galileo's
eyeball or of the stone on Dr Johnson's boot to whatever interpretation they (or
other) parties placed upon it.[22] To be sure, those impacts were 'hard in the
relevant sense', i.e., the purely physicalist sense that they involved some
objective (real-world) causal process that was not yet (in Davidsonian parlance)
'under a description'. However, this is just Rorty's point: that one can be as
'realist' as one likes with respect to such brute physical goings-on while denying
that this has any implications for our thinking about science or philosophy of
science.

So when Galileo pointed his telescope toward the moons of Jupiter '[t]he
astronomers of Padua took it as merely one more anomaly which had somehow
to be worked into a more or less Aristotelian cosmology, whereas Galileo's
admirers took it as shattering the crystalline spheres once and for all'.[23] To be
sure, one could argue that 'the datum *itself* . . . is utterly real quite apart from the
interpretation it receives'. But in that case one will also have to concede that
such 'reality' is neither here nor there when it comes to working up scientific
theories on the basis of observational data or even – at the most everyday level –
distinguishing those objects that we 'really' perceive from various alternative
constructions placed upon the range of incoming sensory stimuli. Thus the
Rortian pragmatist

> sees no way of transferring this nonlinguistic brutality to *facts*, to the truth
> of sentences . . . To say that we must have respect for facts is just to say
> that we must, if we are to play a certain language game, play by the rules.
> To say that we must have respect for unmediated causal forces is pointless.
> It is like saying that the blank must have respect for the impressed die.
> The blank has no choice, nor do we.[24]

Davidson has vacillated over the years as to whether his arguments can fairly be
co-opted for Rorty's neo-pragmatist purposes.[25] That is to say, he has often
seemed somewhat perplexed as to whether his Tarskian truth-talk is indeed
pretty much redundant when cashed out in neo-pragmatist terms, or again,
whether his point about explanations (as distinct from causes) being always
'under a description' is such as to license Rorty's idea that 'the truth of a
sentence' is wholly unconstrained by 'the event which the sentence is about'.[26] It
is evident enough why he should wish to hold out against this line of argument,
amounting as it does – despite Rorty's sanguine assurances – to a full-scale anti-
realist or paradigm-relativist approach that finds no room for notions of truth or

for causal explanations except in so far as they allow us to 'play a certain language game'. However it is just as evident that Davidson has laid himself open to Rorty's appropriative move through the odd conjunction of a formalized truth-based semantic theory devoid of empirical content with his casual talk of those 'familiar objects whose antics make our sentences and opinions true or false'.

The problem as to how one should interpret such claims – whether as expressing a kind of direct realism or a species of radical empiricism – is compounded by the various ambiguities elsewhere in his essay. Thus, for instance, Davidson appears to switch from rejecting 'the very idea' of a conceptual scheme as one that engenders all sorts of intractable problems to readmitting that same idea in a supposedly innocuous form. Hence his laconic statement that truth may indeed be 'relative to language' but that this is 'as objective as can be' since any language will need to utilize the truth-predicate along with those various truth-functional devices (for conjunction, disjunction, negation, quantification, and so forth) in the absence of which it could not possibly fulfil the most basic communicative tasks.[27] Still one may doubt, given what Rorty makes of it, whether this line of argument is really up to the task. After all, a chief problem with Quine's 'Two Dogmas' is to see how his outlook of radical empiricism and his consequent revisionist policy with regard to certain putative 'laws' of classical logic can possibly provide any rational or normative basis for the process of scientific theory-change.

It is this dilemma that Rorty can so easily exploit with his talk of 'brute' physical stimuli that are under no description (hence 'real' in some ultimate sense of the word) yet which *for just that reason* are incapable of deciding the issue between Galileo and the astronomers of Padua or Dr Johnson and Bishop Berkeley. Kuhn confronts it when attempting to answer various critics in his second-edition Afterword to *The Structure of Scientific Revolutions*.[28] Here he follows Quine in distinguishing between 'stimuli' and 'perceptions', the former (supposedly) holding firm for observers of 'the same' object across different paradigms or conceptual schemes, while the latter he takes to vary with the content of theoretically informed perception from one observer to the next. This is Kuhn's chief line of defence against critics who had deplored his book for undermining the most basic standards of scientific rationality and truth. However his distinction runs up against several problems, among them the fact (as Rorty would be quick to point out) that if stimuli are as 'brute' as all that – so much so as to render them neutral with regard to differing perceptions, let alone rival theories – then it is hard to conceive how they could save Kuhn's approach from the charges of wholesale paradigm-relativism often brought against it. And again, if theoretically informed perceptions are always (like theories) under-determined by the best available evidence – as seems inescapable on Kuhn's Quinean account – then that evidence must itself be a matter of perceptual warrant and hence under-determined by any given range of physical stimuli. In which case these latter can hardly do the job required of them, that is, provide a solid guarantee that ontological relativity (or paradigm-relativism) can be held within rational bounds by supposing that – in this rock-bottom physicalist sense – different observers 'see the same thing'.[29]

In the end Quine's scepticism is just too strong for his own and, more strikingly, for Kuhn's purposes. That is, it leaves them stuck for any adequate answer when the Davidsonian question is raised as to how we could possibly locate or understand the points of divergence between languages, paradigms, conceptual schemes, ontological frameworks, and so forth, if the only hedge against full-fledged relativism is the notional appeal to 'stimuli' as holding firm across differences of perceptual response. Nor is Davidson himself much better placed to resolve this problem, given his twofold reliance on a Tarskian truth-based semantics whose formal apparatus gives little purchase on issues of natural-language interpretation and an outlook of bluff, commonsense realism according to which, quite simply, we can always regain 'unmediated touch' with those 'familiar objects' of perceptual acquaintance 'whose antics make our sentences true or false'. What this shows, I would suggest, is the lingering influence of logical empiricism and the fact that Davidson, despite his strictures on Quine's adherence to the 'third dogma', is himself just as much in thrall to a version of the old scheme/content dichotomy. Also (to repeat) it explains why Rorty can so easily co-opt Davidson's argument in support of his claim that realism about 'brute' physical stimuli or causal impacts has no bearing whatsoever on normative issues of the sort that arise when it comes to evaluating rival descriptive, theoretical, or explanatory hypotheses. For if the stimuli are subject to no rational constraints save those that apply to the general business of linguistic understanding – i.e., those in the absence of which we couldn't make a start on the Quinean business of 'radical translation' – then this offers only the vaguest assurance that large-scale communicative breakdowns are unlikely to occur since we can't make sense of the notion of conceptual schemes so radically different from ours as to render the prospect plausible.

Thus '[t]he method [Davidson's truth-based approach] is not designed to eliminate disagreement, nor can it; its purpose is to make meaningful dis-agreement possible, and this depends entirely on a foundation – *some* foundation – in agreement'.[30] What it leaves wholly unexplained is how substantive dis-agreements can and do arise between parties – scientists and others – who share enough in the way of basic beliefs and linguistic resources to make their dif-ferences mutually intelligible yet concerning whom it may rightly be said that truth lies on one side rather than the other. To be sure, '[s]ince knowledge of beliefs comes only with the ability to interpret words, the only possibility at the start is to assume general agreement on beliefs' ('Very Idea', p. 196). But this policy of maximizing common interpretative ground by assuming the largest degree of rationality in those we seek to understand – Davidson's 'principle of charity' – is one that makes problems for any normative account of knowledge and the growth of knowledge. On his account, quite simply, '[c]harity is forced upon us; whether we like it or not, if we want to understand others, we must count them right in most matters' ('Very Idea', p. 197). And again: '[i]f we can produce a theory that reconciles charity and the formal conditions for a theory, we have done all that could be done to ensure communication. Nothing more is possible, and nothing more is needed' (ibid.). However this conspicuously evades the issue of false beliefs, erroneous scientific hypotheses, mistaken interpretive conjectures, and a whole range of similar cases where the principle of charity just won't do except (again) as a vague source of reassurance that things can't have gone linguistically so far wrong as to produce a state of downright mutual incomprehension. No doubt, as Davidson is careful to allow, there is always the distinct possibility (for us and for others) of somehow getting things wrong and hence of standing open to correction when all the evidence is in. So if charity – counting them right 'in most matters' – is the best (indeed only viable) approach if we want to understand other people at all then still '[t]he guiding policy is to do this as far as possible, subject to considerations of simplicity, hunches about the effects of social conditioning, and of course our common-sense, or scientific, knowledge of explicable error' ('Very Idea', p. 196). All the same this latter qualification sits awkwardly with Davidson's argument that we cannot make sense of what they say except on the twofold charitable assumption (1) that most of their sayings are genuine expressions of belief, and (2) that most of their entailed beliefs are true *simpliciter* and not just 'true for them' in some speaker-relative, culture-specific, or framework-internal sense.

To be sure, as Davidson remarks, this argument acquires extra support if we reflect on 'the close relations between language and the attribution of attitudes such as belief, desire, and intention' ('Very Idea', p. 186). That is to say, such attitudes are scarcely conceivable – except maybe in their simplest (non-human animal) form – apart from certain basic means of linguistic articulation and, beyond that, a conception of truth which specifies their content (just *what it is* that we believe, desire, or intend) in propositional terms. Thus Davidson's argument may be thought to go through since, after all, 'it seems unlikely that we can intelligibly attribute attitudes as complex as these to a speaker unless we can translate his words into ours' (ibid.). However this still begs the crucial question as to whether we ourselves are getting him right – attributing the correct (intended) purport to his attitudes, intentions, and beliefs – and also as to whether he is correct (i.e., justified or rationally warranted) in believing this or that to be the case. This is not to deny Davidson's cardinal point that 'the interdependence of belief and meaning springs from the interdependence of two aspects of the interpretation of speech behaviour: the attribution of beliefs and the interpretation of sentences' ('Very Idea', p. 195). What it *does* call into question is the legitimacy of moving from this basic point about the way that we typically get along in the mostly reliable but still error-prone business of lin-guistic understanding to such generalized (quasi-transcendental) claims as those that Davidson advances on the strength of his Tarskian truth-based semantic theory. On this view, quite simply, 'there is no chance that someone can take up a vantage point for comparing conceptual schemes by temporarily shedding his own'. In which case, Davidson rhetorically asks, '[c]an we say that two people have different conceptual schemes if they speak languages that fail of inter-translatability?' (ibid., p. 185). However this (apparently) knockdown argument turns out to have no very strong implications when it comes to the central issue concerning linguistic or framework relativism. Thus 'what sounded at first like a thrilling discovery – that truth is relative to a conceptual scheme – has not so far been shown to be anything more than the pedestrian and familiar fact that the truth of a sentence is relative to (among other things) the language to which it belongs' (ibid., p. 189). Yet how should we interpret this curious passage if not as yielding crucial ground on just the point that Davidson is out to establish, i.e., the logical priority of truth (or the attitude of holding-true) *vis-à-vis* any second-order issues of translation, linguistic understanding, or communicative grasp?

Of course it may be said that 'relative to language' doesn't mean 'relative to this or that conceptual scheme' since a main purpose of Davidson's essay is to show that if we drop all that otiose scheme-content talk then the problem will resolve itself simply enough into the straightforward idea that 'truth of sentences remains relative to language, but that is as objective as can be'. Thus: '[g]iven the dogma of a dualism of scheme and content, we get conceptual relativity, and truth relative to a scheme', [whereas] '[w]ithout the dogma, this kind of rela-tivity goes by the board' ('Very Idea', p. 198). Yet it is hard to see how anything much is gained, from Davidson's standpoint, by replacing one kind of dualism with another, that is to say, the bad (conceptual-scheme) sort with the good (relative-to-language) sort wherein – supposedly – such problems cannot arise. What the issue amounts to is the question whether Tarski's definition of truth as 'truth-in-L' along with its recursive application to every biconditional of the standard type ' "Snow is white" is true if and only if snow is white' can indeed be extended (as Davidson claims) to the case of natural as well as formal or logically regimented languages. The trouble with this is that Tarski's theory was devised quite explicitly for the latter purpose, i.e., as a formal (meta-linguistic) schema for applying the truth-predicate to each and every veridical sentence of some given (first-order) language.[31] Thus it had to be expressed as a strictly excep-tionless (since true-by-definition) formula whose logical structure was such as to exclude any possibility of a truth-value mismatch between the left- and right-hand sides of the biconditional. It is therefore no valid objection to the Tarskian theory *as originally conceived* that it amounts to a species of trivial, circular, or merely tautologous statement which acquires its undoubted force of logical self-evidence only at the cost of giving up any claim to substantive content.[32] That is to say, the theory works – in the way intended – just on condition that the two sentences (the first one in quote-marks, the second without) simply cannot come apart as concerns their truth-value since, after all, they are two tokens of the self-same sentence-type. Hence the possibility, in every such case, of running the standard 'disquotational' technique whereby one simply relieves sentence one of its quote-marks, deletes sentence two altogether, and is then left with just the statement itself unaffected save in virtue of its now forming part of a language for which one has established an adequate (i.e., formally and recursively specifiable) theory of truth.

However it is far from clear that such a theory could be of any use when it comes to the interpretation of natural language. For in this context it is always possible that such comings-apart may occur, whether through instances of mistranslation, failures of communicative grasp, mistakes with regard to speaker's intention, erroneous attributions of belief, conceptual divergence, informational mismatch, or the fact that we ourselves, like other people, might always be wrong with respect to this or that presumptively veridical statement. Perhaps, as Davidson says, charity is in some sense 'forced upon us' to the extent that, 'whether we like it or not, if we want to understand others, we must count them right in most matters' ('Very Idea', p. 197). However this agreement-optimizing strategy comes up against its limit in the above-mentioned sorts of case where counting them right as concerns the particular matter in hand must involve *either* giving up any claim to get things right on our own account *or* adopting – what Davidson firmly rejects – a *laissez-faire* outlook according to which truth must be thought of as relative to belief and belief, in turn, to those various conceptual schemes that decide what counts as such for different speakers or communities. At any rate there is not much help to be had from a Tarskian truth-theoretic approach, even (or especially) when combined with the principle of charity, which applies only at a large formal remove from the business of actually figuring out the various ways in which things can go right or wrong with our efforts to understand others, as well as with our own (and their) best endeavours to maximize the truth-content of beliefs. For that theory is *by its very nature* incapable of distinguishing between the sorts of case where any problem is most likely down to some failure of linguistic-communicative grasp and those other sorts of case where most likely it involves a substantive difference of views or conflict of beliefs. As regards these latter the issue is primarily one of statements and their truth-value rather than their optimal meaning when treated in accordance with a principle of charity which aims so far as possible to maximize agreement or bring them out 'true' by our own interpretative lights.

No doubt this principle holds as a matter of pragmatic convenience – even as a kind of baseline methodological rule – when trying to grasp the gist of what others are saying. Thus, in Davidson's view, 'we must say much the same thing about differences in conceptual scheme as we say about differences in belief: we improve the clarity and bite of declarations of difference, whether of scheme or opinion, by enlarging the basis of shared (translatable) language or of shared opinion' ('Very Idea', p. 197). However, once again, this cannot get us far in deciding whether those differences stem from problems of communicative grasp or whether they turn on substantive (truth-evaluable) conflicts of belief where we wouldn't – or shouldn't – want to smooth them out through the enlargement of mutual understanding, 'shared opinion', or maximal convergence in beliefs-held-true. For if charity is carried to this point then it becomes just a kind of good-willed or vaguely ecumenical attempt to resolve such disputes on the default assumption that they have more to do with linguistic-communicative hitches than with large-scale, systematic errors of interpretation or with downright mistaken beliefs.

Davidson may say that this is to get the matter backwards since 'knowledge of beliefs comes only with the ability to interpret words', in which case 'the only possibility at the start is to assume general agreement on beliefs' ('Very Idea', p. 196). And again: '[g]iven the underlying methodology of interpretation, we could not be in a position to judge that others had concepts or beliefs radically different from our own' (p. 197). To be sure, there is a sense – a sense of the phrase 'radically different' – in which this statement amounts to no more than a plain, self-evident truth. Nevertheless we can (just about) imagine the case of two interlocutors whose worldviews, ontologies, metaphysical commitments, conceptual schemes, linguistic repertoires, and so forth were so drastically out of kilter as to render them each totally incapable of judging where the differences lay. Of course Davidson maintains that no such situation could possibly arise given the necessity that all languages – in order to fulfil their communicative role – must have in common certain basic (language-constitutive) structural and logico-semantic features. Since we cannot make sense of such a wildly implausible scenario therefore we should see that commonality of meanings, concepts and beliefs is the very precondition for making sense across other, less 'radical' differences of language or culture. Such agreement 'may take the form of widespread sharing of sentences held true by speakers of "the same language", or agreement in the large mediated by a theory of truth contrived by an interpreter for speakers of another language' ('Very Idea', p. 197). However if this claim is to have any bite – any force against wholesale scheme-relativist talk – then it will need to take far more detailed account of those genuine problems of translatability (whether between languages, paradigms, or theories) whose occurrence is sufficiently a matter of record to provide ample grist to the mill of thinkers like Quine, Kuhn and Rorty. Also it will need to distinguish between cases where the problem is wholly or chiefly linguistic in character, cases (such as those of most interest to cultural historians) where it results from some widespread shift in the currency of belief, and cases – among them major episodes of scientific theory-change – where any adequate treatment must involve normative criteria of truth, rationality, or inference to the best explanation.

In this respect Davidson's overly generalized truth-theoretic approach can be seen to suffer from the same kind of problem – the same normativity-deficit – which, on his diagnosis, leads directly from talk of conceptual schemes to talk of ontological or paradigm relativism. No doubt it offers a powerful argument against extreme versions of that doctrine, such as Kuhn's idea of scientists before and after some major revolution in thought living 'in different worlds', or Quine's claim that if quantum physics turned out to require a radical adjustment to the ground rules of classical logic then this would be a shift of much the same order as that 'whereby Kepler superseded Ptolemy, or Einstein Newton, or Darwin Aristotle'.[33] Such notions will appear misguided, Davidson argues, if one starts out from the concept of truth as a logical primitive and then asks what sorts of basic function any language must necessarily perform if it is to serve for the range of everyday-communicative as well as for more specialized, e.g., scientific purposes. Where relativism most often gets a hold is through its over-emphasis on *semantic* differences between languages and its under-emphasis on what they have in common – what they *must* be supposed to share – as regards their underlying logical structure. Thus it may well be that they diverge widely with respect to their various ways of dividing up the colour spectrum or of picking out objects, properties, or events that possess some particular salience for members of the language-community concerned. (The best-known, though maybe apocryphal, cases are the manifold words for different shades or hues of 'white' that figure in Eskimo vocabularies and the likewise highly discriminate nuances of 'green' that play a kindred orienteering role in the language of certain nomadic pastoral tribes.) Such differences will often have a perfectly good explanation in terms of their socio-cultural function or their plain usefulness in finding one's way around the world. However, as Davidson remarks, they are not the best guide when it comes to matters of interlingual translatability or of explaining how communication can possibly occur across otherwise large (as it might seem unbridgeable) differences of culture, language, or 'conceptual scheme'.

What is required in order to offset this relativist conception is a grasp of the point that semantics *doesn't* go all the way down, that different languages must have a good deal in common, and that the best place to look is at the range of logico-syntactic features – the devices for conjunction, disjunction, negation, cross-reference, anaphora, quantification, and so forth – in the absence of which no language could communicate even the most basic attitudes or beliefs. Hence Davidson's central claim *contra* the scheme-relativists: that truth (or the attitude of holding-true) is the precondition for whatever we are able to grasp in the way of differing, language-specific meanings or semantic conventions. Which is also to say that thinkers such as Quine, Whorf, Kuhn, Feyerabend *et al* are demonstrably wrong – putting the semantic cart before the logico-syntactic horse – in supposing that such differences might constitute a block to inter-lingual, intercultural, or trans-paradigm understanding. Rather it is the case that they could not even show up or register as such were it not for the background of shared and logically expressible presuppositions which must necessarily be grasped by any competent speaker/interpreter of any language that can itself be thought of as meeting the above sorts of requirement. In short, '[p]hilosophers who make convention a necessary element in language have the matter backwards. The truth is rather that language is a condition for having conventions.'[34] Once admit this, Davidson urges, and a whole range of philo-sophic pseudo-problems fall away, among them (not least) the Quinean problem of 'radical translation' and the idea that we or others might be 'massively in error' with regard to our mutual understanding of each other's beliefs. Quite simply we couldn't make rational sense of their utterances or expect them to make rational sense of our own were it not for the threefold enabling pre-sumption (1) that truth is logically prior to meaning, (2) that truth-conditions can be specified in terms of propositional contents and attitudes, and (3) that this provides an adequate basis for deciding between rival translations, theories, or interpretive hypotheses. Otherwise we should be wholly at a loss to explain not only how it does quite often come about that we are able to achieve some measure of success in matters of interlingual translation or trans-paradigm understanding but also how we are sometimes made uncomfortably aware of failures to attain that goal. For such awareness could scarcely arise except against a shared background of statements-held-true and a grasp of the operative standards – of rationality, logical structure, empirical warrant, and so forth – that apply in evaluating truth-apt statements.

Thus, on Davidson's sanguine prognosis, 'we may without circularity or unwarranted assumptions accept certain very general attitudes towards sentences as the basic evidence for a theory of radical translation' ('Very Idea', p. 195). That theory might seem excessively abstract or question-begging in so far as it detaches truth in general from the truth-content of particular beliefs or utterances, and in so far as it fails to specify just which attitudes (and contents or objects thereof) are justified or warranted in any given case. However this objection is off the point, Davidson thinks, since 'if we merely know that someone holds a certain sentence to be true, we know neither what he means by the sentence nor what belief his holding it true represents' (ibid., p. 196). Nor should we need to possess such knowledge if truth is indeed a logically primitive concept and utterance-meaning therefore a derivative function which may harmlessly be treated as language- or scheme-relative just so long as we respect that basic order of priority. That is to say, for any given speaker, '[h]is holding the sentence true is thus the vector of two forces: the problem of interpretation is to abstract from the evidence a workable theory of meaning and an acceptable theory of belief' (ibid., p. 196). Combine this with the 'principle of charity' – that on the whole we do best (by other people and ourselves) if we maximize the range of agreed-upon truths, the scope of shared rationality, and hence the translatability of their utterances into our own – and what results is a general assurance that neither we nor they could be 'massively in error' with respect to the purport of any given utterance. In which case (to repeat): 'if we can produce a theory that reconciles charity and the formal conditions for a theory, we have done all that could be done to ensure communication ... Nothing more is possible, and nothing more is needed' (ibid., p. 197).

IV

Still one may doubt that these two criteria provide anything like an adequate account of the truth-conditions that properly apply either in the context of everyday (natural-language) translation and communication or in the more specialized contexts of scientific and philosophical debate. For one thing they ignore the plentiful evidence that misunderstandings often occur, whether as a consequence of getting things wrong (sometimes drastically so) with regard to other people's meanings, intentions, or communicative gist, or again, in consequence of applying some false scientific theory that appears to account for our present-best range of empirical evidence but which later turns out to have rested on mistaken premises or presuppositions. There are just too many examples of this – in the everyday-anecdotal as well as in the history-of-science literature – for Davidson's argument to carry much force as a knockdown rejoinder against the scheme-relativist claim. That is to say, there is always the distinct possibility – borne out by any number of communicative breakdowns, cross-purpose exchanges, false hypotheses, erroneous theories, misconstruals of the evidence, and so forth – that Davidsonian across-the-board charity may not be the best or most reliable guide when assessing what counts as a rational (i.e., truth-maximizing) guide in such matters. Nor is the Tarskian 'formal theory' much help in this regard. For if the notion of truth cashes out as nothing more than truth 'relative to L' where L must be conceived as some particular language, conceptual scheme, Kuhnian paradigm, Quinean ontological framework, or whatever, then clearly we are plunged straight back into all the problems (chief among them that of radical translation) that Davidson hopes to resolve.[35]

No doubt, as he says, the case for such a truth-based semantic approach gains strength when we reflect on the close relationship between language and various propositional attitudes, among them primarily the interlinked attitudes of belief, desire and intention. Thus it does seem improbable, on the face of it, 'that we can intelligibly attribute attitudes as complex as these to a speaker unless we can translate his words into our own' ('Very Idea', p. 186). However this argument still applies – as might be expected, given its Tarskian provenance – at a high level of formalized abstraction from the business of actually figuring out what other people have in mind and whether *we or they* have adequate (rational or causal-explanatory) grounds for adopting some particular set of such attitudes with regard to some particular range of evidence, desired outcomes, intentional strategies, and so on. For the principle of charity must surely have certain limits, whatever its usefulness as a default assumption (i.e., the premise that interpreting other people's meanings and beliefs goes best if we hold them 'right in most matters') or as a means of avoiding the familiar slide from scheme-relativism into notions of wholesale untranslatability across languages or paradigms. Where those limits show up most clearly is through reflection on the various instances of large-scale or systematic error – in the natural sciences, historical enquiry, intercultural understanding, interpersonal exchange, and so forth – that have often occurred in the past and whose present and future possibility cannot be ruled out by any talk of Davidsonian 'agreement in the large'.

Such talk may nonetheless have its place in the *psychology* of language and communication, that is to say, as a kind of enabling device which helps to assure speakers and interpreters that they are not the victims of cross-purpose exchange or total communicative breakdown. This is I think what Davidson means (or can best be interpreted to mean) when he remarks that 'charity is forced upon us', and that 'whether we like it or not, if we want to understand others, we must count them right in most matters' ('Very Idea', p. 197). It is also what motivates his further claim that conceptual-scheme relativism is incoherent, and just as much so 'when based on partial failure of translation [as] when based on total failure' (ibid.). Clearly there is some room for debate at this point as to just what constitutes 'partial failure' on Davidson's account, not least because he then goes on to state that, 'given the underlying methodology of interpretation, we could not be in a position to judge that others had concepts or beliefs radically different from our own'. It is odd that any argument from partial failure should be taken to involve such drastic (and, as Davidson would have it, such plainly self-refuting) relativist consequences, however one assesses the strength of his case against the thesis in its full-strength, 'total failure' form. What this brings out, I suggest, is Davidson's habit of posing the issue in such sharply dichotomous terms that we are sure to run into all the problems of radical scheme-relativism unless we adopt the full-strength contrary thesis, i.e., that which maximizes truth and rationality even with regard to certain *prima facie* false statements, irrational beliefs, or scientifically discredited theories and worldviews.[36]

Of course Davidson is not denying the possibility of genuine advances in our state of knowledge, or the occurrence of progressive theory-changes such as those whereby (in Quine's phrase) 'Kepler superseded Ptolemy, or Einstein Newton, or Darwin Aristotle'. Indeed, as I have said, it is a chief aim of his truth-based, logico-semantic approach that it should offer an alternative to Quine's argument (taken up by Kuhn) that these episodes of 'progress' were perceived as such only as a consequence of their finding a place in some new, presumptively more adequate conceptual framework. Thus Davidson comes out very firmly against any overt form of scheme-relativism or any version of the case for regarding truth as 'internal' to this or that Quinean ontology, Kuhnian paradigm, or whatever. Yet it is far from clear that this purpose is well served by his use of the Tarskian truth-schema as a device for ensuring communicative grasp and enabling mutual intelligibility – as well as meaningful comparison – across and despite any differences of (so-called) conceptual scheme. For when extended beyond its primary domain, i.e., that of formal logic and applied (as Davidson's theory requires) to the domain of natural-language interpretation this approach runs the risk of falling prey to another, no less problematical form of scheme-relativism, namely that whereby truth comes out as *whatever it takes* by way of charitable licence to count other people 'right in most matters'.

Thus there is not, after all, such a great difference between the kinds of semantic-scheme relativism espoused by thinkers like Quine, Kuhn, Whorf *et al* and the schema-based conception of truth-in-L as Davidson adapts it from Tarski. To be sure, the latter gives reason to suppose that the former approach goes wrong – and lays itself open to the standard forms of anti-relativist riposte – by ignoring certain truth-functional components of language, chief among them the logical connectives, quantifiers, devices for negation, conjunction, disjunction, and so forth. However it offers no adequate account of how these features might plausibly link up with a reliable means of distinguishing different sorts of linguistic and conceptual misunderstanding. That is to say, it fails to differentiate instances where *we ourselves* have gone wrong through misinterpreting other people's rationally justified statements or beliefs and instances where we have got them pretty much right as regards their intended gist but where *they themselves* happen to be wrong (misinformed, confused, or in the grip of some false theory) to the extent of creating barriers to mutual comprehension. Charity plus the formal theory may help in assuring us that 'massive error' is unlikely in either case. However, it offers no help either in explaining how large-scale failures of grasp can and do sometimes occur, in showing how their occurrence can best be put down to some particular range of language-related, theoretically induced, or causal-explanatory factors. For this would involve far more in the way of detailed, case-specific treatment than could ever be supplied by a Davidsonian theory which takes as its rule the max-imization of imputed truth-content for any statement or utterance that we happen to find opaque or resistant to our efforts of comprehension.

No doubt one can best make a start by adopting something like that theory as a source of generalized assurance that we are not, by and large, in the unfortunate predicament of Quine's 'radical translator' whose hypotheses have nothing more to go on than the noises produced by a native informant when subject to various ambient stimuli.[37] That is, one can take Davidson's point – as against this extravagant thought-experimental scenario – that 'the interdependence of belief and meaning springs from the interdependence of two aspects of the inter-pretation of speech behaviour: the attribution of beliefs and the interpretation of sentences' ('Very Idea', p. 195). Still such assurance is of limited value when we are faced with some particular communicative problem or perhaps some radical (even 'massive') breakdown in the process of mutual understanding across dif-ferences of language, culture, ideology, or scientific paradigm. After all, the sorts of 'shift' that Quine calls to witness – like that which led from Ptolemaic to post-Copernican astronomy – are surely describable in just such terms, whether on account of the mind-wrenching obstacles confronted by those who first encountered the new theory and its shock to their received worldview or, again, as a matter of 'translatability' (i.e., of mutual comprehension) between parties to the rival hypotheses. What Davidson offers is a pretty strong argument on a priori grounds for thinking that such radical differences of Quinean 'conceptual scheme' or Kuhnian scientific 'paradigm' cannot constitute an ultimate, in-principle block to the process of rational adjustment whereby such parties manage to achieve a fair measure of common argumentative ground. What drops out of this account, however, is the well-attested fact that some disagreements – like those instanced by Quine – go well beyond the limits envisaged by a theory which takes it that the structure and content of truth can be adequately specified in formal (logico-syntactic) terms.

This is where Davidson's approach most clearly reveals its residual adherence to just those elements in the programme of logical empiricism which he expressly sets out to challenge. It is the kind of thinking that leads him to jump straight across from assertions of a radically 'commonsense' empiricist outlook (talk of 're-establish[ing] unmediated touch with the familiar objects whose antics make our sentences and opinions true or false') to arguments from the logical conditions of possibility for holding this or that to be a truth-apt statement or a sentence up for evaluation by shared standards of rational judgement. Thus: '[w]hatever plurality we take experience to consist in – events like losing a button or stubbing a toe, having a sensation of warmth or hearing an oboe – we will have to individuate according to familiar principles'. In which case, Davidson concludes, '[a] language that organises *such* entities must be a language very like our own' ('Very Idea', p. 192). However the force of that italicized *such* is apt to raise certain crucial questions with regard to Davidson's entire truth-based logico-semantic approach. That is to say, it introduces the idea that what actually 'makes our sentences and opinions true or false' (at least in a good many cases) is their success in picking out *just those kinds* of entity – along with their kind-constitutive features, properties, causal powers, and so forth – which constitute the relevant object-domain and are hence able to occupy that truth-making role.

However this takes us on to very different ground as concerns the relationship between truth, meaning and reference or the various ways in which communicative uptake occurs despite and across paradigm-shifts, divergences of worldview, or problems of interlingual translatability. What it requires, in short, is that the basic Davidsonian approach (i.e., charity plus the Tarski-derived truth-theoretic apparatus) be extended to incorporate an externalist theory of reference-fixing and, besides that, some adequate causal-explanatory account of just how it is that our sentences and beliefs hook up with whatever they purport to describe or represent. Such is of course the kind of theory developed by Saul Kripke, Hilary Putnam, and others since the early 1970s and reinforced by a great variety of arguments from modal logic, philosophical semantics, and the history and philosophy of science.[38] Moreover it receives additional support from advocates of an alternative, non-Quinean form of 'naturalized' epistemology which avoids the dead-end of a radically empiricist (or physicalist) approach and instead makes room for those normative values – of truth, reason and inference to the best explanation – that found no place in Quine's drastically reductionist programme.[39]

I have written at length about these topics elsewhere (as have a good many other commentators) so will here do no more than briefly indicate their usefulness in pointing a way beyond the problems with Davidson's truth-theoretic approach.[40] Most important is the fact that they accord equal weight to the 'structure' and 'content' of truth, that is to say, the two aspects of a theory of interpretation which Davidson addressed in a sequence of essays under just that title.[41] Those essays started out by espousing a substantive notion of 'content' which rejected any outright deflationist version of the Tarskian formula – such that the truth-predicate would figure as a merely redundant or place-filling term – and which instead (like Tarski himself on occasion) endorsed something more akin to a full-fledged correspondence-theory.[42] At this stage Davidson also makes clear his disagreement with Rorty over the latter's neopragmatist claim that Davidsonian 'truth' is likewise just convenient shorthand for whatever is currently and contingently 'good in the way of belief'. Yet by the end he seems to have pretty much abandoned that position and become at least halfway convinced that the truth-content of our sentences, beliefs and attitudes cannot be accorded any such substantive (i.e., non-circular or other-than-formal) specification.

What continues to dog his thought – like Quine's before him – is that vexing dichotomy between scheme and content which the logical empiricists inherited from Kant and which shows up again in these two thinkers' work despite their claims (Davidson's especially) to have come out on the far side of all such misconceived dualist talk. Hence the impression he often gives of going straight to the heart of the matter with regard to these and related problems. However that impression soon gives way to a sense that they have not so much been resolved as sharpened yet further through Davidson's constant veering about between a truth-theoretic approach devoid of empirical content and a radically empiricist outlook which lacks any rational or normative bearings. If this puts one in mind of Kant's famous dictum that 'concepts without intuitions are empty' while 'intuitions without concepts are blind' then the echo is scarcely fortuitous.[43] Just as Kant went some lengthy, complex and often tortuous ways around in seeking to explain how intuitions could be 'brought under' adequate concepts, so philosophers in the wake of logical empiricism have proposed different ways of mending the rift while in fact producing yet further variations on that old Kantian theme. These latter range all the way from Quinean ontological relativity to Kuhnian paradigm-relativism, Rortian 'strong' descriptivism, or Davidson's curious blend of a naïvely empiricist (or perhaps direct-realist) outlook with a Tarskian formal specification which floats altogether free of empirical or real-world evidential constraints.

V

Nor is there much help to be had from a 'naturalized' Kantian approach to these issues, like that proposed by John McDowell, which purports to overcome all such dualisms by talking Kant down from his own 'metaphysical' illusions and declaring that the problem of knowledge simply disappears once we grasp his single most important insight.[44] This was, in McDowell's formulation, that

> empirical knowledge results from a co-operation between receptivity and spontaneity. (Here 'spontaneity' can be simply a label for the involvement of conceptual capacities.) We can dismount from the seesaw if we can achieve a firm grip on this thought: receptivity does not make an even notionally separable contribution to the co-operation.[45]

However there is more than a hint of hand-waving in this claim that all the well-known problems with Kant's attempt to reconcile sensuous intuitions with concepts of understanding via the faculty of judgement – itself bound up with the yet more mysterious agency of 'imagination' – can be somehow made to vanish through a switch of preferential terms in favour of 'receptivity' and 'spontaneity'. What is 'notional' here, one is inclined to think, is the belief that merely stating their inseparable character as a matter of philosophic fiat can suffice to establish that we have now come out safely on the far side of all such dualist conceptions. For as becomes evident in the course of McDowell's argument there is just no way that substituting one pair of terms for the other can repair the deep-laid rift between a logicist approach by which concepts are emptied of empirical content and an empiricist approach that renders our experience and knowledge effectively devoid of rational or normative bearings. To be sure, McDowell is quite right in asserting that this is a bad (philosophically disastrous) state of affairs and that there *must* be something wrong with any theory – such as Kant's on one (as he thinks mistaken) reading and that of logical empiricism – which produces so dire a result. Yet it is hard to credit McDowell's claims to have finally dismounted from the see-saw if one observes the sheer lengths of complex and often tortuous argumentation to which he is driven in his various attempts to talk Kant down from the heights of metaphysical abstraction, or to resolve these issues in terms that would respect the objectivity of logic, mathematics, and the formal sciences while allowing them a role in our communal practices of reason-giving or knowledge-acquisition.[46] For there seems little hope of achieving that wished-for deliverance unless one accepts – as McDowell seems oddly unable to do – that even the most abstract and rigorously formalized branches of those disciplines have their ultimate source and justification in empirical procedures such as counting, collecting, and empirically based inductive reasoning.

Hence his Wittgenstein-derived idea that this whole set of problems results from our adopting a 'sublimated' conception of truth, one that supposes the existence of 'super-rigid rails' that would somehow (impossibly) lay down the conditions of correctness in rule-following for any range of applications beyond our finite power to specify that range in advance.[47] McDowell is torn – unresolvably so – between a strong pull toward the realist (i.e., objectivist) view that those conditions must surely transcend any communal or practice-based criterion of correctness and a nagging sense that any such claim must surely run into the standard range of Wittgensteinian counter-arguments.[48] What creates this dilemma – as so often in the rule-following debate – is the idea that truth-values objectively conceived are *ex hypothesi* recognition-transcendent and hence lie beyond our utmost powers of acquisition or manifestation. That is to say, it is a more extreme sceptical version of the standard anti-realist line of argument which substitutes truth-talk with talk of 'warranted assertibility', and which restricts this latter to the class of sentences for which we are able to produce some adequate empirical or formal proof.[49] Where Wittgenstein – at least on Kripke's reading – pushes yet further in a sceptical direction is by requiring that we should somehow have advance knowledge of the way that any formal (recursive) rule should properly apply or any arithmetical procedure be correctly carried out with respect to cases that we haven't yet encountered or calculations that are just too large or difficult to fall within our present ratiocinative grasp.[50] Failing that, we cannot know for sure what it means to 'follow a rule' consistently from one application to the next, or even be certain whether our present application is in accord with what we take (perhaps erroneously) to have been our own past practice or standard of correctness in just that regard.

I have argued elsewhere that this is nothing more than a pseudo-dilemma resulting from a false *tertium non datur*, i.e., the strictly absurd thesis that if we don't already know the correct results in advance then we can't know what would lead us to arrive at those results, i.e., possess an adequate working grasp of such basic concepts as recursivity or continuing a number-series by constant incremental steps.[51] One line of response – that adopted by realists with respect to abstract objects such as those which figure in mathematics, logic and the formal sciences – is to maintain that we can indeed have knowledge of them though not through any kind of 'sublimated' quasi-perceptual grasp like that which Plato envisaged in his doctrine of forms, and which thus gives a hold for anti-realists to press their standard sceptical case. Another is the lesson drawn by semantic externalists, proponents of a non-Quinean naturalized epistemology with adequate normative content, and those who would maintain – *contra* Frege[52] – that an appeal to the process of empirical knowledge-acquisition has its place even in philosophy of logic, mathematics, and the formal sciences.[53] This latter case has been powerfully argued by, among others, Philip Kitcher in his description of how mathematics can be thought of as advancing through progressive stages of abstraction from elementary operations such as counting or grouping objects into sets to the furthest, most speculative kinds of number-theory or formalized proof-procedure.[54]

No doubt there is a deep, philosophically challenging issue with regard to what Eugene Wigner has described as 'the unreasonable effectiveness' of mathematics in the physical sciences.[55] That is to say, it is the puzzle as to how a discourse on such abstract entities as numbers, sets, classes, functions, etc., can so often have produced so impressive a match with all kinds of empirically based observational and predictive data. According to some sceptically inclined philosophers of mathematics this is a problem that intrinsically eludes any adequate conceptual solution. Thus we can either have objective, recognition-transcendent mathematical truth (which would then *ex hypothesi* lie beyond reach of our utmost cognitive powers) or mathematical knowledge in some humanly attainable form (which would then fall short of objectivist truth since by very definition it must lie within those same epistemic limits).[56] Anti-realists about mathematics – Michael Dummett most prominent among them – take the view that this issue had better be resolved in favour of a verificationist account which treats hypothetical, i.e., so far exceptionless yet formally unproven statements (such as Goldbach's conjecture that every even number is the sum of two primes) as strictly neither true nor false just so long as no proof is forthcoming.[57] Mathematical realists reject this view and assert that a statement such as 'Goldbach's conjecture is true' has its truth-value fixed by the way things stand in mathematical reality quite apart from our present or even (at the limit) our future best-possible means of proof or ascertainment. Moreover, they can claim philosophical support from certain (on the face of it) unlikely quarters, such as Kurt Gödel's insistence that his incompleteness-proof – briefly stated: that any logical system sufficiently complex to generate the axioms of elementary arithmetic will contain at least one theorem that cannot be proved within that system – is itself proof of our somehow having access to objective mathematical truths which inherently transcend the limits of computability or formal demonstration.[58] For we should otherwise be wholly at a loss to explain how Gödel was able to arrive at his result or how its truth should be evident to anyone capable of following Gödel's argument.

At any rate it is clear enough from the history of post-Galilean science that mathematics has provided a singularly powerful resource in the development of various physical theories whose predictions were impressively borne out by the results of empirical research. Any theory which rejects that claim on sceptical or anti-realist grounds is one that flies so strongly in the face of all our scientific evidence to date that it must, on any sensible reckoning, count among the class of empirically disproven hypotheses. In which case, to repeat, there seems little hope for an approach to issues in epistemology, logic and philosophy of science which continues to maintain some version – however nuanced or qualified – of the Kantian split between sensuous intuitions and concepts of understanding. What has continued to make trouble for philosophers like Davidson and McDowell is just the kind of difficulty that Kant faced when he sought to explain how two such disparate faculties could possibly be reconciled or shown to constitute different ways of talking about the self-same process, i.e., that involved in our jointly 'receptive' and 'spontaneous' knowledge of the world. In Kant it takes the form of some notoriously obscure passages where this synthesizing power is attributed first to the role of intermediary 'judgement', and then to the exercise of 'imagination', itself conceived as 'a blind but indispensable function of the soul, without which we should have no knowledge whatsoever, but of which we are scarcely ever conscious'.[59] McDowell thinks that we can readily avoid such regressive, obscurantist talk and dismount from the dualist (scheme/content or concept/intuition) 'see-saw' by taking up Kant's alternative idea of 'receptivity' and 'spontaneity' as strictly inseparable powers of mind which cooperate in every act of cognitive or epistemic judgement.[60] Yet, as I have argued elsewhere, this amounts to no more than a preferential switch of terms that substitutes one dualism for another and which still gives rise to all the same problems despite McDowell's many, often tortuously phrased attempts to persuade us otherwise.[61]

Indeed one could write a plausible account of the major debates in analytic philosophy since the demise of logical empiricism that would view them as resulting precisely from the grip of this deep-laid dualist inheritance. That story would perhaps go furthest toward explaining their failure to develop an alternative approach that involved no such disabling rift between Davidsonian 'structure' and 'content', or knowledge in its formal (truth-theoretic or logico-semantic) mode and knowledge as a matter of empirical warrant or observational-predictive power. For if one thing is clear about the 'problem of knowledge' as conceived by philosophers from Plato down it is that any adequate account must somehow explain how logic, mathematics and the formal sciences should possess so remarkably high a degree of proven empirical-predictive warrant despite our conviction of their holding true (necessarily so) quite apart from any such considerations. Adorno puts the case with typically acerbic yet melancholy force in a passage from *Minima Moralia* concerning the relationship between 1940s' logical positivism and various symptoms of latter-day cultural decline. Among them he cites, improbably enough, the US craze for television quiz shows and the practice of IQ testing. Thus:

> [t]he modes of behaviour appropriate to the most advanced state of technical development are not confined to the sectors in which they are actually required. So thinking submits to the social checks on its performance not merely where they are professionally imposed, but adapts them to its whole complexion. Because thought has by now been perverted into the solving of assigned problems, even what is not assigned is processed like a problem ... Just as for neo-positivists knowledge is split into accumulated sense-experience and logical formalism, the mental activity of the type for whom unitary knowledge is made to measure is polarized into the inventory of what he knows and the spot-check on his thinking-power: every thought becomes for him a quiz either of his knowledgeability or his aptitude. Somewhere the right answers must already be recorded ... While thought has forgotten how to think itself, it has at the same time become its own watchdog. Thinking no longer means anything more than checking at each moment whether one can indeed think.[62]

Adorno's diagnosis will no doubt strike most analytic philosophers as absurdly off the point or as a blatant instance of importing extraneous (socio-political) concerns into areas – such as philosophy of science, language or logic – where they have no legitimate place. However it may well ring disturbingly true for anyone who takes a more detached, less professionally involved view of the matter. What is then liable to strike them is the extent to which debate in those areas is still following the same basic agenda laid down by logical positivism, even (or especially) where it claims to have effected some decisive shift of philosophic ground.[63]

This whole issue has been somewhat confused by the widespread sceptical retreat from a priori truth-claims of whatever sort that has come about very largely through reflection on mathematico-scientific developments such as non-Euclidean geometry, quantum mechanics, and the paradoxes of classical set-theory.[64] All the same those developments have not so much rendered the problem obsolete as posed it with yet greater pertinence and force. Hence, *inter alia*, the long-running and inconclusive debate as to whether the various conceptual dilemmas thrown up by the orthodox (Copenhagen) quantum theory might require some more or less drastic revision to the ground rules of classical logic or some change to our most basic ideas about the nature and structure of physical reality.[65] What emerges once again is the dualism of scheme and content that has created such a deal of trouble from Kant, via logical empiricism, to the present day. Only by rethinking the whole vexed issue of naturalized versus normative epistemology – an issue often posed yet scarcely resolved in the wake of Quine's 'Two Dogmas' – can philosophy hope to overcome that seeming impasse.

NOTES

1 W. V. Quine, 'Two Dogmas of Empiricism', *Philosophical Review*, Vol. 60 (1951), pp. 20–43; reprinted with various detailed revisions in Quine, *From a Logical Point of View*, 2nd edn (Cambridge, MA: Harvard University Press, 1961), pp. 20–46.

2 Donald Davidson, 'On the Very Idea of a Conceptual Scheme', in *Inquiries into Truth and Interpretation* (Oxford: Oxford University Press, 1984), pp. 183–98.

3 See especially Quine, 'Reference and Modality', in Leonard Linsky (ed.), *Reference and Modality* (Oxford: Oxford University Press, 1971), pp. 17–34.

4 Quine, 'Epistemology Naturalized', in *Ontological Relativity and Other Essays* (New York: Columbia University Press, 1969), pp. 69–90; also *From a Logical Point of View* (op. cit.) and *Word and Object* (Cambridge, MA: MIT Press, 1960).

5 See especially Robert B. Barrett and Roger F. Gibson (eds), *Perspectives on Quine* (Oxford: Blackwell, 1990); Donald Davidson and Jaakko Hintikka (eds), *Words and Objections: Essays on the Work of W. V. Quine* (Dordrecht: D. Reidel, 1975); Lewis E. Hahn and Paul A. Schilpp (eds), *The Philosophy of W. V. Quine* (Chicago: Open Court, 1998); Robert Kirk, *Translation Determined* (Oxford: Clarendon Press, 1986).

6 See Linsky (ed.), *Reference and Modality* (op. cit.); also Ruth Barcan Marcus, *Modalities: Philosophical Essays* (New York: Oxford University Press, 1993).

7 Quine, 'Reference and Modality' (op. cit.).

8 See Raymond Bradley and Norman Swarz, *Possible Worlds: An Introduction to Logic and its Philosophy* (Oxford: Blackwell, 1979); Charles S. Chihara, *The Worlds of Possibility: Modal Realism and the Semantics of Modal Logic* (Oxford: Clarendon Press, 2001); G. Hughes and M. Cresswell, *A New Introduction to Modal Logic* (London: Routledge, 1996); M. Loux (ed.), *The Possible and the Actual: Readings in the Metaphysics of Modality* (Ithaca, NY: Cornell University Press, 1979).

9 Quine, *Methods of Logic* (New York: Henry Holt, 1950); *Philosophy of Logic* (Englewood Cliffs, NJ: Prentice-Hall, 1970); *Selected Logic Papers* (Cambridge, MA: Harvard University Press, 1995).

10 See also Jaegwon Kim, *Supervenience and Mind: Selected Philosophical Essays* (Cambridge: Cambridge University Press, 1993); Christopher Norris, *Truth Matters: Realism, Anti-Realism, and Response-Dependence* (Edinburgh: Edinburgh University Press, 2002) and *Philosophy of Language and the Challenge to Scientific Realism* (London: Routledge, 2004).

11 Thomas S. Kuhn, *The Structure of Scientific Revolutions*, 2nd edn. (Chicago: University of Chicago Press, 1970).

12 Davidson, 'On the Very Idea of a Conceptual Scheme' (op. cit.), p. 183.

13 Alfred Tarski 'The Concept of Truth in Formalised Languages', in *Logic, Semantics and Metamathematics*, trans. J. H. Woodger (Oxford: Oxford University Press, 1956), pp. 152–278; also Davidson, 'In Defence of Convention T', in *Inquiries into Truth and Interpretation* (op. cit.), pp. 65–75.

14 See various contributions to Lewis Edwin Hahn (ed.), *The Philosophy of Donald Davidson* (Chicago: Open Court, 1999); Kirk Ludwig (ed.), *Donald Davidson* (Cambridge: Cambridge University Press, 2003); Ursula M. Zegle'n (ed.), *Donald Davidson: Truth, Meaning, and Knowledge* (London: Routledge, 1999).

15 Davidson, 'On the Very Idea of a Conceptual Scheme' (op. cit.), p. 198.

16 Quine, 'Two Dogmas of Empiricism' (op. cit.); also entries under Note 10, above.

17 See especially Richard Rorty, *Consequences of Pragmatism* (Brighton: Harvester, 1982); *Objectivity, Relativism, and Truth* (Cambridge: Cambridge University Press, 1991); *Truth and Progress* (Cambridge University Press, 1998).

18 Rorty, 'Pragmatism, Davidson and Truth', in *Objectivity, Relativism, and Truth* (op. cit.), pp. 126–50; also in Ernest LePore (ed.), *Truth and Interpretation: Perspectives on the Philosophy of Donald Davidson* (Oxford: Blackwell, 1986), pp. 333–55.

19 See also Davidson, 'The Structure and Content of Truth', *The Journal of Philosophy*, Vol. 87 (1990), pp. 279–328 and 'Afterthoughts, 1987', in Alan R. Malachowski (ed.), *Reading Rorty: Critical Responses to* Philosophy and the Mirror of Nature, *and Beyond* (Oxford: Blackwell, 1990), pp. 134–8.

20 Rorty, 'Is Truth a Goal of Inquiry? Donald Davidson versus Crispin Wright', in *Truth and Progress* (op. cit.), pp. 19–42.

21 Rorty, 'Texts and Lumps', in *Objectivity, Relativism, and Truth* (op. cit.), pp. 78–92; p. 81.

22 Ibid., p. 81.

23 Ibid., p. 81.

24 Ibid., p. 81.

25 See entries under Note 19, above.

26 Ibid., p. 80.

27 Davidson, *Inquiries into Truth and Interpretation* (op. cit.).

28 Note 12, above; also Kuhn, *The Road Since Structure: Philosophical Essays, 1970–1993*, eds James Conant and John Haugeland (Chicago: University of Chicago Press, 2000).

29 See Ian Hacking (ed.), *Scientific Revolutions* (Oxford: Oxford University Press, 1981) and Paul Horwich (ed.), *World Changes: Thomas Kuhn and the Nature of Science* (Cambridge, MA: MIT Press, 1993).

30 Davidson, 'On the Very Idea of a Conceptual Scheme' (op. cit.), pp. 196–7. All further references given by 'Very Idea' and page number in the text.

31 See Note 14, above.

32 For further discussion, see Barry Allen, *Truth in Philosophy* (Cambridge, MA: Harvard University Press, 1993); Simon Blackburn and Keith Simmons (eds), *Truth* (Oxford: Oxford University Press, 1999); Paul Horwich, *Truth* (Oxford: Blackwell, 1990); Richard L. Kirkham, *Theories of Truth: A Critical Introduction* (Cambridge, MA: MIT Press, 1992).

33 Quine, 'Two Dogmas of Empiricism' (op. cit.), p. 43.

34 Davidson, 'Communication and Convention', in *Inquiries into Truth and Interpretation* (op. cit.), pp. 265–80; p. 280.

35 See Notes 14 and 32, above.

36 See also Christopher Norris, *Resources of Realism: Prospects for 'Post-Analytic' Philosophy* (London: Macmillan, 1997) and *New Idols of the Cave: On the Limits of Anti-Realism* (Manchester: Manchester University Press, 1997).

37 See Quine, *Ontological Relativity and Other Essays* and *Word and Object* (Note 4, above); also Kirk, *Translation Determined* (Note 5).

38 See especially Saul Kripke, *Naming and Necessity* (Oxford: Blackwell, 1980); Hilary Putnam, 'Is Semantics Possible?', 'Explanation and Reference', 'The Meaning of Meaning', and 'Language and Reality', in *Mind, Language and Reality* (Cambridge: Cambridge University Press, 1975), pp. 139–52, 196–214, 215–71, 272–90; also J. L. Aronson, R. Harré and E. Way, *Realism Rescued: How Scientific Progress is Possible* (London: Duckworth, 1994); Richard Boyd, 'The Current Status of Scientific Realism', in Jarrett Leplin (ed.), *Scientific Realism* (Berkeley and Los Angeles: University of California Press,

1984), pp. 41–82; Peter Lipton, *Inference to the Best Explanation* (London: Routledge, 1993); Stathis Psillos, *Scientific Realism: How Science Tracks Truth* (London: Routledge, 1999).

39 See, for instance, Alvin Goldman, *Epistemology and Cognition* (Cambridge, MA: Harvard University Press, 1986); Hilary Kornblith, *Inductive Inference and its Natural Ground* (Cambridge, MA: MIT Press, 1993) and *Knowledge and Its Place in Nature* (Oxford: Clarendon Press, 2002); Kornblith (ed.), *Naturalizing Epistemology*, 2nd edn (Cambridge, MA: MIT Press, 1994) and *Epistemology: Internalism and Externalism* (Oxford: Blackwell, 2001).

40 See entries under Notes 10, 36 and 39, above.

41 Davidson, 'The Structure and Content of Truth' (op. cit.).

42 See Kirkham, *Theories of Truth* (op. cit.) for some illuminating further discussion.

43 Immanuel Kant, *Critique of Pure Reason*, trans. Norman Kemp Smith (London: Macmillan, 1964).

44 John McDowell, *Mind and World* (Cambridge, MA: Harvard University Press, 1994). For further discussion see Norris, 'McDowell on Kant: Redrawing the Bounds of Sense' and 'The Limits of Naturalism: Further Thoughts on McDowell's *Mind and World*', in *Minding the Gap: Epistemology and Philosophy of Science in the Two Traditions* (Amherst, MA: University of Massachusetts Press, 2000), pp. 172–96, 197–230.

45 McDowell, *Mind and World* (op. cit.), p. 9.

46 For further discussion see Norris, 'McDowell on Kant' and 'The Limits of Naturalism' (Note 44, above).

47 See especially McDowell, 'Intentionality and Interiority in Wittgenstein', in K. Puhl (ed.), *Meaning Scepticism* (Berlin: de Gruyter, 1991), pp. 148–69 and 'Meaning and Intentionality in Wittgenstein's Later Philosophy', *Midwest Studies in Philosophy*, Vol. 17 (1992), pp. 40–52; also Saul Kripke, *Wittgenstein on Rules and Private Language* (Oxford: Blackwell, 1982); Alexander Miller and Crispin Wright (eds), *Rule-following and Meaning* (Chesham: Acumen, 2002).

48 See Ludwig Wittgenstein, *Philosophical Investigations*, trans. G. E. M. Anscombe (Oxford: Blackwell, 1953), Part I, Sections 201–92 *passim*.

49 See especially Michael Dummett, *Truth and Other Enigmas* (London: Duckworth, 1978), *The Logical Basis of Metaphysics* (Duckworth, 1991), and *The Seas of Language* (Oxford: Clarendon Press, 1993); also Neil Tennant, *Anti-Realism and Logic* (Oxford: Clarendon Press, 1987) and *The Taming of the True* (Oxford: Oxford University Press, 1997); Crispin Wright, *Truth and Objectivity* (Cambridge, MA: Harvard University Press, 1992).

50 See Notes 47 and 48, above.

51 See Norris, *Truth Matters* (op. cit.); also 'The Limits of *Whose* Language? Wittgenstein on Logic, Mathematics, and Science', in *Language, Logic and Epistemology: A Modal-Realist Approach* (London: Macmillan, 2004), pp. 66–110.

52 See especially Gottlob Frege, 'The Thought: A Logical Enquiry', in Robert M. Harnish (ed.), *Basic Topics in the Philosophy of Language* (Hemel Hempstead: Harvester-Wheatsheaf, 1994), pp. 517–35; also Frege, *Collected Papers on Mathematics, Logic and Philosophy*, ed. Brian McGuiness, trans. Max Black *et al* (Oxford: Blackwell, 1984); Michael Dummett, *Frege: Philosophy of Mathematics* (London: Duckworth, 1991); Bob Hale and Crispin Wright, *The Reason's Proper Study: Essays Toward a Neo-Fregean Philosophy of Mathematics* (Oxford: Clarendon Press, 2001).

53 See Notes 38 and 39, above; also Penelope Maddy, *Naturalism in Mathematics* (Oxford: Clarendon Press, 2000).

54 Philip Kitcher, *The Nature of Mathematical Knowledge* (Oxford: Oxford University Press, 1984).

55 Eugene Wigner, 'The Unreasonable Effectiveness of Mathematics', *Communications in Pure and Applied Mathematics*, Vol. 13 (1960), pp. 1–14.

56 See especially Paul Benacerraf, 'What Numbers Could Not Be', in Benacerraf and Hilary

Putnam (eds), *The Philosophy of Mathematics: Selected Essays*, 2nd edn (Cambridge: Cambridge University Press, 1983), pp. 272–94; also Michael Detlefson (ed.), *Proof and Knowledge in Mathematics* (London: Routledge, 1992); W. D. Hart (ed.), *The Philosophy of Mathematics* (Oxford: Oxford University Press, 1996); Hilary Putnam, *Mathematics, Matter and Method* (Cambridge: Cambridge University Press, 1975).

57 See Note 49, above.

58 Kurt Gödel, 'On Formally Undecidable Propositions of *Principia Mathematica* and Related Systems', trans. B. Meltzer (New York: Basic Books, 1962) and 'What is Cantor's Continuum Problem?', in Benacerraf and Putnam (eds), *The Philosophy of Mathematics* (op. cit.), pp. 470–85; also Ernest Nagel and James Newman, *Gödel's Theorem* (London: Routledge & Kegan Paul, 1971) and S. G. Shanker (ed.), *Gödel's Theorem in Focus* (London: Routledge, 1987).

59 Kant, *Critique of Pure Reason* (op. cit.), p. 112.

60 McDowell, *Mind and World* (op. cit.).

61 Note 44, above.

62 Theodor W. Adorno, *Minima Moralia: Reflections from a Damaged Life*, trans. E. F. N. Jephcott (London: Verso, 1974), pp. 196–7; see also Adorno *et al*, *The Positivism Dispute in German Sociology*, trans. Glyn Adey and David Frisby (London: Heinemann, 1976).

63 For further argument to this effect, see Norris, *Truth Matters*, *Minding the Gap*, and *Language, Logic and Epistemology* (Notes 10, 44 and 51, above).

64 See especially Hilary Putnam, *Realism and Reason* (Cambridge: Cambridge University Press, 1983); also Paul Boghossian and Christopher Peacocke (eds), *New Essays on the A Priori* (Oxford: Clarendon Press, 2000); Paul K. Moser (ed.), *A Priori Knowledge* (Oxford: Oxford University Press, 1987); J. Alberto Coffa, *The Semantic Tradition from Kant to Carnap: To the Vienna Station* (Cambridge University Press, 1991).

65 See, for instance, Peter Gibbins, *Particles and Paradoxes: The Limits of Quantum Logic* (Cambridge: Cambridge University Press, 1987); Max Jammer, *Philosophy of Quantum Mechanics: The Interpretations in Historical Perspective* (New York: Wiley, 1974); Christopher Norris, *Quantum Theory and the Flight from Realism: Philosophical Responses to Quantum Mechanics* (London: Routledge, 2000); Hilary Putnam, *Mathematics, Matter and Method* (Cambridge: Cambridge University Press, 1979).

5

Ethics, Autonomy, and the Grounds of Belief

I

How far can or should we be held responsible for what we believe? From one point of view – call it 'doxastic voluntarism' – such responsibility is the *sine qua non* of any approach that would take due account of our various intellectual and ethical obligations, that is to say, our proper concern as rational agents with the business of sorting true from false or morally acceptable from unacceptable beliefs. From another, more inclined toward some form of doxastic determinism, it has seemed nothing short of self-evident that beliefs are to a large extent non-volitional, or subject to various kinds of causal or socio-cultural influence. Where the former stakes its claim on our capacity for freely willed, autonomous choice in keeping with the dictates of moral or intellectual conscience the latter requires that we take more account of those other (heteronomous) factors that may limit or constrain the extent of our responsibility in this regard. Moreover, the determinist will then remark that there is a problem for the advocate of free will or doxastic autonomy if their exercise is taken to involve submission to overriding imperatives such as those of dedication to truth, valid inference, evidential warrant, or openness to persuasion by the best (most rational) argument. For in that case they would be subject to constraints of a different but no less binding character, namely to the norms of epistemic good conduct or respect for those same (in this sense heteronomous) standards of rational debate.

At its crudest this response takes the form of postmodernist jibes to the effect that Kant's great watchword *sapere aude* – 'dare to think for yourself', 'let reason be your guide' – is a plain performative contradiction, proclaiming the virtues of intellectual freedom while enjoining a strict compliance with its own demand.[1] It is not hard to see the confusion here between the general advice that we should strive so far as possible to exercise our powers of reflective, self-critical, conscientious thought and the specific injunction – no part of Kant's claim – that we should think just like him. However there are real problems to be faced when the advocate of free will (or doxastic responsibility) attempts to explain how we can reconcile those values with the fact that any freedom of intellectual conscience worth having must involve a commitment to reasons or principles that will then play a crucial determining role in our various beliefs and actions. Otherwise the notion of freedom will reduce to that of sheer randomness or unmotivated chance occurrence, as with certain, in my view misconceived arguments that adduce the indeterminate or probabilistic character of events on the subatomic (quantum) scale as evidence that moral philosophy no longer has anything to fear from the old Newtonian bugbear of iron-cast physical determinism.[2] Quite apart from their dubious scientific credentials such arguments clearly invite the charge of leaving no room for the exercise of a responsible freedom, as opposed to just a notional 'freedom from' the otherwise all-encompassing laws of physical cause and effect. Still the autonomist may be hard put to make her case against various objections that are apt to arise when considering the extent to which cultural, religious, ideological, or other such formative influences may play a predisposing or determining role even – or especially – in the case of our most deeply held principles and beliefs.

Elsewhere, among followers of Wittgenstein, it is argued that the problem will simply disappear (like all such 'metaphysical' quandaries) if one sees that there are two different language-games involved, those of reason-based justification on the one hand and causal explanation on the other.[3] Or again, it can be conjured away through a 'naturalized' (or de-transcendentalized) reading of Kant which recommends that we jettison a great deal of his outmoded metaphysical machinery but retain the basic distinction between a physical realm where causal explanations are perfectly in order and a 'space of reasons' where the pertinent criteria are those of valid inference, well-formed argument, or justificatory warrant.[4] However, these strategies are no more effective in resolving the central issue – to put it bluntly, no less of a philosophic cop-out – than the idea that both sorts of talk make sense on their own terms and therefore cannot possibly get into conflict just so long as we regard them as belonging to disparate language-games or modes of thought. For this recourse to language as a means of escape from all our philosophic perplexities is one that leaves the conceptual problem firmly in place, amounting as it does to a placid assurance that 'everything is in order' with our accustomed linguistic practices. Yet the free will/determinism issue is just as pressing or worrisome when couched in everyday, non-specialist terms as when subject to a full-scale 'metaphysical' treatment in the Kantian manner. Quite simply, such problems cannot be wished away by any amount of linguistic therapy or Wittgensteinian attempts to persuade us that they are really just a form of self-induced philosophic bewitchment. Besides, these approaches are always at risk of implicitly espousing a cultural-determinist view – and thus belying their professions of even-handedness – in so far as they entail the idea that beliefs are intelligible only within some language-game or communal 'form of life'. For then it follows that the freedom to question or to challenge doxastic norms must *ipso facto* be limited to whatever makes sense by those same communal lights.

Outside the analytic line of descent these issues have received some very different kinds of treatment. Among them is Sartre's existentialist idea of human consciousness as the locus of an ultimate, unqualified freedom (a 'hole' in being or a region of absolute 'nothingness') which marks the sole point of interruption in a physical universe otherwise governed by the iron laws of physical-causal determinism.[5] There is much of great interest and value in Sartre's approach to these topics, as likewise in the work of those – like Merleau-Ponty – who have sought to offer a viable account of human moral autonomy while criticizing Sartre for his all-or-nothing view and insisting that we recognize the practical constraints on our freedom in any given real-world context.[6] One strength of their analyses is the fact that they provide a good range of real or imagined test-case scenarios in order to flesh out the issues and bring us flat up against the kinds of dilemma confronted not only by human agents in various sorts of complex moral predicament but also by philosophers who seek to engage – and not evade – their more intractable aspects. Still the basic problem re-emerges very sharply in Sartre's later acknowledgement that if the idea of freedom is to have any genuine, as opposed to merely notional content then it will need to be specified in terms that take adequate account of those numerous factors (whether physical, historical, socio-cultural, psycho-biographical, or whatever) that in practice must be seen as placing certain limits on our scope for moral autonomy.[7]

This allowance becomes more explicit in his politically engaged writings where it is a chief premise of Sartre's Marxist-dialectical approach that human beings make their own history, but not in circumstances or under conditions of their own choosing. However it is also present in his existentialist works to the extent that freedom is here thought of as exercised in a context – that of our relationship to other people under certain, often highly fraught circumstances – which itself requires allowance for just such constraints, though here of a more interpersonal than large-scale collective, class-based, or group-dynamic kind. Indeed the very notion – so crucial to Sartre's early existentialist thinking – that freedom always entails responsibility even when manifested in selfish, morally or socially irresponsible ways is one that must likewise impose significant restrictions in that regard. And the same applies to the issue of doxastic voluntarism, free as we are (in principle at least) to adopt any number of possible beliefs on any given topic yet constrained as we are (by factors ranging from passive indoctrination to rational conviction on the basis of empirical evidence or cogent demonstrative grounds) to believe what we do as a matter of involuntary assent. Thus the problems with Sartre's existentialist ethic and his notion of absolute, unqualified freedom can be seen to work out as a close analogue – albeit more dramatically expressed – of those which have constantly resurfaced in the 'other', i.e., Anglophone or mainstream analytic tradition.

If one thing is clear, to repeat, it is that these problems cannot be resolved by any kind of linguistic therapy aimed toward talking us down from the heights of 'metaphysical' abstraction and leading us back to a sensible acceptance of the different language-games involved. This Wittgensteinian approach is really just a line of least resistance or a strategy adopted in order to evade what is surely among the most pressing issues in philosophy of mind, epistemology and ethics. That is to say, it avoids facing up to the fact that we are inevitably tugged both ways between the powerful conviction that people *can and should* be held responsible for their beliefs and the knowledge – just as much a part of our basic moral-evaluative competence – that such responsibility is never exercised in total isolation from the various causes, influences, pressures of circumstance, or acculturated modes of thinking that predispose us toward one or another doxastic commitment. In the face of this dilemma it is tempting to adopt a standpoint analogous to that of some philosophers who have 'answered' the problem about consciousness by suggesting that it is just too difficult (or too far beyond our innate powers of conceptual grasp) to allow of any adequate scientific or indeed philosophical solution.[8] However, as opponents have been quick to remark, this 'mysterian' argument has nothing to commend it except the appeal – perhaps more evident to philosophers than scientists – of preserving a space where causal explanations necessarily run out and philosophy continues to set the rules for what counts as a valid or admissible hypothesis.[9] Besides, there is something intellectually disreputable about any theory that declares straight off as a matter of stipulative fiat that phenomenon x – whether quantum mechanics or human consciousness – is something that by its very nature exceeds our utmost powers of conceptual-explanatory grasp. Such arguments are not so very different from those items of orthodox Christian doctrine that J. S. Mill denounces with splendid moral vigour when he states his refusal to believe in any God whose ways are so profoundly mysterious (for instance, in the matter of eternal damnation) as to lie beyond reach of mere human understanding.[10] To raise the problem of doxastic voluntarism to a high point of philosophic bafflement is in effect to concede the irrelevance or downright uselessness of philosophy when it comes a matter of the greatest importance for our conceptions of moral, political, legal and intellectual responsibility.

II

So where have we arrived at this preliminary stage in our discussion? Not, to be sure, on the verge of suggesting any confident answer or adequate solution. Indeed it might seem that the prospect has receded even further as a result of having canvassed some views on the topic – some more or less qualified defences of doxastic voluntarism and the contrary (non-volitionist) stance – and having found them open to various kinds of philosophically cogent or intuitively powerful rejoinder. Now one is faced with a choice between four possible ways of proceeding. First there is the option that would most likely be favoured by hardline 'analytic' types who see no virtue in continuing to fret over age-old metaphysical issues where the lack of any widely agreed-upon solution shows that they were ill formed to begin with and had therefore better be shelved or recast in some suitably modified, e.g., linguistic or logico-semantic guise. To this way of thinking the antinomies thrown up by debates about doxastic voluntarism – like those that have bedevilled the free-will/determinism issue in philosophy of action – are such as to call for treatment in the mode of *reductio ad absurdum*, that is, as showing that they must derive from some one or more false (since deadlock-producing) premises. However this 'solution' is rather like Russell's famous but philosophically unconvincing Theory of Types which advised that we could best get over the paradoxes of classical set-theory – those of self-reference or self-inclusion – by laying it down as a rule of good mathematical and logical conduct that systems be constructed and distinctions maintained in such a way that those paradoxes simply could not arise. Still they are apt to strike home with undiminished force for anyone who tries to get her mind around Russell's various examples of the kind, just as the problem about doxastic voluntarism won't go away – or show up as a mere pseudo-problem engendered by false 'metaphysical' premises – simply through flat declarations to that effect. Nor can it be any more effectively dissolved through the second, Wittgensteinian option according to which it is only on account of our (i.e., philosophers') chronic 'bewitchment by language' that these dilemmas have come to exert such a hold. For here again no amount of linguistic therapy – of patiently coaxing those philosophers down from the giddy heights of metaphysical abstraction – can be of much use when we come to reflect on the real, not illusory or language-induced problem of reconciling moral-intellectual responsibility with a due allowance for the various constraints on our own and other people's modes of belief-formation.

The third option takes a lead from Kant in pressing those antinomies not to the point of a self-refuting *reductio* but rather to the point where they are taken to entail a very different way of conceiving the issue.[11] This confines our knowledge of causality to the realm of phenomenal (perceptual) experience, conceptual understanding, and physical science while conserving a strictly separate domain – or 'space of reasons' – for the exercise of ethical choice under no compulsion save that of the requirement to respect the universal dictates of moral law. Yet there is an obvious problem here in so far as compliance with that law is supposed to be a matter *both* of freely willed, autonomous assent *and* of something more like a passive acquiescence in maxims or principles that brook no exception and would hence seem to leave no room for such moral autonomy. Thus the Kantian 'solution' turns out to be just another variant on the same old dilemma, one that is by no means resolved – rather sharpened – by those revisionist (naturalized or 'de-transcendentalized') readings of Kant that have lately emerged by way of response to the defects and anomalies of old-style logical empiricism.[12] For such readings still have to face the choice of either reproducing that absolute Kantian distinction of realms, in which case they will hardly be rid of transcendental motifs, or else pushing right through with the naturalistic treatment of Kantian epistemology and ethics, in which case they will produce a version of Kant which cuts out some crucial load-bearing segments of his argument. Among these latter – most damagingly for the revisionist case – are just those passages that claim to establish the possibility of free will and moral autonomy in a world that is otherwise subject to causal determinism in every last detail of every last event. Kant's legacy is plainly visible across a wide range of latter-day responses to this problem, from John McDowell's halfway naturalized and (in my view) deeply problematical version of Kantian epistemology to Donald Davidson's idea of 'anomalous monism', itself – despite the somewhat misleading description – a dualist doctrine that dare not quite speak its name.[13] So there seems little hope of an answer from purported solutions of this third (Kantian or quasi-Kantian) kind, even though they are more responsive to the philosophic depth of the problem and the sheer unlikelihood that it might be laid to rest through some straightforward logical *reductio* or application of linguistic therapy in the Wittgensteinian mode.

So the question remains: what hope of an answer (a fourth-way alternative) if the best efforts of philosophy to date have produced nothing more than a series of dilemmas, deadlocked antinomies, conflicting intuitions, and conceptual dead-ends? Still things may not be as hopeless as this suggests if one just hangs on to the basic principle that whatever else philosophy may claim to do it cannot depart from certain indubitable axioms of human thought and experience. These are axioms – not just convenient working hypotheses – in so far as they serve both as a starting-point for further, more detailed and rigorous reflection and also as a check on the tendency to press toward doctrinal extremes (such as wholesale determinism or radical voluntarism) that are plainly at odds with much of what we know as a matter of self-understanding and shared experience. This tells us that Plato must have been wrong – in the grip of a false theory of mind and ethical motivation – when he argued that knowledge of the good must infallibly lead to virtuous behaviour, or that bad actions could result only from ignorance, stupidity, or misunderstanding. By the same token we are inclined to agree with Aristotle when he makes allowance for *akrasia* (weakness of will) as a complicating factor that often intervenes to prevent our following the straightforward dictates of duty or moral conscience. So likewise with the standard objections to Kantian deontological ethics, i.e., that such thinking both under-estimates the complexity of human predicaments and motives, and over-estimates the binding character of any such abstract-universalist moral creed. Yet at the same time – and here the familiar dilemma crops up once again – we are compelled to acknowledge that there *must* be some basis for ethical values beyond this potentially all-licensing appeal to the range of qualifying clauses required for any statement concerning the scope and limits of moral responsibility. Thus it is one thing to argue that Plato and Kant got it wrong – albeit on different metaphysical grounds – when they took such a sternly uncompromising line as regards the absolute status of moral truths and the requirement that ethical reasoning not be deflected by merely 'pathological' considerations of this sort. Yet it is another thing entirely to push so far in the opposite direction that one is left with the idea of ethical judgement as involving nothing more than a shared (even if community-wide) consensus as to what should count, in any given case, as a reasonable, decent, or morally acceptable view of the matter. In striving so hard to avoid all the problems with Kantian moral rigorism this approach runs the risk of becoming just another variant on a well-worn cultural-relativist theme, or confusing what is true, justified, or right in the way of belief with what passes as such according to our own communal practices and values. For then we are stuck with another form of determinism that is no less degrading to our basic conceptions of moral autonomy and selfhood in so far as it involves a socio-cultural rather than a causal or physicalist theory of belief-formation.

Still there is no denying the force of our conviction that we *do* have a significant measure of choice in the matter of what we believe and, moreover, that such choice is not drastically compromised or shown up as just a kind of willing self-delusion by the fact that our opting for one or another doxastic commitment can often quite plausibly be traced back to some prior influence, whatever its precise nature. After all, there is a vast (non-denumerable) range of such variously weighted influences that impinge at any moment on any individual in any given life-context and it is absurd to suppose that, even (*per impossibile*) with all the evidence to hand, one could ever predict the future course of that person's actions and beliefs. Yet as a putative solution to the free-will/determinism problem this fares no better, philosophically speaking, than the standard response to Laplace's claim that from a complete knowledge of the present state of the universe right down to its ultimate physical constituents one could in principle retrodict its entire previous history and likewise predict its entire future development. That 'solution' consists in saying quite simply that we don't possess and could never attain such an ultimate state of knowledge, and therefore that Laplace's determinist claim is beside the point for all practical as well as genuine philosophic purposes. However this just won't do as an answer – least of all a philosophical answer – since it fails to take the crucial point that determinism might conceivably be true (as a matter of fact) quite aside from any merely contingent limits on our powers of comprehension or ability to figure out the whole, endlessly complex concatenation of causes and effects. Nor is there much comfort to be had for the hard-pressed anti-determinist from the idea that science has now moved on to a stage where such claims no longer present any threat in so far as they have been superseded by developments like chaos theory, mathematical undecidability, or (in quantum-physical terms) the uncertainty relations and limits on our powers of precise, objective measurement. For such arguments are open to the threefold charge of (1) confusing ontological with epistemological issues, (2) presupposing the truth of certain highly questionable (e.g., quantum-theoretical) conjectures, and (3) trivializing the whole debate by making it hinge on the outcome of random events – say quantum goings-on in the brain – that would surely do nothing to explain our capacities for rational belief-formation or autonomous action.[14] For there seems little point in advancing this sort of case if the only result is to exchange one philosophically unpalatable view (hard-line psycho-physical determinism) for another, equally unwelcome idea (that rationality and free will are just illusions engendered by our post-hoc attempts to make sense of such sheerly random, unmotivated goings-on).

III

The reader will perhaps have noticed a recurrent pattern in the last few paragraphs, namely the way that they each start out with a statement of the need to move beyond these vexing antinomies, only to end with a reformulation of the same basic problem in different terms. My excuse is that the problem is a tough one – among the most philosophically recalcitrant – and that any attempted solution is obliged in good conscience to register the various counter-arguments or likely objections that rise up against it at every turn. There is a curious example of this in Benjamin Libet's much-discussed findings with regard to the neurophysiology of decision-making and the temporal relationship or order of dependence between brain-states and conscious mind-states.[15] Most controversial was the fact, as he at first claimed, that neural-imaging experiments had shown a distinct, measurable time-lag between the occurrence of physical events in the brain that correlated with certain apparently willed or deliberate actions and the moment when subjects reported their decision to execute those same actions. From this it seemed to follow that their 'choices' of action were really no such thing but, on the contrary, epiphenomenal events that occurred only *after* the brain had entered into a certain state whose results were first manifest in overt behaviour and then became accessible to consciousness only as a kind of passive delayed effect. However Libet subsequently modified his claim by allowing that any act 'determined' by any given brain-state could always somehow be revoked or countermanded by a further, split-second intervening decision not to proceed in that particular way but to fix on some alternative outcome. Of course there is still the option, for diehard determinists, of arguing that Libet's revised claim complicates but doesn't in the least undermine his original thesis, i.e., that it is a change in brain-state and not some immaterial change of purpose or mind-set that produces the switch. However this argument is open to various further objections from the voluntarist quarter. Among them is the point that it leads to a form of vicious regress – since the countermanding impulse may itself be subject to further countermanding, and so forth ad infinitum – and also that this process cannot be described without at some stage having recourse to an intentionalist idiom, one that involves the ascription of motivating interests, desires, or beliefs.

So there is an odd but revealing and symptomatic sense in which Libet's retreat from the first (strong-determinist) version of his thesis re-enacts precisely that complicating moment – that same split-second intervention of a contrary, action-inhibiting force – which he now incorporates, no doubt on the basis of certain empirical observations, but also (one suspects) partly in deference to our standing intuitions in that regard. For it is a demonstrable feature of all arguments in philosophy of mind, cognitive psychology, and other areas where this issue arises that any statement of the case for hard-line physical determinism will at some point involve a more or less covert or surreptitious appeal to the language of agency, volition and choice. Nor is this merely, as Wittgensteinians would have it, a matter of our using different language-games in different contexts of utterance, e.g., that of causal explanation (including empirical psychology) on the one hand and reason-based, normative, or justificatory talk on the other.[16] Rather it is a question of our total inability to make any sense of human actions and beliefs unless by accepting – whether explicitly or (as very often in the case of determinist arguments) through various tell-tale nuances of word and phrase – those basic voluntarist premises which between them constitute *just what it is* to understand our own as well as other people's motivating interests and concerns. Chief among them, as I have said, and absolutely central to the issue about doxastic responsibility is our understanding that beliefs can be arrived at in a great many ways, some of which render them fit candidates for assessment in rational and moral-evaluative terms while others seem to call for explanatory treatment in an altogether different, more diagnostic mode. Of the latter kind are beliefs acquired (or absorbed) through passive exposure to various modes of causal, cultural, or ideological conditioning. In the former case we have to do with those other, more reflective or adequately reasoned forms of doxastic commitment that have taken due account of such factors, allowed for their possible distorting effect, and thereby achieved both a greater degree of self-knowledge and an outlook in matters of moral or intellectual conscience that is more reliable or truth-conducive since less in the grip of unexamined prejudice.

Of course these descriptions apply only to the twin extremes on a scale of doxastic responsibility that includes a great many intermediate degrees, that is to say, cases where it is hard, maybe impossible, to distinguish the workings of causal influence from those of rational belief-formation, whether for the individual concerned or for those who seek to make intelligible sense of that individual's sayings and doings. Also there is a marked asymmetry between our readiness to fall back on causal hypotheses, i.e., imputations of rationally under-motivated thought and action in the case of other people and our much higher level of resistance to any such suggestion as regards our own most cherished or deep-laid beliefs. After all, there is something basically absurd – a kind of performative contradiction – about saying 'I believe *x* to be the case but this belief of mine is most likely a product of my upbringing, cultural background, ideological formation', or whatever. Thus causal explanations of why people think and behave as they do are much likelier to carry conviction when applied to others (especially to people remote from us in time, geographical locale, or socio-cultural background) than when applied to ourselves and those nearest to us in these respects. Nevertheless that resistance has been quite appreciably lowered, at least among the more educated sectors of society, as a result of various diffuse yet powerful influences such as psychoanalysis, comparative anthropology, and the whole range of present-day social sciences that have stressed the sheer multiplicity of human beliefs and value-systems. Even if one wishes to hold the line well short of wholesale cultural relativism – including its more philosophically 'respectable', e.g., Wittgensteinian variants – still there is no denying the extent to which developments like these have altered (and expanded) our sense of what may count as a rational, or at any rate rationally intelligible item of belief. Besides, it is only from the most dogmatic of voluntarist viewpoints that philosophy could afford simply to disregard the latest findings of neurophysiology, cognitive science, evolutionary psychology, and other disciplines with an arguable bearing on the issues here addressed.

What is called for, in short, is an approach that manages to take these developments on board whilst not leaning over too far in one or the other direction. That is to say, it should avoid the kind of inertly 'culturalist' perspective wherein all beliefs and practices are deemed to make sense by their own communal lights, in which case they must be held immune from any form of 'outside' criticism, but also the opposite error of supposing that standards of doxastic responsibility can be applied without regard to the cultural conditions under which those beliefs and practices emerged. In so far as it is difficult to hold this balance – to weigh the strong claims of moral-intellectual autonomy against the need for a thoughtful and sensitive reckoning with such heteronomous conditions – the difficulty is one that will surely arise in all attempts to resolve the free-will/determinism issue. So we might now seem to be back with the same old dilemma and to have shown nothing more than the unfortunate proneness of philosophy constantly to rehearse familiar problems in a range of alternative but equally futile (since non-problem-solving) ways. However this is to take an excessively sceptical or pessimistic view of the matter. What the arguments and counter-arguments bring out is not so much the ultimate impasse engendered by two conflicting (causal-explanatory and rational-justificatory) modes of thought but rather the conclusion that there *must* be some way of reconciling them – albeit one at present beyond our best powers of conceptual grasp – since they both play a strictly indispensable role in all our thinking about issues of doxastic responsibility. What should also have emerged from this discussion is the impossibility of pushing either case (i.e., for the volitional or non-volitional character of belief) to a point where it would play the other clean off the field by establishing its own irresistible claim to have finally resolved those issues.

Thus it might appear that any hope of progress must lie in the direction of a *via media* between the two extremes, that is, an approach that sensibly acknowledges the limits on our freedom of will as well as the problems that always arise with any full-fledged determinist, causal-explanatory, or anti-voluntarist account. Where this latter goes wrong is in failing to allow for all the evidence we have – not only through intuitive, first-person experience but also in the contexts of social exchange and reflection on other people's acts and beliefs – that there does exist a margin for the free exercise of moral and intellectual conscience whatever the extent of those causal or more broadly socio-cultural constraints. Any theory is sure to be a non-starter if it has to discount the example of various heterodox thinkers or reformers whose moral-intellectual conscience has revolted against the kinds of taken-for-granted belief that defined the currency of 'knowledge' or 'truth' in their own time and place. It is on this objection that determinist arguments must ultimately run aground, as indeed must those other, on the face of it strongly anti-determinist arguments – among them Wittgensteinian appeals to communal 'agreement in judgement' as the furthest one can get by way of rational or moral justification – which likewise leave no room for the values of intellectual and moral autonomy. However these antinomies cannot be resolved (as I suggested above, though prefaced by the cautionary phrase '. . . it might appear . . .') through some kind of compromise or middle-ground approach that would seek to prevent them from arising in the first place by adopting a suitably qualified conception of doxastic voluntarism on the one hand and of doxastic determinism on the other. No doubt it is often best policy in various contexts – law, practical ethics, interpersonal relations, ascriptions of motive to culturally distant (including historical) agents – to work on a generalized 'principle of humanity' which does involve some such compromise stance as a matter of trying to see all around other people's epistemic situations or moral predicaments and not jump straight to a dismissive or critical verdict. That is, we often make this sort of good-willed effort to maximize the imputed rational content of other people's beliefs by achieving an optimum balance between the claims of autonomy and those of due allowance for certain causally or socio-culturally explicable sources of error. Yet philosophically speaking – as Kant recognized, unlike some who purport to have left all those old worries behind – there is a large problem here and one that can only be addressed in metaphysical terms, or anyway in terms that admit of no such straightforward compromise solution. For it remains the case – whether a misfortune or a stroke of good luck from the philosopher's standpoint – that these are *antinomies* in the strict Kantian sense, rather than *paralogisms* (again as defined by Kant) that can be shown to result from some category-mistake or illicit transposition of concepts and categories from one to another topic-domain.[17] In other words they are the kinds of genuine, deep-laid problem that are sure to confront any thinker who seriously engages with the issue of doxastic responsibility.

Not that I should wish to hold Kant up as the likeliest source of deliverance from all our perplexities in this regard. Indeed, it is very largely as a consequence of the various drastic dualisms bequeathed by Kant that philosophy has so often tended to recoil into likewise drastic oscillations from one to another doctrinal extreme on a range of epistemological and ethical issues. Among them are those between the noumenal and the phenomenal, between concepts of understanding and sensuous intuitions, and (most of all) between the realm of autonomous practical reason and that other realm of 'heteronomous' desires, inclinations, affections, and suchlike 'pathological' factors which for Kant have no legitimate bearing whatsoever on issues of moral conscience, especially when they are adduced in order to extenuate or mitigate some wrongful action that would otherwise call for outright moral censure. So if Kant poses the relevant issues with a clarity and force that are often lacking in current debate, he does so in a way that places them forever and intrinsically beyond hope of any adequate solution. This is because he conceives the 'space of reasons' – of our distinctively human intellectual capacities, as opposed to our mere creaturely existence within the chain of concatenated cause and effect – in those same, drastically dichotomous terms. It is a very fine distinction I am trying to draw but one that makes all the difference between an outlook which counts this dilemma as *by its very nature* unresolvable and an outlook on which it remains deeply problematic by our present-best conceptual lights but not, for that reason, to be treated as an ultimate mystery or as requiring the kind of Kantian dualist approach that has found many sublimated echoes in recent debate.

Least of all can it be justified to adopt the kind of sheerly a priori approach that would view any attempt to achieve a perspective atop these vexing antinomies as symptomatic of a basic failure to grasp the irreducibility of mental to physical or – in the currently preferred idiom – intentional to causal modes of describing our beliefs, attitudes, doxastic commitments, moral dispositions, and so forth. Such arguments typically issue in dogmatic claims like that of John Searle with respect to what he sees as the absolute, in-principle impossibility that the 'strong' programme in Artificial Intelligence (AI) might ever be successfully carried through, i.e., to the point where some silicon-based and computer-run system might be thought to manifest all the attributes of human consciousness or intentionality.[18] The main problems with this kind of reasoning are firstly its neo-Cartesian assumption that there *must* be something so utterly distinctive about human mental states that they could not conceivably be realized in any other physical form, and secondly its downright refusal to acknowledge that the brain *just is* one such physically embodied, albeit massively complex and – in our current state of scientific understanding – causally inexplicable entity. To be sure, some philosophers may choose to grasp this nettle (whether in its downright substance-dualist or updated property-dualist form) and thereby reject or at least draw the sting of the mind/brain identity thesis. Otherwise they may resort to some saving compromise like Davidson's 'anomalous monism' or the notion of mind as 'emergent from' ('supervenient upon') the physical brain-states that are found to accompany this or that item of conscious or affective experience.[19] However such arguments amount to no more than a handy but somewhat shifty device for avoiding the central issue about consciousness and its relation to whatever is going on in neuro-chemical terms.

Hence the ease with which opponents of Searle – hard-line physicalists like the Churchlands – can turn his case right around and object to his saying that mental states are somehow 'caused by' brain-states (that is, the sorts of state that can exist only in carbon-based, organic life-forms such as ourselves), rather than saying that mental states *just are* brain-states under a different, folk-psychological description.[20] Dragging in such redundant causal talk is an example of what they dub the 'Betty Crocker Microwave Cookbook' fallacy. This alludes to a passage where the domestic guru explains that heat is *caused by* the kinetic energy of molecules, rather than saying (correctly) that 'heat' *just is* everyday, phenomenological parlance for what physicists term 'kinetic energy of molecules'. Thus Searle's apparent concession to physicalism – his allowance that there is indeed a strict and exceptionless causal correlation between brain-states and mind-states – can nonetheless be seen to underwrite his claim (*contra* the advocates of strong AI) that this link exists only in creatures like ourselves with the right kind of neurophysical architecture and just the sorts of conscious or intentional experience that invariably go along with it. Once rid of this residual dualism, so the Churchlands maintain, we shall see that there is nothing unique or *sui generis* about mind, brain, or the relationship between them. Rather we shall come to treat such mentalist talk as just another item of soon-to-be-discarded since scientifically retrograde belief, along with all the other metaphysical baggage handed down by a long tradition of jointly philosophic and folk-psychological thought.

My point is not so much to take sides on this issue of Searle versus the Churchands but rather to bring out the irony of a situation where Searle's hard-headed causal talk – his overt refusal of Cartesian dualism and insistence on the physical embodiment (i.e., the brain-dependence) of consciousness and inten-tionality – can be used to charge him with falling into precisely such a dualist trap. It seems to me that Searle is here hung up on yet another of those Kantian antinomies that have typified this whole debate and whose effect is to leave thinkers very often exposed to criticisms and objections which are all the more powerful since arising unnoticed from their own arguments. Thus Searle's attempt to carve out a space for the distinctive attributes of human (i.e., con-scious, intentional and organically based) experience while at the same time rebutting any dualist charge is one that leads him to adopt a position – the mind-brain causal dependence thesis – which the Churchlands can treat (not without justification) as a form of epiphenomenalist doctrine that, so far from resolving the Cartesian dilemma, leaves it all the more firmly entrenched. For it then becomes a double mystery (1) by what remotely intelligible process mind-states could 'emerge from' or 'supervene upon' (let alone be 'caused by') physical states of the brain, and (2), if so, how there could be any genuine, rather than notional, appeal to a realm of irreducibly conscious or intentional experience that would constitute a standing refutation of reductive physicalism in the Churchland mode.

This is why Searle's purportedly knockdown case against strong AI – a case advanced mainly on thought-experimental and hence a priori grounds – cannot bear anything like the requisite weight of demonstrative evidence or proof. On the one hand it runs into all the above-described conceptual and logical prob-lems, while on the other it invites the charge of dogmatically denying what must surely be a matter for continued scientific investigation, that is, the pos-sibility that conscious and intentional mind-states might eventually be realized in other-than-human (e.g., silicon-based) systems. Thus, according to Searle's famous 'Chinese Room' thought-experiment, this prospect is a priori ruled out by the fact that we could never know for sure whether the English-Chinese 'translator' inside the room (for which read: the 'conscious and intelligent' AI device) was actually translating the messages handed in or merely responding in mechanical fashion by comparing the word-shapes and sequences with those contained in his data-bank (for which read: a software programme set up to give the impression of thinking 'like us' but in fact quite devoid of any such pow-ers).[21] However, despite its intuitive force, this argument falls to the twofold objection that it holds just as much for our transaction with human subjects – as witness the perennial issue of scepticism vis-à-vis 'other minds' – and that it flies in the face of Searle's own argument that mind-states are causally dependent on brain-states. For if this is the case and if brains are themselves (no doubt fan-tastically complex) computational devices then there is just no rational moti-vation for Searle's claim that mind-states of a nature qualitatively identical to those experienced by human beings cannot conceivably be produced or supported by different kinds of physical system. Besides, there is something decidedly premature – given the current rate of advance in allied fields like neurophysiology and cognitive science – about any argument that claims to deduce the impossibility of further such advances on a basis of purely a priori reasoning and with minimal reference to what's going on in just those pertinent fields.

IV

As I have said, this should not for one moment be taken to suggest that philosophers had better now vacate the high ground of expert debate in these matters and give way to others (the neuroscientists and cognitive psychologists) who really know what they are talking about. If Searle's style of argument exemplifies the dangers of an attitude that grants philosophy the right to decide what shall count as relevant, admissible scientific evidence then it is equally the case that proponents of an out-and-out physicalist approach, like the Churchlands, push so far in the opposite direction as to lay themselves open to the charge of just ignoring – rather than genuinely seeking to resolve – the very real philosophic problems that arise with any such programme. Thus they reject as just a remnant of 'folk-psychology' the idea that there is a whole dimension of subjective experience – 'what it is like' to see the colour red, to suffer pain, to hear an oboe, to undergo the gamut of feelings from elation to despair – which cannot and could not be explained in physicalist terms, even were we to possess a completed science of the brain and its neuro-chemical or cognitive-psychological workings.[22] This is not the place for a detailed discussion of the various arguments for and against the existence of such strictly irreducible qualia or modes of first-person perceptual, affective, or phenomenological experience which supposedly elude any possible description in the terms of a drastically reductionist approach like that espoused by the Churchlands. Sufficient to say, in the present context, that this debate is just as far from any prospect of being effectively resolved either way as are the closely related issues of free will versus determinism or – my chief concern here – doxastic voluntarism versus the claim that beliefs are not volitional and hence not subject to moral blame or approbation. What gives them their distinctly philosophic character is the fact that they produce such deeply held yet sharply conflicting intuitions which dispose us to believe that they *must* be somehow resolvable, while their effect is to render the issue more perplexing and its solution more elusive the harder we think about it.

This is not, as it might well appear, just a recipe for endless equivocation or a pretext for philosophers to sit back and contemplate an ever-deepening (and action-absolving) series of conceptual quandaries. On the contrary: the main purpose of raising such issues is to keep them constantly and clearly in view when we are tempted to adopt some other way of thinking that involves less challenge to our normal, unexamined, or communally warranted habits of belief.

Thus, for instance, the case for regarding our beliefs as not (or not entirely) subject to our powers of conscious, deliberative will is one that has been made – and that still needs making – at times of rampant doctrinal, religious, or political persecution. In this respect, though not in others, it may be seen as the doxastic equivalent of the moral or legal case for treating certain agents as not fully accountable for certain actions, whether in consequence of social factors, intellectual impairment, mitigating circumstance, or a whole range of causal (among them psychopathological) conditions that are felt to justify the plea of 'diminished responsibility'. Of course the big difference is that here we are dealing with various kinds and degrees of unfreedom, that is, of restriction on the subject's scope for intellectual and moral autonomy, whereas in the former case – paradoxically enough – freedom of belief is upheld as a matter of socio-political right on the grounds that people are often to some extent *not* responsible for what they believe, and should hence not be subject to penalty or blame on that account. Indeed one can see the paradox emerging at full force in those two occurrences of the word 'subject' in my previous sentence, first with the active-autonomist sense: 'subject (noun) = locus of freely willed choice and rational accountability', and second with the passive-determinist sense: 'subject (adj.) = under some constraint or compulsion that places limits on the exercise of just those powers'. This is not the sort of problem that might be cleared up by a more precise definition of terms, nor by application of the standard Wittgensteinian therapeutic treatment. Rather, it is one that is apt to strike any thinking individual who considers the arguments on both sides not only from a philosophic standpoint but also in the wider context of debates about law, ethics, and the proper limits – if such there be – on the conscientious freedom to express ideas that go against some existing currency of values and beliefs. For these are questions that are nowhere close to being resolved and which might well be thought – at any rate by those of a sceptical, defeatist, or 'mysterian' mind – as lying beyond reach of any adequate solution.

While the latter view amounts to a strategy of last resort it is nonetheless important to remind ourselves and others of how complex and intractable these questions remain and also how we are prone to fall into errors of judgement – even, as I have argued, miscarriages of justice – by opting too readily for one or the other standpoint. After all, it is among the chief functions of a properly trained philosophical intelligence to supply such reminders when required, as they often are in situations (like those instanced above) where social and political incentives or pressures may override the call for such fine discriminations in the matter of moral and doxastic responsibility. This is one area in which analytic philosophers have something to learn from their 'continental' (i.e., post-Kantian mainland-European) counterparts, whatever the degree of mutual mistrust and downright intellectual antagonism that has marked many of their dealings over the past half-century and more.[23] That is to say, this sense of irreducible complexity – of the objections that arise against any too quick or confident solution – is a prominent feature of much mainland-European philosophy, even (or especially) those aspects of it that analytic thinkers are apt to write off as extravagant, linguistically undisciplined, or overly speculative. I have made the point elsewhere with reference to recent interpretations of Kant and the contrast between, on the one hand, broadly 'continental' readings that engage deeply with problems in Kantian epistemology and ethics and, on the other hand, revisionist readings in the broadly analytic tradition that contrive to keep such complicating factors safely out of view.[24]

Of course this is not to suggest that the 'linguistic turn' in its various forms has rendered mainstream Anglophone philosophy devoid of resources for addressing such topics. One need only look to a thinker like J. L. Austin, in particular his essay 'A Plea for Excuses', if one wishes to find a striking example of the way that 'ordinary-language' analysis can illuminate questions of moral judgement or offer new ways of conceiving the free-will/determinism issue through a patient and meticulous attentiveness to nuances of verbal implication.[25] This is nowhere more apparent than in Austin's reflections on the range of finely tuned adverbial modifiers – 'he did it "wilfully", "deliberately", "knowingly", "consciously", "intentionally", "absent-mindedly", "inadvertently", "carelessly", "accidentally", "unwittingly"', and so on – by which we signal our intuitive grasp of just such nuances and use them to indicate varying degrees of moral culpability. All the same his critics do have a point when they suggest that there is something distinctly parochial about Austin's brand of 'ordinary language' philosophy, an odd mixture of Oxonian *hauteur* and complacent acquiescence in the habits of thought – the linguistically encoded mores – of his own cultural locale.[26] Indeed, one result of the linguistic turn in analytic philosophy since the 1950s – and arguably since the Moore/Russell revolt against 'idealist' or 'metaphysical' excesses of whatever kind – has been to rule out any deeper engagement with such issues except in so far as they are taken to involve some category-mistake, some conceptual error, or (after Wittgenstein) some symptomatic instance of the 'bewitchment of our intelligence by language'. For if philosophy is best, most usefully (or least harmfully) employed in clearing away or therapeutically dissolving those old – e.g., Kantian – dilemmas then the free-will issue itself becomes just another suitable case for treatment. And yet, as I have said, it is an issue that cannot be finessed by any amount of conceptual analysis or any number of placid assurances that 'everything is order' with our language as it stands and that philosophers must therefore be mistaken – in the grip of some (again typically Kantian) metaphysical or transcendental illusion – if they seek to raise problems where no such problems exist.

If Kant famously credited Hume with having shaken him out of his dogmatic slumbers and thereby set him on the path toward a full-scale critical reconstruction of epistemology and ethics then at present what is needed, or so I would suggest, is a similar revitalizing impulse in the opposite direction. Thus analytic philosophy might very well benefit from a willingness to abandon its defensive posture and take some account of those developments in 'continental' thought – from Husserlian phenomenology, via Sartrean existentialism, to Derridean deconstruction – that have kept alive certain crucial questions (or provocative ways of framing them) beyond what counts as proper or legitimate by its own self-assured criteria. If there is one characteristic that chiefly distinguishes the 'two traditions' it is this greater awareness, on the continental side, of the need to pursue problematical issues – like the Kantian antinomies – to a point where they engage the genuine dilemmas of human existence, rather than supposing that these can best be kept from causing trouble through a mode of conceptual or linguistic analysis that effectively sweeps them under the carpet. Perhaps the most striking example of this latter tendency is the work of Gilbert Ryle where it is pretty much assumed that any problems of so seemingly intractable or deep-laid a character must, for that very reason, be put down to some 'category-mistake' or failure to perceive where thinking has been misled by its proneness to various forms of conceptual imprecision or false analogy.[27] Ryle is a particularly interesting case since he published a number of critical yet well-informed essays on Husserlian phenomenology during the 1930s, but later swung across to the received (analytic) view that all the talk of 'intentionality', 'eidetic essences', the 'transcendental ego', and so forth, was in truth just a thinly disguised version of psychologism.[28] Another tantalizing hint of this path not taken – or abandoned after a brief reconnoitre of the alternative prospects on offer – is Austin's passing remark to the effect that his kind of ordinary-language approach could also fairly be described as a form of 'linguistic phenomenology'.[29] However he, like Ryle, showed no inclination to pursue this idea any further, unless one construes the term 'phenomenology' in a scaled-down (normalized analytic) sense that would leave it quite devoid of any distinctive or substantive implications. That is to say, if the remit of phenomenological enquiry is confined to a purely descriptive account of our everyday linguistic practices – no matter how sharp-eyed, detailed, or meticulous – then it will find no room for those other, doubtless more 'metaphysical' sorts of question that have continued to preoccupy thinkers in the post-Kantian European line of descent.

V

It has been my contention throughout this chapter that such issues are absolutely central to any philosophical enterprise worthy of the name, and that they cannot be analysed away by some well-practised technique of conceptual or linguistic problem-control. Nor is there much benefit to be had from those recent attempts at a partial *rapprochement* – like McDowell's semi-naturalized, de-transcendentalized, Wittgenstein-influenced and studiously non-'metaphysical' reading of Kant – which evade the most challenging aspects of that 'other' tradition while they simply reproduce all its unresolved dilemmas in a different, less overt but no less troublesome guise.[30] Philosophy does best in relation to intractable issues like those of free will/determinism or doxastic responsibility by keeping the problems firmly in view, resisting any premature claim to have resolved them decisively either way, but also holding out against the twin temptations of a drive to dissolve them through conceptual analysis and a placid assurance that they cannot arise so long as our language stays in touch with the norms of communal usage. For these counsels cannot get us very far – whether in philosophy or in thinking more clearly about questions of an ethical, legal, social, or political import – when their effect is to close off precisely the kinds of engaged and responsible thought that constitute philosophy's chief claim to attention in such matters. Thus, for instance, Kant's passages in the First and Second *Critiques* concerning the Antinomies of Pure and Practical Reason are germane to any debate about issues of doxastic and moral responsibility, whatever one may think of his proposed 'solution' and the various dilemmas to which it gave rise. My point, to repeat, is that philosophy risks inviting the charge of triviality or downright irrelevance if it adheres too closely to the mainstream-analytic, i.e., problem-solving (or problem-dissolving) mode of address to these issues and hence fails to register the depth and extent of their bearing on our moral, social, and intellectual lives.

That Kant in some sense got it wrong about ethics – that any too rigid (that is to say, *echt*-Kantian) application of his strict universalist claims might be apt to produce morally repugnant consequences in certain situations – is a case that has been rehearsed by a good many recent commentators, among them advocates of a communitarian approach with strong Wittgensteinian leanings.[31] However there are ways of getting it wrong whilst nonetheless posing the crucial questions in a sharply focused and provocative form that has more to teach us than any such recourse to anodyne, philosophically and morally evasive talk about shared language-games or communal practices. The same applies, as I have said, to Sartrean existentialism and its raising of the claim for human autonomy and free will to such a high point of absolute, intransigent principle that we encounter just the kind of choice that Sartre is so good at depicting in his works of philosophy and fiction alike.[32] That is, we are confronted with the need either to accept his extreme voluntarist position – along with its likewise extreme demands on our allegiance in the face of strong counter-arguments – or else to frame some viable, philosophically cogent alternative that would allow for certain kinds and degrees of unfreedom while nonetheless resisting any form of determinist doctrine. If relations had been less strained then analytic philosophers would hardly need telling that this debate has been carried forward to instructive effect by thinkers in the post-war French tradition, from Merleau-Ponty (whose critique of Sartre raises precisely these issues) to Derrida's later writings on the ethics and politics of deconstruction.[33] Moreover – no doubt through its acute responsiveness to episodes in recent French history – it has achieved a far wider and deeper socio-political resonance, as likewise with those various debates within post-war German (especially Frankfurt School) philosophy where epistemological and ethical issues are often inseparably bound up with reflection on the problems and prospects of the German federal state.[34]

This is *not* for one moment to go along with that other, 'continentally' inspired variant of the two-traditions story which would have it that analytic philosophy is a narrowly technical, politically disengaged mode of discourse concerned only with footling matters of linguistic or logico-semantic exegesis.

Even if, as I have suggested, that charge has some force with regard to certain developments on the analytic side, still it is very clearly wide of the mark when applied to the kinds of conceptual clarification and teasing-out of unnoticed complications in our political as well as ethical thinking that has characterized such work at its best. Among the many examples that might be offered I would mention in particular Jonathan Glover's *Humanity: A Moral History of the Twentieth Century*, a book that most impressively combines breadth of historical coverage with depth of philosophical reflection and a keen sense of how our moral judgements can be educated – rendered more acute but also less prone to habits of response – with the aid of such reflection. In cases like this it becomes just a pointless labelling exercise and one with profoundly misleading implications to place it on one or the other side of the Great Analytic/Continental Rift. What emerges, rather, is the two-way relationship between philosophy's need constantly to strive for a more adequate, that is, more intellectually responsible grasp of its own operative concepts and the need that those concepts should be exercised on matters of substantive (which will often mean complex, difficult, and at times sharply divisive) ethical import.

I have suggested here that both interests could be best served by a far more open and mutually responsive attitude in each quarter, though not without the kind of productive friction that comes of their different histories, interests, and modes of development since the time of that (albeit much exaggerated) parting of the ways after Kant. The main cause of such friction so far – and the reason, no doubt, for its having up to now generated more heat than light – is the belief among many analytic philosophers that the other lot are more in the business of creating unnecessary trouble than of solving genuine problems, and the converse belief among many continentals that analytic philosophy amounts to no more than a set of well-practised but evasive techniques for denying the existence of just those problems. The *loci classici* here would include some that I have mentioned already such as Ryle's drastic change of mind with regard to the issues raised by Husserlian transcendental phenomenology and Austin's idea that the problem of knowledge (with its main source in Kant) could best be answered by recourse to the commonsense wisdom enshrined in 'ordinary language'. It is a notion that cuts across some otherwise deep divergences of view, as for instance between the Frege-Russell claim that such language stands in need of logical analysis so as to clarify or disambiguate its surface confusions and the Wittgensteinian assurance that all such problems can be conjured away through the straightforward appeal to whatever makes sense by our own (or other people's) communal lights.[35] Then again, these stereotypical conceptions can be seen emerging at full force in the encounter – the 'determined non-encounter', as Derrida mock-ruefully declared it – between Derrida and Searle on the topic of Austinian speech-act philosophy.[36] They can also be traced through the history of differing responses to Kant's Antinomies of Pure and Practical Reason, that is to say, the issue as to whether these should be regarded as conceptual (or linguistic) aberrations in need of coaxing down from the giddy metaphysical heights or as genuine, deep-laid problems with a crucial bearing on the scope and limits of our freedom. Since that issue is central to the debate concerning doxastic voluntarism – the question as to whether or just how far we can be held intellectually and morally responsible for the content of our various beliefs, convictions, ideological commitments, and so forth – it is one that cannot be raised without reference (however guarded or oblique) to the kinds of discussion carried on within the 'other', post-Kantian continental tradition. In other words it is a distinctly *metaphysical* issue in so far as it involves considerations beyond anything resolvable (or even discussible) on the terms laid down by analytic philosophy either in its 'ordinary-language' (descriptivist) or its logico-semantic (revisionist) mode. To this extent it requires both the kind of far-reaching speculative thought that has characterized philosophy in the Kantian line of descent and (as a necessary complement to that) the kind of meticulous conceptual and linguistic analysis which has typified a good deal of mainstream analytic work. Thus the question of how best to reconcile our often conflicting intuitions in this regard – our sense that beliefs are (or ought to be) purely volitional with our countervailing sense of the need to make allowance for various limiting, e.g., causal or circumstantial factors – is a question that can and should cut right across these conventional boundary-markers.

At present, as I have said, there are strong signs of this awareness in the work of thinkers like McDowell who propose a return to Kant (or to certain select topics and passages in Kant) as offering a useful way forward from the perceived impasse of analytic philosophy in the wake of old-style logical empiricism and of Quine's root-and-branch attack on its governing assumptions.[37] However this proposal is often couched in terms – like those specified by P. F. Strawson in an earlier episode of 'back-to-Kant' thinking – which go so far toward scaling down the metaphysical or transcendental dimensions of Kantian epistemology and ethics that what remains is more like a warmed-over version of the logical-empiricist programme.[38] Thus it tends to work out as yet another exercise in stipulative boundary-drawing whereby Kant's more unfortunate (metaphysically loaded) kinds of talk can be adapted to the norms of a discourse which remains well within the bounds of analytic acceptability. Such, for instance, is McDowell's idea (derived from Wilfrid Sellars) of a 'space of reasons' wherein thinking can exercise its due prerogatives – those having to do with matters of humanly intelligible motive, meaning, or intent – as opposed to the domain of empirical enquiry which is likewise subject to the normative standards and constraints of rational inference, but not (or not directly) to those of moral-intellectual autonomy and freedom.[39] According to McDowell it is possible to maintain this distinction – and thereby conserve an adequate 'space' for the exercise of such freedom – without falling into the kinds of vicious dualism which have plagued Kantian and much post-Kantian philosophy, e.g., those between sensuous intuitions and concepts of understanding or the promptings of mere 'inclination', no matter how well disposed, and the absolute dictates of moral law. We can best achieve this, he thinks, by switching attention to Kant's talk of 'receptivity' and 'spontaneity', the latter conceived as 'only notionally separate' (since they are bound up in a relation of strict mutual dependence) and hence as offering a means of escape from the dualist impasse.

However, as I have argued at length elsewhere, when McDowell attempts to spell out the case in detail – to explain just how the autonomous-sounding claims of 'spontaneity' can be reconciled with those of 'empirical constraint from the outside world' – then it begins to look more like just another variant of that same old Kantian dilemma, one that has if anything been sharpened (not resolved or even somewhat clarified) by its recasting in these different terms.[40] 'If we restrict ourselves to the standpoint of experience itself', he suggests, then

> what we find in Kant is precisely the picture I have been recommending: a picture in which reality is not located outside a boundary that encloses the conceptual sphere . . . The fact that experience involves receptivity ensures the required constraint from outside thinking and judging. But since the deliverances of receptivity already draw on capacities that belong to spontaneity, we can coherently suppose that the constraint is rational; that is how the picture avoids the pitfall of the Given.[41]

One may question whether the claim of 'coherence' is aptly applied to so tortuous and convoluted a passage of reasoning. How 'reality' can possibly be thought of as exerting an external (empirical) constraint on any knowledge we can gain concerning it while all the same 'not located outside a boundary that encloses the conceptual sphere' is quite as problematic as anything encountered in Kant's murkier ruminations on the topic. At any rate, if one thing is clear, it is the fact that McDowell is very far from having finally dismounted from what he calls the 'see-saw' – the chronic oscillation – that has been such a hallmark of epistemology from Kant to the present. Indeed, what gives his attempted solution its particular diagnostic value is the conceptual strain that emerges so vividly in passages like that cited above. Nor are these problems by any means confined to the epistemological sphere, since the issue of knowledge (of its normative claims or justificatory grounds) is one that cannot possibly be set aside in any adequate, i.e., reasoned and responsible treatment of ethical questions. I have made this case specifically with regard to the debate about doxastic voluntarism since it is here – at the point of maximal conflict between autonomist and cultural-determinist views – that philosophy is brought up against the greatest challenge to its powers of rational arbitration. That is to say, there is little merit in any approach that fails to acknowledge the strength or intuitive force of arguments on both sides of this issue, or which treats it as merely a pseudo-dilemma brought about by our unfortunate proneness to forms of conceptual or metaphysical 'bewitchment'. On the contrary: it is one that often arises in contexts ranging from the most rarefied levels of meta-ethical debate to other, more 'applied' or practical dimensions of moral philosophy and – beyond that – in the public domain where it bears directly on various concerns of a social, political, and legal character. Confronted with such difficulties thinking most frequently tends to react in one or other of the opposite ways I have outlined above. Thus it veers either toward the kind of briskly problem-solving approach that plays them down for the sake of conceptual clarity or deference to common linguistic usage, or else toward a mode of address which keeps them firmly in view though at risk of raising the resultant dilemmas to a high point of paradox and ultimate undecidability.

No doubt it would grossly simplify the issue to identify these two contrasting attitudes with the 'analytic' (i.e., mainstream Anglo-American) and 'continental' (i.e., post-Kantian mainland-European) lines of descent. Still this idea will do less harm if it is taken not, in the customary fashion, as a mark of reciprocal hostility or mutual indifference but rather as describing the tense yet productive – since in certain ways strongly antithetical – relationship between them. Such is the attitude adopted by some philosophers of a broadly 'analytic' persuasion when they read Sartre and register the force of certain existentialist claims even though predisposed by their background culture and intellectual training to cast a somewhat quizzical or sceptical eye on the more extreme statements of that doctrine.[42] With Derrida likewise one can take his point about the irreducibility of ethical choice to rule, precedent, or formal prescription without endorsing the kind of full-fledged decisionist approach that would leave no room for the exercise of rational-deliberative thought.[43] This is not to treat Derrida, or indeed Sartre, as mere *provocateurs* or intellectual gadflies whose sole claim on our interest is their knack of coming up with sharply turned paradoxical formulations or skilfully contrived (often fictive) scenarios which may serve to administer a salutary jolt to our more routine or regimented habits of thought. To be sure, there is a prominent aspect of their writing that would seem to justify this rough characterization, as likewise with a good deal of other work – some of it by Anglophone philosophers – which would count as 'continental' in terms of its distinctive thematic, stylistic, or generic attributes.[44] Still there is a crucial divergence of outlook between those who regard such work as *merely* a standing provocation when judged by the norms of rational, commonsense, responsible discourse and those who see in it the kind of provocation that Socrates offered when he challenged the conventional mores of his time, or that Hume put up against a whole range of orthodox philosophic and religious beliefs, or that Kant acknowledged when he credited Hume with having 'aroused me from my dogmatic slumbers'.

It is this latter, more constructive and open-minded sort of response that holds out the best prospect of advance, not only as a matter of productive (mutually provocative) exchange between the 'two traditions' but also as concerns our central topic of doxastic responsibility. For if their difference can be summarized briefly yet without undue simplification it is the difference between a 'continental' way of proceeding that measures itself against the limits and extremities of philosophic thought and an 'analytic' discourse whose regulative principle – albeit with some leeway for testing or stretching – is to draw such anomalies back within the compass of conceptual or linguistic normality. Such is also the tension that Derrida brings out through his early, meticulously detailed and rigorous (and in this sense properly 'analytic') readings of philosophers from

Plato to Husserl.[45] Thus on the one hand he remarks that 'a certain structuralism has always been philosophy's most spontaneous gesture' while on the other he acknowledges 'the principled, essential, and structural impossibility of closing a structural phenomenology'.[46] Otherwise put, it is the constant oscillation between 'hyperbole and finite structure', or a thinking that challenges philosophy's powers of self-assured conceptual grasp and a mode of thought – no less 'principled and essential' – which strives to contain that hyperbolic impulse within the bounds of established rational or logico-semantic intelligibility. This seems to me the most fruitful way of conceiving the relationship between 'continental' and 'analytic' philosophy as that relationship has developed since Kant and, more pointedly, since the two traditions broke step over issues raised by Frege's well-known criticisms of Husserl.[47] At the same time it offers a revealing approach to questions concerning the scope and limits of our moral-intellectual autonomy, whether raised (as by Sartre) in an overtly thematic existentialist mode or (as by Derrida) in terms of philosophy's freedom – within certain specified procedural constraints – to challenge or to radically revise our understanding of canonical texts. What is involved in each case is a highly self-conscious and self-critical reflection on the character of those constraints and on the ways that such freedom can be exercised responsibly despite and against other, more orthodox (restrictive or coercive) habits of belief.

NOTES

1   See, for instance, Jean-François Lyotard, *The Postmodern Condition: A Report on Knowledge*, trans. Geoff Bennington and Brian Massumi (Manchester: Manchester University Press, 1984); also – for a critique of such thinking – Christopher Norris, *The Truth About Postmodernism* (Oxford: Blackwell, 1993).

2   See especially G. E. M. Anscombe, 'Causality and Determinism', in Ernest Sosa (ed.), *Causation and Conditionals* (Oxford: Oxford University Press, 1975), pp. 63–81. I put the case against such extrapolations from the micro- to the macrophysical domain in Norris, *Quantum Theory and the Flight from Realism: Philosophical Responses to Quantum Mechanics* (London: Routledge, 2000), esp. pp. 134–64.

3   Ludwig Wittgenstein, *Philosophical Investigations*, trans. G. E. M. Anscombe (Oxford: Blackwell, 1951).

4   See John McDowell, *Mind and World* (Cambridge, MA: Harvard University Press, 1994); also Robert Brandom, *Making It Explicit: Reasoning, Representing, and Discursive Commitment* (Harvard University Press, 1994); Wilfrid Sellars, 'Empiricism and the Philosophy of Mind', in Herbert Feigl and Michael Scriven (eds), *Minnesota Studies in the Philosophy of Science*, Vol. 1 (Minneapolis: University of Minnesota Press, 1956), pp. 253–329.

5   Jean-Paul Sartre, *Being and Nothingness: An Essay on Phenomenological Ontology*, trans. Hazel E. Barnes (London: Methuen, 1966).

6   See especially Maurice Merleau-Ponty, *Adventures of the Dialectic*, trans. Joseph Bien (Evanston, IL: Northwestern University Press, 1973) and *The Prose of the World*, trans. John O'Neill (Northwestern University Press, 1974); also Jon Stewart (ed.), *The Debate Between Sartre and Merleau-Ponty* (Northwestern University Press, 1998).

7   Sartre, *Critique of Dialectical Reason*, Vol. 1 (*Theory of Practical Ensembles*), trans. A. Sheridan-Smith (London: New Left Books, 1976); Vol. 2 (*The Intelligibility of History*), trans. Quintin Hoare (London: Verso, 1991).

8 See, for instance, Colin McGinn, *The Mysterious Flame: Conscious Minds in a Material World* (New York: Basic Books, 1999).

9 See especially Paul M. Churchland and Patricia S. Churchland, *On the Contrary: Critical Essays, 1987–1997* (Cambridge, MA: MIT Press, 1998).

10 J. S. Mill, *An Examination of Sir William Hamilton's Philosophy, and of the Principal Philosophical Questions Raised in His Writings* (London: Longmans, Green and Dyer, 1878).

11 Immanuel Kant, *Critique of Pure Reason*, trans. N. Kemp Smith (London: Macmillan, 1964).

12 See, for instance, McDowell, *Mind and World* (op. cit.).

13 Christopher Norris, 'McDowell on Kant: Redrawing the Bounds of Sense' and 'The Limits of Naturalism: Further Thoughts on McDowell's *Mind and World*', in *Minding the Gap: Epistemology and Philosophy of Science in the Two Traditions* (Amherst, MA: University of Massachusetts Press, 2000), pp. 172–96, 197–230.

14 See Note 2, above.

15 Benjamin Libet, *Mind Time: The Temporal Factor in Consciousness* (Cambridge, MA: Harvard University Press, 2004); also Libet, Anthony Freeman and Keith Sutherland (eds), *The Volitional Brain: Towards a Neuroscience of Free Will* (New York: Imprint Academic, 2000).

16 See especially Wittgenstein, *Lectures and Conversations on Aesthetics, Psychology and Religious Belief*, ed. C. Barrett (Oxford: Blackwell, 1966); also *Last Writings on the Philosophy of Psychology*, Vols 1 and 2, eds G. H. von Wright and Heikki Nyman (Oxford: Blackwell, 1990 and 1993).

17 Kant, 'The Paralogisms of Pure Reason', in *Critique of Pure Reason* (op. cit.), pp. 328–68.

18 See John R. Searle, *Intentionality: An Essay in the Philosophy of Mind* (Cambridge: Cambridge University Press, 1983) and *Minds, Brains and Science* (Cambridge, MA: Harvard University Press, 1984).

19 See, for instance, Donald Davidson, *Essays on Actions and Events* (Oxford: Clarendon Press, 1980); also Jaegwon Kim (ed.), *Supervenience* (Aldershot: Ashgate, 2002).

20 See Note 9, above.

21 John Preston and Mark Bishop (eds), *View Into the Chinese Room: New Essays on Searle and Artificial Intelligence* (Oxford: Clarendon Press, 2002).

22 For further discussion, see Joseph Levine, *Purple Haze: The Puzzle of Consciousness* (Oxford: Oxford University Press, 2002); Quentin Smith and Aleksandar Jokic (eds), *Consciousness: New Philosophical Perspectives* (Oxford: Oxford University Press, 2003).

23 See also Norris, *Minding the Gap* (op. cit.).

24 See Note 13, above.

25 J. L. Austin, 'A Plea for Excuses', in *Philosophical Papers* (Oxford: Oxford University Press, 1961), pp. 123–52.

26 See, for instance, Keith Graham, *J. L. Austin: A Critique of Ordinary Language Philosophy* (Hassocks: Harvester Press, 1977).

27 Gilbert Ryle, *Dilemmas* (Cambridge: Cambridge University Press, 1954).

28 Ryle, 'Phenomenology', 'Review of Martin Farber, *The Foundations of Phenomenology*', and 'Phenomenology versus *The Concept of Mind*', in Ryle, *Collected Papers*, Vol. 1 (London: Hutchinson, 1971), pp. 167–78, 215–24, 179–96.

29 See Austin, *Philosophical Papers* (op. cit.), p. 182.

30 See Notes 4 and 13, above.

31 For an early and highly influential statement of this view see Peter Winch, *The Idea of a Social Science and Its Relation to Philosophy* (London: Routledge & Kegan Paul, 1958) and *Trying to Make Sense* (Oxford: Blackwell, 1987).

32 See Note 5, above.

33 See Note 6, above; also Jacques Derrida, *Aporias: Dying – Awaiting (One Another at) the 'Limits of Truth'*, trans. Thomas Dutoit (Stanford, CA: Stanford University Press, 1993); 'Force of Law: The "Mystical Foundation of Authority"', trans. Mary Quaintance, *Cardoso*

Law Review, Vol. XI (1990), pp. 999–1045; 'At This Very Moment in This Work Here I Am', trans. Ruben Berezdivin, in Robert Bernasconi and Simon Critchley (eds), *Re-Reading Levinas* (Bloomington, IN: Indiana University Press, 1991), pp. 11–40.

34 See especially Jürgen Habermas, *Justification and Application: Remarks on Discourse Ethics*, trans. C. P. Cronin (Cambridge, MA: MIT Press, 1993) and *Between Facts and Norms: Contributions to a Discourse Theory of Law and Democracy*, trans. W. Rehg (Cambridge, MA: MIT Press, 1996); also J. Bohmann and W. Rehg (eds), *Deliberative Democracy: Essays on Reason and Politics* (Cambridge, MA: MIT Press, 1997).

35 Gottlob Frege, 'On Sense and Reference', in Peter Geach and Max Black (eds), *Translations from the Philosophical Writings of Gottlob Frege* (Oxford: Blackwell, 1952), pp. 56–78; Bertrand Russell, 'On Denoting', *Mind*, Vol. XIV (1905), pp. 479–93; Wittgenstein, *Philosophical Investigations* (op. cit.).

36 See Jacques Derrida, 'Signature Event Context', *Glyph*, Vol. 1 (Baltimore: Johns Hopkins University Press, 1975), pp. 172–97; John R. Searle, 'Reiterating the Differences', ibid., pp. 198–208; Derrida, 'Limited Inc. abc', *Glyph*, Vol. 2 (1977), pp. 75–176; also Derrida, 'Afterword: Toward an Ethic of Conversation', in Gerald Graff (ed.), *Limited Inc* (Evanston, IL: Northwestern University Press, 1989), pp. 111–54.

37 McDowell, *Mind and World* (op. cit.); W. V. Quine, 'Two Dogmas of Empiricism', in *From a Logical Point of View*, 2nd edn (Cambridge, MA: Harvard University Press, 1961), pp. 20–46.

38 See P. F. Strawson, *Individuals: An Essay in Descriptive Metaphysics* (London: Methuen, 1959) and *The Bounds of Sense: An Essay on Kant's Critique of Pure Reason* (London: Methuen, 1966).

39 See especially Wilfrid Sellars, 'Empiricism and the Philosophy of Mind', McDowell, *Mind and World*, and other references under Note 4, above.

40 See Note 13, above.

41 McDowell, *Mind and World* (op. cit.), p. 41.

42 See especially Gregory McCulloch, *Using Sartre: An Analytical Introduction to Early Sartrean Themes* (London: Routledge, 1994).

43 See Note 33, above.

44 For further discussion, see Christopher Norris, *Minding the Gap* (op. cit.).

45 See especially Derrida, *'Speech and Phenomena' and Other Essays on Husserl's Theory of Signs*, trans. David B. Allison (Evanston, IL: Northwestern University Press, 1973); *Writing and Difference*, trans Alan Bass (London: Routledge & Kegan Paul, 1978); *Dissemination*, trans. Barbara Johnson (London: Athlone Press, 1981).

46 Derrida, *Writing and Difference* (op. cit.), p. 162.

47 See Gottlob Frege, review of Edmund Husserl's *Philosophie der Arithmetik*, translated by E.-H. W. Kluge, *Mind*, Vol. LXXXI (1972), pp. 321–37; Gilbert Ryle, 'Phenomenology', 'Review of Martin Farber, *The Foundations of Phenomenology*', and 'Phenomenology versus *The Concept of Mind*' (Note 28, above); also Derrida, '"Genesis and Structure" and Phenomenology', in *Writing and Difference* (op. cit.), pp. 154–68 and *La problème de la genèse dans la philosophie de Husserl* (Paris: Presses Universitaires de France, 1990).

6

Kripkenstein's Monsters: Anti-realism, Scepticism, and the Rule-Following Debate

I

No thinker in recent times has exerted so powerful, so widespread, and (I shall argue) so predominantly negative an influence on the conduct of mainstream philosophical debate as Ludwig Wittgenstein. Let me justify this somewhat provocative opening sentence by briefly unpacking a few of its salient terms. 'Mainstream' I define, for present purposes, as the kind of philosophy that emerged in the wake of old-style logical positivism/empiricism, that gained its ascendance partly through the impact of Wittgenstein's later writings, and which nowadays pretty much decides what counts as serious (academically acceptable) debate in various core regions, among them epistemology, ethics, and philosophy of mind, logic and language. 'Powerful' and 'widespread' I take to be borne out by the constant barrage of references to Wittgenstein not only by self-professed disciples but also by those who adopt a range of philosophical positions that would otherwise seem, on the face of it, flatly opposed to Wittgenstein's way of thinking. 'Negative' takes us on to different, no doubt more controversial terrain and will thus have to wait a bit longer for its justification. At this stage I shall simply venture the hypothesis that Wittgenstein has succeeded, no doubt *malgré lui*, in promoting an orthodox philosophic creed whose grip is all the stronger for its claiming to be no such thing but rather to provide a means of deliverance from all our needless philosophical quandaries. So far from therapeutically showing the fly a way out of the fly-bottle the chief effect of Wittgenstein's later writings has been to keep philosophers obsessively buzzing around a number of set-piece topics – such as the 'private-language' and 'rule-following' debates – which permit no solution save on the terms (or on something very like the terms) laid down by Wittgenstein himself.[1] Moreover, that effect has been most pronounced among those who dissent in various ways from the orthodox or fideist Wittgensteinian approach, yet who find themselves ineluctably drawn back into the same closed circle of argument.

Thus anyone surveying the current scene in analytic philosophy from a fairly detached, i.e., doctrinally uncommitted standpoint would surely be struck by the sheer amount of time, effort, and subtlety devoted to fine points of Wittgensteinian textual exegesis and to staking out some minor variation on this or that canonical theme. Moreover, they might well conclude that by far the greater part of this effort was directed toward certain pseudo-dilemmas or hypercultivated problems which have acquired such prominence – and such a power to induce philosophical bewilderment – only through a kind of widespread intellectual contagion with its source in Wittgenstein's peculiar knack for projecting his own worries on to the philosophic community at large. Hence, I would suggest, the strange inverse effect whereby a discourse purporting to cure us of all those neurotic obsessions (among them, not least, the problem of 'other minds' and the sceptic's hyperbolical doubt concerning the existence of an 'external world') should since have given rise to a huge volume of commentary itself manifesting distinct obsessional traits and offering no answer to those problems save a recommendation that we lay them to rest through further doses of the same therapy. This is not the place, nor have I the inclination, for some speculative venture into psycho-biography that would trawl through the many, well-documented episodes in Wittgenstein's personal and social life which might give a hold for diagnosing the source of his own compulsive anxieties.[2] That argument would risk looking absurd if taken to imply that any philosopher who found such topics challenging, intriguing, or worth detailed attention should on those grounds qualify for the same treatment. Besides, it would run perilously close to a further endorsement of the therapeutic line – the idea that they arise from a chronic (even pathological) 'bewitchment of our intelligence by language' – which typifies Wittgenstein's later thinking and that of his orthodox followers.

Still there is something oddly selective (not to say highly prejudicial) about a doctrine that holds philosophical problems to be fit subjects for therapy just so long as they are *not* the sorts of problem that engaged Wittgenstein's interest in a serious way, such as those thrown up by his reflections on rule-following and private language.[3] All the more so, one is tempted to add, since the latter are marked by a peculiar degree of specialized self-absorption and by a regular failure to conceive of alternative possibilities that lie outside their pre-established terms of debate. My own view, as will shortly appear, is that a good deal of recent analytic philosophy has become bogged down in a range of issues which invite not only the charge of triviality but also – what amounts to much the same thing – the charge of inventing ever more complex and ingenious 'solutions' to non-existent or merely notional problems. Moreover I shall contend that this situation has developed in large part through Wittgenstein's influence, more specifically, through his way of conjuring doubt or evoking sceptical qualms even while professing to lead us back to a sane (philosophically unburdened) sense of their futile and self-defeating character. The result has been not only a vast literature devoted to expounding Wittgenstein's views but also a curious compulsion on the part of many otherwise dissident thinkers to run their case past the standard range of likely Wittgensteinian objections and hence, very often, to surround that case with so many caveats and scruples as to bring it out pretty much in conformity with his. This tendency is most clearly visible when advocates of a realist position in various contexts – among them epistemology, philosophy of science, mathematics, and ethics – attempt to find some workable *modus vivendi* with the kinds of anti-realist argument developed on the basis of Wittgenstein's thoughts about rule-following and related topics.[4] What very often results is a tortuous attempt to explain how one can have all the 'realism' one needs – or all the 'truth' and 'objectivity' that realists demand of any discourse proof against the charge of socio-cultural-linguistic relativism – while accepting the force of those passages in Wittgenstein that speak of communal 'agreement in judgement' as the furthest one can get in such matters.[5]

It seems to me that philosophers who take this line are attempting to square the circle and that there is just no way of reconciling Wittgenstein's claims with a due regard for the basic premises of realism. These are (1) the alethic principle that truth is epistemically unconstrained; (2) the objectivist principle that the range of truths necessarily exceeds the range of propositions that can be verified (or falsified) by the best means at our disposal; and (3) the rejection of any approach – like that adopted by anti-realists of various technical persuasion – which assimilates truth to assertoric warrant and the latter, in turn, to whatever kinds of knowledge we are able to acquire or to manifest through forms of reliably shared communicative grasp.[6] This is where the Wittgensteinian influence – the appeal to 'language-games' and 'forms of life' – joins up with the anti-realist claim (as argued by thinkers like Michael Dummett) that quite simply it *cannot make sense* to conceive of truths that somehow transcend our utmost powers of proof, ascertainment, or verification.[7] That is to say, the objectivist about this or that area of discourse must be in the grip of a false ('metaphysical') conception which leads him to suppose – deludedly – that we can somehow be in a position to know that there exist certain truths for which we possess no possible means of finding them out. Hence Dummett's thesis that statements of the so-called 'disputed class' (whether in mathematics, the physical sciences, or areas of discourse such as history and ethics) are neither true nor false to the best of our knowledge and thus neither true nor false *sans phrase*. To which the realist will respond that this is a piece of sheer philosophical confusion that mistakes the perfectly valid claim: 'I know that there exist various true (or false) statements whose truth-value I am unable to establish' for the patently absurd claim: 'I know the truth-value of various statements whose truth-conditions presently elude my utmost powers of ascertainment.'

On Dummett's account, in the case of well-formed, massively corroborated yet so far strictly unproven mathematical theorems such as Goldbach's Conjecture (that every even number is the sum of two primes) or of unverifiable statements concerning historical events – such as 'Napoleon sneezed six times on the eve of Waterloo' – the realist is deluded if she thinks that there must be some ultimate, objective, verification-transcendent truth of the matter. Rather she should take Wittgenstein's point that ascriptions of truth and falsehood can make sense only in so far as they play some specified role in our communal procedures for assessing such claims. What this involves is the twofold condition, first that they be acquired through a grasp of the relevant linguistic practices, and second that they be duly manifested – and capable of recognition – through the kinds of shared understanding that constitute the practice in question. So clearly the realist is out on a limb when she holds that truth is recognition-transcendent, or that we have good reason for maintaining the existence of truths that outrun our present-best (or even best-possible) means of proof or verification. To which the realist will once again reply that this is an absurd and self-refuting argument given our knowledge of the growth of knowledge, that is to say, our grasp of the plain (scientifically evidenced) truth that certain past theories have been proven false – in the grip of various deluded or 'commonsense' errors – and hence our rational conviction that the same most likely applies to a great deal of our currently accepted (both commonsense and scientific) lore.

Thus the realist and the anti-realist place two flatly opposite constructions on the same basic 'argument from error'. For the realist this works out as a case for taking it that truth *cannot possibly* equate with any (past or present) state of knowledge since all the evidence so far points in a contrary direction, i.e., as supporting the objectivist claim that truth is epistemically unconstrained or verification-transcendent.[8] For the anti-realist this is to get the lesson precisely back to front since what the argument from error shows beyond doubt is that 'truth' can never be anything more than what counts as such according to this or that range of (however optimized) epistemic criteria.[9] Where the realist errs is in vainly conceiving that we might have an ultimate touchstone for truth that somehow (impossibly) allowed us to judge the truth-value of statements for which we possessed no means of proof or adequate justification. Where the realist takes the anti-realist to err, conversely, is in failing to grasp how truth might transcend any such constraints on our present or future powers of ascertainment. For this argument either collapses into manifest triviality by equating truth with idealized epistemic warrant – i.e., 'whatever it takes' for knowledge to attain that limit – or else falls back to some version of the claim that truth *just is* what we determine it to be by our best, currently accepted communal lights. The only alternative, these thinkers maintain, is to adopt the realist view that truth is indeed recognition-transcendent and hence that the truth-value of our various statements, theories, hypotheses, and so forth is fixed by whether or not they correspond to some objectively existent state of affairs that can always, in principle, obtain quite apart from our various available proof-procedures and methods of verification. However, once again, this invites the standard anti-realist riposte that such arguments lie wide open to sceptical attack since they place a strictly unbridgeable gulf between truth and knowledge, or what is really (objectively) the case and whatever we are able to establish concerning it.

This dilemma is pushed hardest by philosophers of mathematics – the traditional home-ground of Platonism – who insist quite simply that *tertium non datur* since we can either have truth objectively conceived, or humanly attainable knowledge, but surely not both unless through some quasi-mystical idea of our gaining epistemic access to abstract entities (such as numbers, sets and classes) which by very definition transcend the utmost limits of perceptual or cognitive grasp.[10] No doubt there are deep philosophical problems here, though not

perhaps so deep – or intractable – as is often made out by anti-realists who take the mathematical instance as a means of raising similar doubts with regard to every area of discourse or field of enquiry. Thus Gödel, for one, saw this as a false dilemma and argued that a Platonist conception need not involve any such absurd and self-contradictory claim as that of our somehow making perceptual 'contact' with a realm of suprasensible objects.[11] Rather there existed a different, *sui generis* mode of knowledge that had to do with mathematics, logic, and the formal sciences and which allowed *both* for the objective (recognition-transcendent) status of any truths concerning them *and* for the possibility of our acquiring such knowledge through various investigative methods and proof-procedures. However my chief point in all this is that anti-realism has often been made to look the most sensible (i.e., least scepticism-inducing) option by philosophers who mount some version of the case that we are confronted with a non-negotiable choice between objectivist truth and humanly attainable knowledge. Where scepticism always gets a hold, they claim, is by exploiting the self-evident impossibility that we could ever gain knowledge of truths which by very definition (on the realist account) transcended our utmost powers of verification. This is why, in Thomas Nagel's words, realism stands forever 'under the shadow of scepticism', or again – as Barry Stroud puts it – why 'all possible experience is equally compatible with the existence and the non-existence of the world'.[12] The point is pushed home most forcefully by Michael Williams when he remarks that 'if the world is an objective world, statement about how things appear must be logically unconnected with statements about how they are; this lack of connection is what familiar thought-experiments dramatically illustrate'.[13]

Such is, at any rate, the standard line of argument adopted by anti-realists so as to emphasize their distance from any form of all-out epistemological scepticism that would count reality a world well lost for the sake of indulging various hyperbolic doubts. All that is required, they urge, is a sensible acceptance that we can well do without objectivist notions of truth as recognition-transcendent or epistemically unconstrained and should instead make room for some appropriate degree of human perceptual, epistemic, or cognitive involvement in determining what counts as a valid judgement with respect to different (more or less truth-apt) areas of discourse. Thus philosophers such as Crispin Wright – advocates of a broadly response-dispositional approach – have devoted much effort and ingenuity to distinguishing those various criteria and explaining just how they apply to the kinds of discourse in question.[14] Others, among them John McDowell, have striven to redeem some viable account of objective (supra-communal or discourse-transcendent) truth even while accepting the supposed force of Wittgenstein's arguments against such a view.[15] What these thinkers have in common is a strong sense that there *must* be something more to truth than Wittgensteinian communal 'agreement in judgement' combined with an equally strong sense that if this 'something more' cannot find a place within our shared practices of truth-ascription then it must inevitably open the way to global scepticism. This tension is most evident in Nagel's case when objectivist avowals, for instance with regard to mathematical truth, very often sit awkwardly side by side with passages that seek to avert the sceptical threat by debunking the illusory 'view from nowhere' which would claim such objective (standpoint-independent or non-perspectival) status.[16] Here again the main source of these philosophic scruples seems to be the fixed idea that realism cannot stand up to rigorous scrutiny unless hedged around by qualifying clauses that meet the sceptic on his own chosen ground, that is to say, by bringing truth safely back within the compass of present-best judgement or – at the limit – idealized epistemic warrant.[17] Hence (as I have said) the near-compulsive need among so many otherwise convinced realists about truth to test their arguments against the usual range of set-piece objections from Wittgenstein and, very often, to scale those arguments down to the point where they accord pretty much with the current anti-realist agenda.

Thus when Wright puts forward his various alternative (non-objectivist) criteria – among them the notions of 'superassertibility' and 'cognitive command' – these serve basically as a means of holding the line against full-fledged anti-realism while nonetheless avoiding any challenge from the Wittgensteinian quarter. 'Superassertibility' he defines as applying to some statement of a given discourse 'if and only if it is, or can be, warranted and some warrant for it would survive arbitrarily close scrutiny of its pedigree and arbitrarily extensive increments to or other forms of improvement of our information'.[18] That is to say, it is a criterion very like that of idealized rational acceptability, one that stops well short of objectivist truth though requiring more than consensus belief or 'agreement in judgement' within some existing community. 'Cognitive Command' is a stronger condition in so far as it envisages a standard of correctness outside and beyond any that applies within this or that particular (discourse-relative) context of debate. Thus, according to Wright, 'when a discourse exhibits Cognitive Command, any difference of opinion will be such that there are considerations quite independent of the conflict which, if known about, would mandate withdrawal of one (or both) of the contending views'.[19] This sounds like a large (even decisive) concession to objectivist realism since it accepts that, in certain cases, there will be 'independent' grounds – reasons quite other than those acknowledged by either party – which could serve to adjudicate the issue. That is to say, it appears to go a crucial step further than Wright's notion of 'superassertibility' toward meeting the realist's basic demand that truth be thought of as recognition-transcendent and epistemically unconstrained. Yet this appearance is somewhat misleading, as emerges if one looks a bit harder at Wright's phraseology in the above passage. For to say that there exist 'considerations' which 'if known about' would trump the beliefs or arguments of both parties is *not* of course to say – as the realist would have it – that in such cases (i.e., those warranting ascription of Cognitive Command) statements may possess an objective truth-value regardless of whether their truth-conditions are known. Nor is it in any way surprising that Wright should stop short of this latter claim, given the fact that his entire programme is designed to outflank the sceptical challenge by showing how we just don't need objectivist truth and can perfectly well make do with a range of other, more epistemically nuanced and hence less problematical notions. This in turn reflects his Wittgenstein-derived (and Dummett-reinforced) belief that it can ultimately make no sense to conceive the existence of truths that might always in principle outrun our best powers of proof or verification.

As concerns Wright's criterion of 'superassertibility' it is clear enough that this amounts to a detailed variation on Dummett's idea of assertoric warrant, that is, a duly optimized (or idealized) version of the verificationist case. So if the truth of some claim in a given discourse is properly to count as 'superassertible' then it has to stand up to the most rigorous scrutiny and satisfy the strictest requirements of evidential testing but must also be seen as, 'in a natural sense, an *internal* property of the statements of the discourse – a projection, merely, of the standards, whatever they are, that actually inform assertions within the discourse'.[20] In which case objectivity drops out of the picture, its role taken over by accordance with those same intra-discursive or communally endorsed standards. Thus there is ultimately little to distinguish this approach from Dummett's anti-realist take on Wittgensteinian themes save Wright's more explicit allowance for the ways in which a statement's assertoric warrant may be strengthened through 'arbitrarily close scrutiny of its pedigree' and 'arbitrarily extensive increments to or other forms of improvement of our information'.[21] Despite his desire to come up with some alternative (or range of alternatives) to the full-fledged anti-realist line Wright is still very much in the grip of that nowadays prevalent idea that realism stands 'under the shadow of scepticism', and hence that any adequate answer to the sceptic will have to redefine what 'realism' means in strictly non-objectivist terms. This comes out very plainly when Wright specifies that superassertibility 'supplies no external norm – in a way that truth is classically supposed to do – against which the internal standards might *sub specie Dei* themselves be measured, and might rate as adequate or inadequate'.[22] In other words there is no objective (recognition-transcendent) standard that could possibly determine the truth-value of our various assertions, as apart from those discourse-specific criteria that decide what shall count as assertoric warrant within some given community of authorized usage.

II

It seems to me that Wright – like so many philosophers after Wittgenstein – is caught in the toils of a hopeless attempt to square some workable (suitably qualified or scaled-down) conception of realism with an answer to the sceptic on terms of the sceptic's own canny devising. What results, in his case especially, is a proliferation of quasi-realist concepts and categories which relinquish the idea of objectivist truth and seek to compensate through ever more elaborate alternative specifications. This tendency has no doubt been reinforced by the impact of Kripke's ultra-sceptical reading of those passages in Wittgenstein that have to do with the topics of rule-following and 'private language'.[23] These are widely (in my view mistakenly) thought to have problematized the very notion of correctness in following a rule or in carrying out even the simplest, arithmetical operations. Most remarkable is the power of Wittgenstein's gnomic *obiter dicta* to induce all manner of extravagant doubts and perplexities even whilst claiming – in therapeutic mode – to give philosophy peace. At any rate Kripke's 'sceptical conclusion' has received a vast amount of exegetical treatment from commentators who (like Kripke himself) find it both frankly absurd and weirdly compelling. What he purports to demonstrate is (1) the impossibility of knowing for sure what counts as a correct application of rules such as that for numerical addition; (2) the total absence of any 'fact' about our own or other people's rule-following proclivities that could possibly serve to adjudicate the issue between right and wrong answers in some given case; (3) the fallacy of thinking that we could ever check the consistency of our own arithmetical procedures by comparing our present and past applications of 'the same' rule; and (4) the lack of any ultimate criterion in these and suchlike matters save that of accredited expert belief or existing communal warrant.

These conclusions all follow – or so it is maintained – from the basic Wittgensteinian point that when it comes to applying a given rule there is always room for a vast range of 'deviant' yet (on their own terms) perfectly consistent interpretations which produce answers at variance with ours, or with what we take to be the correct (i.e., rule-accordant) response. Kripke's test-case here is that of a student who seems to have grasped the rule for addition since he has managed to produce all the right (text-book) answers for sums that have so far included no number greater than 57. If he is then asked to add '57 + 68' and produces the answer '5' we shall want to say something like: 'look, you got it right in all those previous cases, so just apply the same rule now'. But what if he responds, somewhat baffled: 'yes, I was applying the same rule, you know, the one that says "any sum containing numbers larger than 57 always gives the product 5"'? And of course the fact of his having offered all those previous (by his and our own lights) correct answers is perfectly accordant with his having always worked on that other (to us) wildly inconsistent or arbitrary rule. Where Kripke's argument pushes yet further into regions of hyperbolic doubt is by raising the question as to whether *we ourselves* can ever be sure that some present calculation is consistent with our past practices, or indeed as to whether those past practices might have been subject to some stipulative limit-point (like that invoked by the student) that we had not yet exceeded in all our calculations to date. Thus perhaps we had all along been working with a 'quus' rule (or rule for 'quaddition') which brought us out right by conventional standards – the standards governing majority usage of the terms 'plus' and 'addition' – up to just that point but which went off the rails (again by conventional standards) when dealing with numbers greater than 57.

At this point someone might reasonably seek to allay our doubts by saying: 'just remember how you used to *count* things "1, 2, 3", etc., and how the process of addition involved nothing more than carrying on in just the same way regardless of any numerical limit'. But then, what proof can we have that we weren't in fact *quounting*, not counting, on all those previous occasions and hence coming up with 'correct' answers while nonetheless applying a different rule from that which our interlocutor had in mind? As Kripke puts it:

> I applied 'count', like 'plus', to only finitely many past cases. Thus the sceptic can question my present interpretation of my past usage of 'count' as he did with 'plus' ... he can claim that by 'count' I formerly meant *'quount'*, where to 'quount' a heap is to count it in the ordinary sense, unless the heap was formed as the union of two heaps, one of which has 57 or more items, in which case one must automatically give the answer '5' ... The point is perfectly general: if 'plus' is explained in terms of 'counting', a non-standard interpretation of the latter will yield a non-standard interpretation of the former.[24]

For Kripke, quite simply, there is no truth of the matter that could ever provide us with a definite decision-procedure for settling the issue of correctness in cases like this. After all, what could that procedure consist in if not some higher-level rule for the proper application of rules, and so on through an infinite (vicious) regress or one that could be halted only by an instance of patently circular argument? Then again, the criterion might be located in some ultimate appeal to our knowledge of just what it is to reason correctly and consistently from one calculation to the next, or in our grasp of the essentially recursive and commutative character of operations like addition and subtraction. However, so the Kripkean thesis holds, this response runs up against the sceptic's reiterated claim that there is no deep further 'fact' about the reasoner's thoughts, intentions, meanings, or other such mental (= 'private') goings-on that could possibly serve to distinguish between their having meant 'plus' or 'quus' – 'addition' or 'quaddition' – on all the evidence so far. To suppose that there is – and that it offers a standard of correctness in rule-following – is to fall into just the kind of error that Wittgenstein exposed in his argument against the possibility of a 'private language', that is to say, an internal language-of-thought which sets the conditions for veridical utterance or valid reasoning and in no way depends on any 'outside' appeal to wider (communally sanctioned) usages and practices. Such would be the error, Wittgenstein suggests, of someone who habitually bought a second copy of the daily newspaper just to make sure that what the first copy said was true.[25] And such – if we are to credit Kripke's account – is the error of those who seek refuge from the rule-following quandary in an appeal to standards of consistent reasoning from one calculation to the next which presuppose the possibility of knowing for sure that what we mean by terms like 'plus' and 'addition' is what we clearly recall having meant by those terms on previous occasions. For there is nothing – no determinate fact about our meanings past or present – that could offer this assurance that we hadn't been working on the 'quus'-rule rather than the 'plus'-rule, or performing acts of 'quaddition' rather than 'addition', on every such occasion to date.

A natural and far from naïve response is to say that Kripke's argument is plainly false since mathematical truths – and certainly those of elementary (Peano) arithmetic – are secure beyond rational doubt. The objector might then go on to remark that any philosophical theory which argues to contrary effect is sure to have gone seriously off the rails, or perhaps – on a more charitable reading – to have been intended as a *reductio ad absurdum* of the sceptical case. Indeed there are passages in Kripke's book where he expresses something like this view, finding his own conclusions bizarre, absurd, unthinkable, and so forth. Yet elsewhere he is firmly committed to the thesis that the sceptical argument does (indeed must) go through if one accepts, as he does, the conjoint force of Wittgenstein's thoughts about rule-following and his case against the possibility of there being any such thing as a 'private language'. What this amounts to, in short, is an unprecedently powerful form of scepticism which denies that we can ever have grounds for supposing that any 'fact' about our past practices, procedures, or rule-following activities could ever provide the least guidance or assurance for our present or future reasonings. No doubt, 'when we consider a mathematical rule like addition, we think of ourselves as being guided in our application of it to each new instance', and assume furthermore that 'past intentions regarding addition determine a unique answer for indefinitely many new cases in the future' (Kripke, pp. 17–18). Yet, if the 'Kripkensteinian' argument holds, then this is the merest of illusions and one that inevitably comes to grief on the above kinds of sceptical argument. Above all Kripke takes it – quite seriously, so far as one can tell – to destroy any assurance we might otherwise have that the standards of correctness for arithmetical and other such recursive operations extend beyond a finite (up-to-now encountered) number of instances and encompass a potentially infinite range of like cases.

This scepticism has its source, yet again, in Wittgenstein's avowedly therapeutic attempt to wean us off the 'super-rigid rail' conception of rule-following, that is, the deluded objectivist idea that any standard which applies to some sample range will also – of strict necessity – apply to all further instances no matter how numerically large or how far beyond the scope of our present conceiving, computational powers, or whatever. Crispin Wright registers the force of such doubts when he asks: '[h]ow can a sentence be undetectably true unless the rule embodied in its content – the condition which the world has to satisfy to confer truth upon it – can permissibly be thought of as extending, so to speak, of itself into areas where we cannot follow it and thus determining, without any contribution from ourselves or our reactive natures, that a certain state of affairs complies with it?'.[26] Like a good many of Wright's more cryptic or elusive passages this sentence leaves one momentarily unsure as to whether it is meant as a rhetorical question – inviting the anti-realist response that no such situation could ever conceivably obtain – or whether it envisages the possibility that certain (e.g., mathematical) statements might satisfy the said condition. However, as we have seen, there is evidence elsewhere in Wright's work that he is sufficiently persuaded by the anti-realist case (at any rate, the case that full-strength [objectivist] realism opens the door to full-strength [global] scepticism) to expend great effort in devising a range of compromise formulas such as 'superassertibility' and 'cognitive command'. Indeed this persuasion comes across in the above-cited passage when Wright signals his doubt with regard to how a sentence can be 'undetectably true', or be thought of as somehow 'extending ... of itself into areas where we cannot follow it'. Here one picks up obvious echoes of Kripke's ultra-sceptical take on Wittgenstein's rule-following considerations, along with a somewhat routine endorsement of Dummett's anti-realist outlook as concerns the issue of recognition-transcendent or unverifiable truths. This impression is reinforced by Wright's further thought that, for any given (truth-apt) sentence, objectivists are faced with the task of explaining how the 'condition that the world has to satisfy to confer truth upon it' is one that can be known or specified 'without any contribution from ourselves or our reactive natures'.[27] Hence his attraction to a duly qualified and nuanced form of the response-dispositional approach according to which different areas of discourse – from mathematics and the physical sciences to morals, sociology, aesthetics, and the language of colour and other perceptual modalities – can best be distinguished with respect to the precise *kind and degree* of that 'reactive' (or responsive) contribution.[28] Only thus, so the argument goes, can philosophy do justice to our strong realist intuitions in some such areas while resisting the siren call of an objectivist realism which places truth beyond our furthest epistemic reach.

However there is a strongly marked bias in Wright's thinking that inclines him toward an anti-realist position even with respect to those 'areas of discourse' that might appear prime candidates for placement at the objectivist end of the scale. This emerges most clearly when he spells out the implications of a response-dispositional approach for philosophy of mathematics and the formal sciences. Thus 'in shifting to a broadly intuitionistic conception of, say, number theory, we do not immediately foreclose on the idea that the series of natural numbers constitutes a real object of mathematical investigation, which it is harmless and correct to think of the number theoretician as explaining'.[29] What is meant by 'intuitionism' in this context is the idea – most influentially pro-pounded by Dummett – that mathematical truth cannot be conceived in objective (recognition-transcendent) terms but must rather be restricted to that class of statements and theorems for which we possess some adequate means of proof or verification.[30] Thus it is a main plank in Dummett's broader anti-realist programme for replacing objectivist talk of 'truth' (according to which any well-formed statement will take the value 'true' or 'false' irrespective of whether or not we are able to establish that value) with talk of 'warranted assertibility' (where the range of assertible statements coincides with the scope and limits of our best available proof-procedures). Here again there are signs in Wright's formulation of the case that he doesn't wish to go all the way with this Dummettian creed, or that he sees some force to the realist objection that there must exist, now as heretofore, a great number of mathematical truths eluding or awaiting discovery. After all, there is something *prima facie* absurd about the notion that any statement to the effect 'Fermat's Last Theorem is true' was itself neither true nor false – that it belonged to Dummett's non-bivalent or 'disputed class' – until Andrew Wiles produced his celebrated proof. Nor does there seem much sense in the idea that a well-formed, massively corroborated, yet so far strictly undecidable theorem such as Goldbach's Conjecture is likewise devoid of any objective truth-value just because it is at present (or maybe forever) incapable of proof by any computational or formal means.

So one can see well enough why Wright should balk at a straightforward endorsement of full-scale mathematical anti-realism. All the same, any scruples of this sort are effectively countermanded by his treating realist talk as 'harmless' even if (in some sense) 'correct', a conjunction of terms which makes it hard to interpret just where he stands on the issue with regard to mathematical truth. Perhaps useful guidance may be had from Wright's point that 'we do not immediately foreclose on the idea that the series of natural numbers constitutes a real object of mathematical investigation'. Yet when taken along with his 'harmless' remark this seems to suggest that he must be adopting some kind of error-theory, that is to say, the view that such talk has a legitimate role in our thinking about mathematics but that the 'objects' concerned have no reality outside that particular (on its own terms perfectly 'correct', i.e., communally sanctioned) discourse. What emerges from Wright's treatment of this topic is the conflict between his residual realist leaning – his sense that there must be *something more* to truth than accordance with our best methods of proof or verification – and his idea that anti-realism (whether in its full-strength Kripkean or milder Dummettian form) has indeed 'foreclosed' on the objectivist case, i.e., the argument that truth might always transcend or elude our optimal means of ascertainment. Hence his seemingly modest proposal – very much like Dummett's – that we test the anti-realist claim across sundry areas of discourse (from mathematics to morals) and in each case seek to establish just where it falls on the scale from 'cognitive command', via 'superassertibility', to something like 'rightness according to the norms of this or that communal usage'.

Hence also Wright's attraction to the response-dispositional (RD) approach which attempts to steer around the supposed problem with realist, that is to say, objectivist truth by adopting a qualified version of the Lockean appeal to 'secondary qualities' – such as colour – which allow for some degree of normalized or optimized human cognitive involvement while avoiding any doctrinaire commitment to anti-realism.[31] However, as I have argued at length elsewhere, this apparent even-handedness – in his case as in Dummett's – goes along with a marked anti-realist bias when it comes to assessing those various kinds of discourse.[32] Thus the RD approach tends to work out either as a mere tautology ('"truth" = that which *by very definition* all parties would presumptively agree upon under conditions of idealized epistemic warrant') or as a hedged-about version of the strong anti-realist case ('"truth" = that which counts as such according to the best judgement of knowers who are favourably placed with regard to the relevant, suitably specified perceptual or cognitive conditions'). The former line of argument is trivially circular – though perfectly acceptable to the realist – since it states nothing more than the self-evident fact that if best judgement is infallibly truth-tracking then truth must *ipso facto* lie within the compass of best judgement. In terms of the Platonic 'Euthyphro Contrast' much invoked by RD theorists it corresponds to Socrates' objectivist position, i.e., that the gods are always right when it comes to moral issues in so far as they possess an unerring power of moral discernment and are therefore perfectly capable of distinguishing pious from impious acts.[33] Such acts are objectively right or wrong — quite apart from what the gods may think — but since the gods are infallibly equipped to tell the difference their authority is beyond reproach. Transposed into the context of RD debate this produces a stopgap 'solution' to the issue about realism which conserves at least a notional role for optimized judgement (or idealized rational warrant) but which defines that role in purely circular terms, that is to say, as involving 'whatever it takes' to ensure that best judgement accords with truth. In which case clearly there is nothing left of the standard Dummettian argument for anti-realism, namely the impossibility of conceiving objective (recognition-transcendent, hence unknowable) truths, but also — by the same token — no useful work for the RD theorist to do by way of spelling out those particular requirements that make for adequate assertoric warrant under specified perceptual, cognitive, or epistemic conditions.

The second line of argument avoids this charge of redundant circularity by insisting that 'best judgement' be defined with reference to genuine (substantive) criteria concerning what would typically, normally, or optimally be agreed upon by those in a good position to know. These latter might include, for instance, perceivers whose colour-judgements were the product of an unimpaired visual and cortical apparatus functioning under normal (non-distorting) ambient conditions, or subjects whose powers of mathematical, logical, scientific, or moral reckoning were exercised to the full and likewise in the absence of deleterious (rationality-impeding) factors.[34] Such specifications can of course be set up in different ways on a scale that runs, roughly speaking, from the sorts of normative criteria which apply to standard (averagely gifted or competent) perceivers and reasoners granted nothing more than averagely good working conditions to the sorts of limit-point criteria which approximate to those of idealized epistemic warrant. However, what keeps these latter types of argument within the limits of an RD-compatible approach is their programmatic allowance for the claim that truth in such matters cannot be *entirely* objective or recognition-transcendent but must always involve some reference to the modalities of human perceptual or cognitive response. Thus, in terms of the Plato analogy, this approach works out as a more or less qualified endorsement of Euthyphro's case (*contra* Socrates) that it is the gods whose strictly omniscient powers of judgement must be taken to determine which should count among the class of pious (or impious) acts. That is to say, what constitutes true moral virtue is precisely the fact that it is approved by the gods and that the gods' approval — embodying as it does the ultimate authority — is sufficient to confer such status beyond rational doubt.

In a sense, as Wright readily concedes, the Euthyphro Contrast may appear something of a philosophic red herring since the class of pious acts is extensionally equivalent on both interpretations. Thus the same acts will be picked

out as virtuous irrespective of whether one takes it (like Socrates) that the gods'
authority derives from their infallibly truth-tracking responsiveness to objective
moral properties or whether one takes it (like Euthyphro) that those properties
derive from – or are constituted by – the gods' infallible judgement. Still there is
a genuine issue here when it comes to the realism/anti-realism debate and the
attempt of RD theorists to stake out some viable alternative (or range of
alternatives) to those starkly polarized positions. For the chief aim of that
approach – as likewise with some of the milder, more moderate or pragmatic
forms of anti-realism – is to explain how truth can be (at least in some degree)
epistemically constrained, i.e., subject to the scope and limits of best judgement
whilst yet leaving room for the widely shared intuition that it can (and often
does) lie beyond the grasp of any present, no matter how expert or optimally
qualified community of knowers. Absent the fiction of divine omniscience – thus
bringing the debate down to earth in epistemic or philosophically relevant terms
– and the Euthyphro Contrast (along with the instance of Locke on secondary
qualities) serves rather neatly to highlight the positions taken up by various
parties to this current debate.

However there is still the issue as to whether any kind of RD approach, no
matter how elaborately qualified, can succeed in delivering a compromise
solution that would satisfy adherents of either view. After all, realists (or
objectivists) about truth cannot settle for anything less – for any degree of
epistemic constraint on the range of admissible (truth-apt) sentences or statements – without letting their whole case go by default. For them, quite simply,
it is self-evident to reason – as well as a fact borne out by the entire history of
human enquiry to date – that there have been, are, and will no doubt continue to
be a great many truths that exceed or transcend the limits of present-best
knowledge. To suppose otherwise is to suppose (absurdly) that the way things
stand in mathematical, physical, historical, or other regions of reality is somehow dependent on the way things stand with our cognitive faculties, range of
information, or powers of intellectual grasp. To this way of thinking any effort,
like Wright's, to defuse the realist/anti-realist conflict by proposing some range
of intermediate positions – such as 'superassertibility' or 'cognitive command' –
is a plain non-starter since it still comes down on the side of warranted
assertibility (as against truth) and of epistemic constraint (as against alethic,
objective, or recognition-transcendent truth-values).

This is why, as Neil Tennant puts it, the realist will often complain that 'the
anti-realist is guilty of epistemic hubris in taking the human mind to be
the measure of reality'.[35] However the anti-realist will just as often respond
'by charging the realist with semantic hubris in claiming to grasp such
propositional contents as could be determinately truth-valued independently of
our means of coming to know what those truth-values are' (ibid.). To which the
realist will typically come back by remarking (in Michael Devitt's phrase)
that this is to 'put the cart before the horse' since there is something strictly
preposterous about taking a highly speculative and far from secure theory in
philosophy of language to undermine the most basic and well-tried procedures

of logico-mathematical thought or scientific, historical, and other such reasoning on the evidence.[36] That is to say, from a realist viewpoint all these various attempts to somehow accommodate our realist intuitions to the range of semantically based anti-realist arguments are so much misplaced effort since no such arguments could possibly (or rationally) outweigh the range of scientific as well as philosophical considerations stacked against them. Thus to take the anti-realist line is to allow a dubious claim from philosophical semantics (one with its source in old-style verificationism, however updated or refined) to dictate the agenda for discussion in areas where that claim runs up against our strongest intuitions regarding truth and the progress of knowledge to date.[37]

III

Among those of broadly anti-realist persuasion Tennant stands out – even more than Wright – for his keen sense of the problems involved in defending that standpoint and his sheer resourcefulness in devising argumentative strategies for getting around them. Thus he shies away from the full-strength anti-realist position, that of the undeterred partisan who 'bites the bullet' and simply refuses to acknowledge the force of those opposing considerations. What such a theorist will need to do, Tennant remarks, is 'provide a far-reaching overhaul of some of our central philosophical concepts (knowledge, truth, possibility and logical implication), so as to accommodate the rather arresting conclusion that every truth is known'.[38] Now on the face of it this is what *all* anti-realists aim to provide in response to Dummett's redefinition of the issue about realism, that is to say, his treatment of it as primarily an issue in philosophy of language and logic rather than an issue in epistemology or ontology, at least as hitherto conceived. So it is – through adopting this particular version of the post-Fregean and post-Wittgensteinian 'linguistic turn' – that Dummett arrives at his cardinal thesis concerning the impossibility that our conception of truth for any given statement in this or that area of discourse should somehow outrun our reliably acquired and publicly manifestable grasp of its truth-conditions.[39] Thus the 'arresting conclusion' which Tennant here disavows (namely, the doctrine that 'every truth is known') cannot be so easily decoupled from anti-realism in its basic, agenda-setting form. Theorists may very well differ between themselves or – as with Wright – from one formulation to the next with respect to the *precise degree* of epistemic constraint or (conversely) the *approximation* to standards of objective truth that characterize some specific area of discourse. Or again, like Tennant, they may go to great lengths of meticulously argued conceptual and logical analysis in order to produce a more moderate (in his case, falsificationist rather than verificationist) version of anti-realism which seemingly offers nothing like so blatant an affront to our normal conceptions of truth and rational warrant. Still they are committed to the basic idea – spelled out in numerous canonical passages from Dummett – that we simply *cannot make sense*

of the objectivist claim that truth might be recognition-transcendent or epistemically unconstrained.

Tennant puts the case that anti-realists often go wrong (and lay themselves
open to powerful forms of realist counter-argument) by extrapolating too
quickly or directly from mathematics, logic and the formal sciences to areas of
discourse where the pertinent criteria are those of empirical warrant rather than
demonstrative proof. After all, '[i]n mathematics, once a statement is proved it
remains proved. In empirical discourse, however, statements are defeasible. That
is, they can be justified on a certain amount of evidence, but may have to be
retracted or even denied on the basis of new evidence accreting on the old'
(Tennant, p. 48). Thus anti-realism stands to lose a good deal of (what Tennant
considers) its intuitive plausibility if proponents follow Dummett too closely in
treating the set-piece mathematical issue of Platonism versus intuitionism as a
paradigm instance for the whole debate. 'When anti-realists generalise from the
mathematical case, with its conditions of constructive proof, they usually look
for appropriate conditions of warranted assertibility. That is, they seek analogues
of the mathematical case of assertion backed by proof' (ibid.). However this
strategy gets them into trouble for just the reason that Tennant has spelled out,
namely the fact that mathematical proofs, once achieved, are unfalsifiable by any
(least of all empirical) means, while empirical statements – those with a claim to
adequate assertoric warrant – cannot be proved but must always be subject to an
ongoing process of assessment and revision in light of the best, most compelling
evidence to hand. So anti-realists are ill advised to make too much of the
Dummettian analogy with intuitionism in the philosophy of mathematics.
Rather,

> one should attend to the main feature of natural scientific theorising to
> which Popper drew our attention: our scientific theories can at best be
> falsified, not verified. Accepting this logical predicament, the anti-realist
> should seek to fashion a notion of warranted denial, or of constructive
> falsity, that appropriately complements the notion of warranted assertion,
> or of constructive truth, already developed for mathematics. (Tennant,
> p. 49)

However this proposal runs aground on the same objection that is often brought
against Popperian (falsificationist) claims to have solved the issue with regard to
induction and old-style positivist verificationism, i.e., that what counts as a
decisive falsification must at some point have recourse to just such verificationist
criteria. In which case the anti-realist (semantical) variant of this same Popperian
argument must itself give rise to a similar range of objections from the realist
quarter.

Besides, Tennant's point about the crucial distinction between mathematical
proofs and matters of empirical warrant is one that the realist – especially the
realist about mathematics – can well turn around to her own (one might think
quite decisive) philosophical advantage. Thus, according to David Lewis, 'it's too

bad for epistemologists if mathematics in its present form baffles them, but it would be hubris to take that as any reason to reform mathematics ... Our knowledge of mathematics is ever so much more secure than our knowledge of the epistemology that seeks to cast doubt on mathematics.'[40] Others – Jerrold Katz among them – have argued to similar effect against any form of anti-realist or response-dispositional approach which trades on the supposed impossibility that we should somehow gain knowledge of, or achieve epistemic 'contact' with, such abstract entities as numbers, sets, or classes. I shall quote the relevant passage from Katz at some length since it shows very clearly how Tennant's line of reasoning can be subject to a downright opposite (i.e., realist) construal. Thus:

> [t]he entire idea that our knowledge of abstract objects might be based on perceptual contact is misguided, since, even if we had contact with abstract objects, the information we could obtain from such contact wouldn't help us in trying to justify our beliefs about them. The episte-mological function of perceptual contact is to provide information about which possibilities are actualities. Perceptual contact thus has a point in the case of empirical propositions. Because natural objects can be otherwise than they actually are (*non obstante* their essential properties), contact is necessary in order to discover how they actually are ... Not so with abstract objects. They could not be otherwise than they are ... Hence there is no question of which mathematical possibilities are actual possi-bilities. In virtue of being a perfect number, six must be a perfect number; in virtue of being the only even prime, two must be the only even prime. Since the epistemic role of contact is to provide us with the information needed to select among the different ways something might be, and since perceptual contact cannot provide information about how something must be, contact has no point in relation to abstract objects. It cannot ground beliefs about them.[41]

According to Tennant it is an error (or at least a high-risk strategy) on the anti-realist's part to treat mathematics as a paradigm case since if the argument is to work for other, empirically grounded areas of discourse then it had better not take its philosophic bearings from a discourse where truth is an all-or-nothing matter of demonstrative proof or rational self-evidence. To this extent he seems in agreement with Katz, that is, on the point that mathematical proofs, if valid, cannot be either disconfirmed or further corroborated through any kind of test-procedure that would seek to strengthen their credentials. In such cases, as Tennant puts it, '[t]he warranting relation is monotonic on its first term, which is the set of evidential premises for the conclusion that is its second term' (p. 44). Thus with regard to mathematics, logic and the formal sciences 'if any state of information I warrants the assertion of $\emptyset$, then any expansion I^* of I warrants the assertion of $\emptyset$'. In the case of empirical statements, conversely, discourse may in some sense aspire to this condition of monotonicity but can never reach it simply by reason of its always being open to possible disconfirmation with the advent of further evidence.

However it is then hard to see what can motivate Tennant's albeit highly qualified (i.e., falsificationist) version of the anti-realist approach. For one can just as well – indeed more plausibly – accommodate his distinction between logico-mathematical and empirical orders of truth-claim by adopting Katz's rationalist-realist outlook and maintaining the objective (falsification-transcendent) status of the former along with the always corrigible, evidentially constrained character of the latter. What's more, this seeming concession to anti-realism as regards the criteria of assertoric warrant for empirical, e.g., physical-scientific or historical statements is in fact no such thing but a due acceptance that what *counts* as truth by the best of our current epistemic or evidential lights is intrinsically subject to revision or correction not only in consequence of improved knowledge but also, ultimately speaking, when set against the objectivist standard of what may in principle exceed or transcend our utmost cognitive endeavours. That is to say, there is something curiously under-motivated about Tennant's heroic attempt to hold the line against realism or objectivism in any form while nonetheless backing off from the basic anti-realist idea that 'all truths are known', or even that 'all truths are knowable'. For on the one hand his falsificationist approach does nothing to temper or to lessen the strength of such counter-intuitive claims, while on the other (as emerges very clearly by contrast with the passage from Katz cited above) it tends to confuse the issue with regard to those different orders of truth-claim involved in the formal and the empirical sciences.

Tennant puts the case for falsifiability – rather than verifiability – as the anti-realist's best line of argument since, on his account, it manages to deflect these intuitively powerful objections from the realist quarter by respecting the Popperian idea that empirical statements are always subject to revision or refutation, and hence making room for some version of the claim that truth might exceed our present-best knowledge or means of ascertainment. Thus: '[i]nstead of working with epistemically diluted grounds for empirical assertion, we should work with epistemically undiluted grounds for empirical denial' (Tennant, p. 45). However, once again, it is hard to make out how this argument could come anywhere near to meeting the realist's objection while also hanging on to the anti-realist's single most effective rejoinder, i.e., that realism must forever stand 'under the shadow' of scepticism since it places truth (objectively conceived) forever beyond our utmost epistemic ken. What one is left with, it seems, is a sharpened version of the well-known problem with Popper's falsificationist doctrine, that is to say, the fact that it scarcely supports his general outlook of scientific realism and indeed creates just as many diffi-culties here as the inductivist doctrine which it aims to supplant. By thus construing the issue between realism and anti-realism in terms of relative degrees of epistemic 'dilution', Tennant is effectively shifting the issue on to well-trodden philosophic ground where anti-realism sets the terms of debate but where it cannot make any (no matter how nuanced or qualified) concession to the realist without either abandoning its own case or rendering that concession entirely nugatory.

Perhaps, as he says, there are certain 'principles in the epistemology of linguistic understanding' which 'make anti-realism the natural starting-point for one's reflections on the relationships between (learnable) language, (substantial) thought and (determinable) reality' (Tennant, p. 47). Those principles are basically the same ones advanced by Dummett, i.e., having to do with the requirement that the conditions of warranted assertibility for any given statement be subject to certain, linguistically manifestable powers of acquisition and recognition. As we have seen, Tennant wants somewhat to soften their impact by adopting a falsificationist approach with regard to empirical statements in place of Dummett's across-the-board verificationism and – in accordance with this – by distinguishing more clearly between the unfalsifiable (once proven) truths of mathematics, logic and the formal sciences and the always defeasible truth-claims of empirical discourse. However, this leaves him in the awkward predicament of striving to uphold what avowedly remains an anti-realist position while both acknowledging the strength of certain, on the face of it decisive realist counter-arguments and in effect conceding its non-applicability to some of those areas (such as mathematics and logic) where Dummett has most vigorously pressed its claims. Thus the realist might very well challenge Tennant's above-cited statement of the case by removing the three parenthetical terms and recasting that sentence to read: 'realism [is] the natural starting-point for one's reflections on the relationships between language, thought, and reality'. This edited version would in fact amount to a full-scale realist rejoinder and a point-for-point rebuttal of the various argumentative moves by which anti-realism typically proceeds. That is to say, it would (1) reject the conflation of 'reality' with the scope and limits of *determinable* reality, (2) deny that 'substantial' thought is definitionally equivalent to something like 'thought concerning just that area of known or knowable truth', and (3) make the case – *contra* such forms of anti-realist thinking – that the operative truth-conditions for well-formed statements may indeed go beyond that particular range whose criteria we have 'learned' in the narrow (verificationist) sense of acquiring, recognizing, or being able to manifest some knowledge of the means by which to ascertain those conditions. To take a contrary stance with regard to each of these claims is once again, as Devitt argues, to 'put the cart before the horse' in so far as it involves a willingness to doubt some deep-laid and scientifically well-attested realist principles in favour of a highly speculative doctrine in philosophical semantics.[42]

Nor is the case significantly altered, so the realist will maintain, if one opts for one among the range of qualified, nuanced, or scaled-down versions of the anti-realist thesis which avoid any flat-out commitment to the (surely absurd) proposition that 'all truths are known'. For no matter how far one modifies this thesis – whether in the epistemic direction of Wright's 'superassertibility' or 'cognitive command' or toward some ultimate (limit-point) conception of idealized rational warrant – it will still fall short of the realist's demand that truth be conceived as always potentially exceeding our present-best or even future-best-possible means of ascertainment. As I have said, Tennant is intensely aware of such objections from the adversary camp and indeed goes as far toward meeting them – or framing his arguments so as to acknowledge their intuitive force – as is possible within the broadest parameters of an anti-realist approach. Thus his claim, like Dummett's and Wright's, is not so much to argue the case for anti-realism as to test that case without prejudice or foregone commitment across a range of candidate areas of discourse and establish just how well or how far it holds up under pressure from the realist challenge. In the current literature nobody has done this job with such exemplary thoroughness or taken that challenge with so acute a sense of the arguments that constantly rise against his own position. All the same it is clear – in Tennant's case as in Dummett's and Wright's – that anti-realism figures as the default option and hence that in so far as there is a burden of proof it falls very squarely on the realist to show that we can somehow conceive the existence of truths that transcend our best methods of proof or verification. This despite the fact that his book comes up with such a range of intuitively powerful objections to its own thesis and with so many cautionary instances – such as Kripke's ultra-sceptical take on the Wittgensteinian rule-following 'paradox' – that it often reads like a full-scale *reductio* of the case.

Nowhere are the problems with Tennant's approach more strikingly apparent than in his dealing with this full-strength Kripkean version of the anti-realist argument as applied to meanings, intentions, standing beliefs, propositional contents, and the very idea that we might know what we are doing when we perform some elementary arithmetical task such as that of addition. About one thing Tennant is in no doubt: that if this line of argument goes through then it completely demolishes his own conception of philosophical enquiry along with that held by the great majority of fellow enquirers, including those of a strongly sceptical disposition. Thus the Kripkean strategy 'would call into question ... the claims of inherence, determinacy, generativity, representation, objectivity and mutual understanding' (Tennant, p. 101). In which case he can only agree with Wright that 'to sustain [this] argument is to uncage a tiger whose depradations there is then no hope of containing'.[43] After all, it is the upshot of Kripke's (quite literally) *ne plus ultra* case that we can have no rational grounds for the belief that in following a basic recursive rule – such as that of addition – we are in fact following the same rule as we applied in previous instances or at earlier stages in 'the same' process of arithmetical calculation. Quite simply there is no deep further fact about our meanings, intentions, dispositions or whatever that could possibly determine whether we are now (or had been in the past) working on the standard rule for addition or working on some other, 'deviant' rule – such as that for *quaddition* – which comports just as well with all our performances to date but might throw up discrepant results at some future stage in the process. All of which follows, so Kripke maintains, from those canonical passages in Wittgenstein that link the manifest impossibility of there existing any such thing as a 'private language' (i.e., a realm of purely apodictic self-certainty) with the likewise demonstrable fact that any 'rule' which we might adduce is itself open to as many different interpretations as there exist alternative (on their own terms perfectly correct) construals of it.[44] As I have said, Kripke himself takes the view – one shared by Tennant, Wright, McDowell, and just about every commentator – that this sceptical upshot is 'bizarre' and 'absurd' beyond the utmost limits of rational acceptability. Yet where Kripke regards it as simply irrefutable and hence as forcing us back on a 'sceptical solution', i.e., that provided by Wittgenstein's appeal to communal warrant as our last, best refuge from all such sceptical doubts, Tennant and the others continue to hope for an alternative way of framing the issue that would somehow resolve those doubts while meeting the Kripkean challenge head-on and also avoiding any too direct clash with our basic realist intuitions. However it is unclear, to say the least, that this wished-for outcome can possibly be achieved without at some point leaning over in one or the other (realist or anti-realist) direction.

One can get some sense of the sheer argumentative strains involved from the following passage where Tennant seeks to explain how his own kind of 'moderate' anti-realism goes along with a perfectly viable conception of what it takes for our meanings, thoughts and beliefs to possess some determinate content.

> In speaking thus of meanings and/or contents one is not committing oneself to reifying them. It is not so much that they have to be taken as objects, but rather that we have to acknowledge the objectivity of meaning-facts (facts 'about' meaning(s)) and can do so without committing ourselves to there having to be such things as meanings for them to be about. The intuitionist is therefore assuming Meaning Objectivity, without committing herself to any picture involving Meanings as Objects. (Tennant, p. 309)

I trust I am not alone in finding this a highly problematical passage and one that exposes certain irresolvable tensions in Tennant's 'moderate' anti-realist position. Indeed it runs uncomfortably close to the kind of 'error theory' adopted by some philosophers who see no way of extirpating talk about certain (in their view) non-existent 'objects' such as meanings or moral values but who still consider such talk to be referentially vacuous.[45] Tennant terms this position 'error-theoretic irrealism' and describes it as one which 'accepts the superficial syntactic appearances of our declarative sentences at face value, allows that our primitive assertions aim at the truth, but maintains that these assertions always miss their target' (p. 68). Quite simply, they are 'false' in the straightforward sense that they 'misrepresent the world', or that in 'mak[ing] an intelligible attempt to tell it like it is' they nevertheless 'get it wrong' (ibid.). Tennant is understandably keen to stake his distance from an error-theoretic or irrealist approach since he sees it as leading – like Kripkean scepticism – to a stage where philosophy would find itself deprived of any genuine (substantive or non-self-deluding) topics for debate. However it is far from clear that he manages to keep that distance or to navigate his middle course between the twin, equally (for him) problematical extremes of objectivist realism and its various flipside (e.g., Kripkean, full-fledged irrealist, or error-theoretic) positions. For what puts Tennant at odds with avowed error-theorists like J. L. Mackie – and what gives the above (inset) passage its decidedly tortuous character – is the fact that he wishes to *espouse and defend* (rather than expose and refute) something very like the sorts of belief in question.[46] At any rate it is hard to unravel the logic of an argument that relies so crucially on various wire-drawn semantic distinctions and alternative phrasings designed to make room for a workable conception of 'Meaning Objectivity' without any realist commitment to the notion of 'Meanings as Objects'. No doubt the very nature of Tennant's project – that of, as he puts it, 'staying on the straight and narrow, and finding a stopping-place in between the two extremes' – is such as to require a good deal of tight philo-sophic manoeuvre (p. 50). All the more so since there is an ever-present risk that in voicing a 'crescendo of concerns' with regard to Kripkensteinian and other forms of flat-out meaning-scepticism he will be led 'further down the primrose path to full-blown realism' (ibid.). However the above-cited passage – like a great many in Tennant's book – gives reason to doubt that this tightrope-walk can be carried off without toppling over in one or the other direction.

Thus the whole project of devising some 'moderate' (so to speak, realistically acceptable) version of the anti-realist case is one that must either make peace with the basic, non-negotiable realist requirement – i.e., the existence of objective truths concerning the areas of discourse in question – or else amount to no more than a minor variation on standard anti-realist themes. Tennant is clear enough about this when he examines Wright's attempt to stake out a range of middle-ground positions (such as 'superassertibility' and 'cognitive command') that would claim to respect our working intuitions while steering well away from the realist primrose path. As he puts it:

> Wright thinks one can 'inflate' the deflationist account of truth, and that the resulting 'inflated' notion, which he calls superassertibility, is not yet what is required for realism. One can agree, in so far as one concedes that superassertibility (if we can make sense of it) is a substantial notion of truth, but not yet a realist one. But can we, as anti-realists, make sense of superassertibility? Or is the earlier and simpler notion of warranted assertibility (with an appropriate account of warrant) the best that the non-realist substantialist can do? (Tennant, p. 42)

However this argument cuts just as strongly against his own more sophisticated efforts to construct an anti-realist *via media* between the claims of full-fledged objectivist realism (or recognition-transcendent truth) on the one hand and, on the other, those of full-fledged irrealism with respect to some particular area of discourse. For in his case also it is matter of backing off as far as possible from the realist Scylla while avoiding any ruinous contact with the Charybdis of

Kripkensteinian or other such forms of extreme and ultimately self-refuting scepticism.

Tennant states the issue with perfect lucidity when he says that '[r]ealism, in the ontological sense in which it is opposed to these irrealisms, is the view that the sector of reality is mind-buffeting, or reflected in the mind. The things in question really are out there, and they will impinge on us if we are suitably aware of and sensitive to them' (ibid., p. 75). Moreover one must take it, on the realist account, that something analogous to this line of argument applies in the case of those abstract entities (like numbers, sets and classes) or the strictly non-denumerable range of propositions concerning them which extend beyond our present or future-best powers of expression or verification.[47] In which case the realist will also maintain that there exists a realm of objective or at any rate sufficiently determinate meanings, intentions, propositional contents, attitudes, and so forth which can meet the criteria of adequate warrant for our various truth-apt sayings, beliefs and theoretical commitments. Otherwise the way is clearly open to the kind of corrosive meaning-scepticism that would wreck the entire philosophical enterprise, not to mention our most basic conceptions of everyday linguistic-communicative grasp. Tennant is at times quite strongly drawn in a realist direction, most of all when it is a matter of heading off arguments from the opposing (e.g., Kripkean or irrealist) quarter. Thus:

> the corresponding irrealism holds that the sector of 'reality' in question is at best mind-built, if it exists at all; and at worst non-existent. The dubious sector of reality is populated by convenient fictions (social individuals; mathematical objects and relations), or by unjustifiable extrapolations (theoretical physical entities and processes), or by posits brought into the picture only in order to satisfy our craving for an objectivity that is, however, not to be had (causal relations, rules, meanings and values). (Tennant, p. 75)

What Tennant needs to do if his argument is to work — that is, if he is to fix a sharp conceptual divide between these various kinds of irrealism and his own moderate anti-realist stance — is establish the precise terms upon which a statement can be counted truth-apt in *something more* than a straightforward verificationist sense but in *something less* than the objectivist sense that would require the existence of unknown or unknowable (i.e., verification-transcendent) truths. However, as I have said, this judicious middle-ground turns out to be highly elusive and — no matter how carefully specified — to offer nothing like the required degree of conceptual stability.

IV

Of course there is a large current literature devoted to the question of whether there 'exist' any such things as meanings, intentions, beliefs, or propositional contents and attitudes toward them. It is a question that divides philosophers along various lines, as for instance – most sharply – with the current debate between those who look forward to the advent of a mature neuroscience that will permit us to eliminate every last remnant of such 'folk-psychological' talk and those who deny that a physicalist language of the kind envisaged could ever provide a remotely adequate substitute.[48] It is also – much closer to Tennant's concerns – the main point at issue between thinkers like Quine who adopt a strictly extensionalist theory of reference (one that rejects any otiose appeal to meanings, intentions, or beliefs as giving rise to the problem of quantification into opaque contexts) and others who maintain that this reductive approach comes nowhere near offering an adequate account of our powers of linguistic or logico-semantic grasp.[49] Tennant is keen to distance himself from such views since he considers the strong anti-realist (or 'irrealist') argument to be one that goes flat against some of our most basic commonsense-intuitive as well as philosophical convictions. Thus '[w]e have to find a sustainable view of the status of semantic discourse itself, if our semantic theory is to be able to serve as a foundation for those anti-realist views and accompanying reforms that are to be pressed for other discourses' (Tennant, p. 6). This is needed both in order to provide 'a certain sort of reflexive stability for the whole enterprise' and in order to distinguish Tennant's form of moderate anti-realism from the full-strength (hence self-refuting) variety espoused by less circumspect or cautious types. However, as we have seen, such stability is not to be had from any approach that takes anti-realism as the default position and which then sets out to render that position more plausible by introducing various adjustments, caveats, and qualifying clauses. For if one thing is clear from recent debates around the rule-following 'paradox' and other central themes of post-Wittgensteinian philosophy of mind and language it is the fact that, once launched on this particular trajectory, there is no holding the line against the most extreme and (as Tennant acknowledges) the most philosophically disabling forms of sceptical counter-argument. Quite simply, the sceptic will always have the last word if the debate is set up so as treat realism – i.e., the thesis that we *can* conceive the existence of objective (verification-transcendent) truths – as an inherently strange or extravagant doctrine which therefore *ipso facto* requires a great deal of subtle and ingenious defence.

This conclusion follows 'logically' enough as soon as one takes the first (and crucial) argumentative step of containing 'truth' within the bounds of know-ability or epistemic warrant and thus ruling out any idea that certain statements may be true or false – objectively so – as a function of the way things stand in reality and quite apart from our more or less adequate state of knowledge concerning them. That is to say, it rejects the cardinal realist claim that our statements, when truth-apt, should be taken as *truth-bearers* whose truth-value is decided independently of any such consideration by certain objective states of affairs or certain abstract (e.g., mathematical or logical) orders of necessity which stand to them in the relation of *truth-makers*. While Tennant very firmly rejects this claim as a drastic deviation from the moderate anti-realist 'straight and narrow' he is also inclined to keep it in view as a check upon the tendency of anti-realism to press too far in an irrealist direction and thus begin the slide toward Kripkean and other varieties of wholesale meaning-scepticism. What he wants – and considers to lie within reach of a falsificationist reworking of the argument – is just the kind of patient, probing, non-dogmatic approach that would live up to Dummett's professed aim and take each 'area of discourse' on its merits as a candidate for treatment somewhere on the scale between objectivist truth and epistemically constrained assertoric warrant. Such would be the chief benefit, as he sees it, of building in the falsifiability (rather than the verifiability) criterion, i.e., that this approach makes greater allowance – by analogy with Popper's claims – for the non-finality of our present-best judgement in these matters and the always revisable character of any distinctions thus drawn. That is to say, Tennant goes about as far as possible (given his working brief) to accommodate certain realist intuitions, especially where these serve to shore up his case against Kripkean scepticism. Nevertheless, as with others like McDowell and Wright, Tennant's desire to meet the realist halfway on these issues about truth and objectivity is more than offset by his fixed idea that it *cannot make sense* to posit the existence of unknown or unknowable truths. In his case, as in theirs, the agenda is fixed by just those kinds of Wittgenstein-derived argument that strike them (and indeed strike Kripke himself) as utterly absurd or bizarre. What has enabled that agenda to exert such a well-nigh compulsive hold on recent debate despite these commonplace expressions of outraged philosophical conscience is a widely shared sense that the Kripkensteinian paradox won't go away until someone comes up with an adequate answer on its own ultra-sceptical terms of reference.

Yet if one thing emerges with daylight clarity from the long history of arguments for and against scepticism it is the fact that no such answer can ever be forthcoming so long as the sceptic sticks to his guns and refuses to concede the force of any claim that his thesis can be shown to produce a whole range of drastically counter-intuitive results. It is the same basic strategy that anti-realists exploit – albeit in a somewhat less extreme or doctrinaire form – when they assert that we can *either* have mathematical knowledge *or* objective mathematical truth but surely not both, or again, when they seek to demonstrate the impossibility of our conceiving that certain statements in the Dummettian 'disputed class' might have objective truth-conditions that transcend the limits of formal proof or empirical verifiability.[50] Such arguments are nowadays so prominent and their force so widely acknowledged as to constitute something like an orthodox position in philosophy of mind and language. Yet to the realist it is nothing less than self-evident that there have been, are, and will forever remain a great many well-formed and truth-apt statements in mathematics, the physical sciences, history, and other areas of discourse whose truth-value is in no way affected by the scope and limits of our present or (conceivably) our future-best means of verification. Thus she will beg to disagree when Tennant defines the 'straight and narrow' of his middle-ground approach as one that allows the moderate anti-realist to enjoy the best of both worlds. From her point of view this betokens not so much a willingness to take the realist's arguments on board as a downright refusal to accept them on any but the terms dictated by an anti-realist conception of truth as epistemically constrained or as ultimately subject to the limiting condition of warranted assertibility.

According to Tennant the realist must always run into trouble – end up by endorsing a strictly untenable (since self-refuting) doctrine – if she ventures to maintain the existence of verification- or recognition-transcendent truths. Thus '[c]oncerning the anti-realist principle (in its present unrestricted form) that all truths are knowable, the realist should simply' refuse to assert it, rather than go so far as to deny it; for [s]he cannot provide any definitive counter-examples' (Tennant, p. 267). However at this point the realist will do best to reply (1) that Tennant's olive-branch proposal merely confuses matters by playing on the ambiguity between 'knowable within the limits of our present-best means of ascertainment' and 'knowable when all the evidence is in and subject to ideally rational assessment', and (2) that in any case such epistemic questions have absolutely nothing to do with the issue as to whether certain statements might be objectively true or false quite apart from our knowing (or not knowing) how to demonstrate their truth or falsity. As Tennant sees it this amounts to a 'rather amusing' stand-off between the realist and the anti-realist since they are each in the odd situation of catching the other out on a weak point of doctrinal over-commitment while not being able to push their own case too far without inviting the same sort of charge. That is to say, the realist's (supposed) embarrassment at finding herself unable to come up with any instance of an unknowable truth 'is not unlike the anti-realist being unable to give any particular counter-examples to the realist's principle of bivalence, on pain of self-contradiction'. And again, just to rub the point in: '[e]ach must play the game of merely refusing to assert the other's favourite principle, while avoiding being lured into citing putative counter-examples' (Tennant, p. 267). Yet it is still open to the realist to claim that this is a misrepresentation of the issue between her and the anti-realist, and moreover one that stacks the cards very heavily in favour of anti-realism, whether understood on a strong (Dummettian) or a 'moderate' (Tennant-style) construal. For in so far as this debate is nowadays conducted in logico-semantic terms, i.e., as a matter of whether or not we can make sense of the idea of objective (recognition-transcendent) truths, it must always entail, for the anti-realist, a rejection of the principle of bivalence for statements belonging to the 'disputed class' of as-yet unproven or empirically unverifiable claims.

Tennant is perfectly clear about this: nonbivalence is basic to the anti-realist case no matter how many or significant the concessions that may be granted to the moderate realist in pursuit of a workable *modus vivendi* with moderate anti-realism. Yet there is something distinctly skewed about the terms on offer, as emerges when Tennant goes on to explain them in more detail. Thus the realist 'may be able to do a little better by his own lights. He may strengthen his refusal to assert the anti-realist principle that all truths are knowable, to an assertion that there are counter-examples to it' (p. 267). However this concession once again turns out to have sharp limits, since any putative counter-example adduced will be subject to the standard (anti-realist) requirement that it fall within the scope of constructive proof or empirical verifiability. Thus 'he [the realist] must have his audience understand the existence claim non-constructively, on pain of self-contradiction. And it is precisely this understanding which the anti-realist is not willing to profess' (ibid.). Yet of course it is on just this cardinal point – the plausibility (or otherwise) of conceiving that truth might always outrun the limits of present or future-best verification – that the realist takes issue with the anti-realist. Where the anti-realist unfailingly scores by his own (no matter how logically sophisticated) verificationist lights is by sticking to the claim that it cannot make sense to conceive the existence of truths that exceed the scope of knowability or optimized epistemic warrant. Where the realist comes back against this whole line of argument is by pointing to the sheer absurdity of any position which restricts truth (or the range of truth-apt statements, theories, or hypotheses) to the compass of whatever we are able to prove or ascertain by the best – including the future-best-possible – means at our epistemic disposal. No doubt the realist will be stuck for an answer if asked to come up with some clinching example of a statement or proposition p in respect of which we can legitimately say 'p is true' or 'p is false' even though its truth-value lies beyond our utmost capacities of formal proof or empirical verification. However it is only on the anti-realist's preferred account of what the realist must be saying that she appears committed to this clearly wrong since self-contradictory position. Otherwise her argument amounts to no more than the unproblematical claim that certain well-formed yet formally unproven or unverifiable statements – those belonging to Dummett's 'disputed class' – can nonetheless be known to possess an objective truth-value despite our incapacity to specify that value either now or even (conceivably) at some limit-point stage of idealized epistemic warrant.

Such would be the case, to repeat, with mathematical theorems like Goldbach's Conjecture or empirically undocumented claims such as 'Napoleon sneezed six times on the eve of Waterloo'. Beyond that it would apply to speculative statements in the physical sciences which we can know to be either true or false quite aside from any issue concerning our present or future-best means of ascertainment. Scott Soames makes this point most tellingly when he asks us to consider statements of the type: 'there exists a duplicate solar system in some region of the expanding universe beyond the furthest reach of terrestrial radio-telescopy'.[51] The example is particularly apt since Dummett very often deploys such metaphors to make just the opposite (anti-realist) point, i.e., that truth-values (or criteria of assertoric warrant) cannot possibly extend beyond the epistemic ken of knowers – like ourselves – whose competence to judge is restricted to a certain range of informational or cognitive resources.[52] Thus, according to Dummett, a realist approach with respect to any given area of discourse will take it that statements of the relevant kind possess a determinate (bivalent) truth-value just in so far as they succeed or fail in asserting some objectively valid proposition quite aside from the issue as to whether or not they

are arrived at on the basis of adequate knowledge or epistemic warrant. For the
realist it is a matter of truths 'out there' to be discovered, like features of a
landscape (mountains or lakes) whose existence and location depends not at all
on the fact of some explorer's having come across them, or again, like that
duplicate solar system far out in the expanding universe whose reality (or
otherwise) is wholly unaffected by our not being able to detect any sign of it.[53]
For the anti-realist, conversely, such claims cannot make sense in so far as they
posit the existence of truths which by very definition lie beyond our furthest
evidential, probative, or epistemic reach. That is to say: since we cannot acquire
or manifest a grasp of the conditions of assertoric warrant for statements that
belong to the 'disputed class', therefore such statements must be taken to lack
any determinate truth-value. Least of all can that value be conceived as pertaining to a realm of objective (recognition-transcendent) truths that would fix
it, i.e., bring the statement out bivalently true or false whatever the limits of our
knowledge. To adopt this view, so the anti-realist maintains, is to court logical
absurdity or downright self-contradiction. For it involves the surely nonsensical
idea that we can somehow have knowledge of or access to truths which *ex
hypothesi* exceed our utmost powers of proof or verification. In which case we
should grasp the anti-realist nettle and accept certain (to the realist) highly
unpalatable consequences, such as the confinement of truth-values within the
limits of human knowability, or even – if this argument is pushed right through
– the retroactive 'bringing-about' of past events through some present or future
change in our state of knowledge concerning them.[54]

Hence – as I have suggested elsewhere – the marked kinship between
Dummett's highly speculative (not to say decidedly *outré*) thoughts in this
regard and the kinds of quantum-based conjecture advanced by astrophysicists
like John Wheeler.[55] Such is the idea, in brief, that the occurrence of certain
celestial events such as supernovae at billions of light-years distance from earth
might itself be 'decided' retrocausally by a momentary switch in our radio-
telescope settings, just as – on a smaller (laboratory) scale – the outcome of
certain delayed-choice quantum experiments seems to involve a drastic affront to
our normal conceptions of temporal and causal sequence.[56] This is not the place
for a detailed discussion of the philosophic issues raised – and (I would argue)
conspicuously fudged or evaded – by these wild extrapolations from the quantum to the macrophysical domain. What I wish to do, rather, is point up their
relevance to the debate currently engaged between realists and anti-realists, and,
in particular, to the sorts of test-case analogy (like those instanced by Soames
and Dummett) which involve a clear-cut conflict of views between knowledge
conceived as a matter of discovering objectively existent worlds (or features
thereof) and knowledge conceived as in some sense a matter of 'bringing about'
such worlds.[57] This latter notion has its main source in Dummett's intuitionist
approach to the philosophy of mathematics where he takes a strong line against
any form of realist (or 'Platonist') commitment to the objective, recognition-
transcendent status of abstract entities such as numbers, sets, classes, functions,
or truth-values concerning them.[58] However it also has a wider bearing on his

tendency to take anti-realism as the default position for every 'area of discourse', including those empirically based disciplines – such as history and the physical sciences – where the problem of knowledge presents itself in a different (one might think, less sharply paradoxical) form. This despite his frequent expressions of a non-partisan approach and his overt methodological stance – one shared with Tennant, Wright, and others – which purportedly involves testing each area so as to establish whether we can best make sense of it on realist or anti-realist terms.

Where the bias shows through most plainly is in Dummett's off-the-point construal of realism as a claim to the self-contradictory effect that we can assign a determinate truth-value to statements of the disputed class despite our possessing no method of proof or means of verification. However this is no part of the realist's argument, at least on any fair (i.e., genuinely non-partisan rather than anti-realistically motivated) account of what she must be saying. Rather her case is more plausibly that, for a wide range of statements across various truth-apt areas of discourse, we may be – indeed most often are – in a position to maintain that statement p must be *either* true *or* false (objectively so) whatever our present state of ignorance in that regard. Tennant follows Dummett in conflating these two, wholly different versions of the realist argument. The first is very clearly a non-starter since it involves (as charged) a patent contradiction, while the second involves nothing more than the claim that there exist many truths (whether those that find expression in statements of the disputed class or those that cannot be expressed for want of any adequate linguistic means) beyond our best possible means of ascertainment. Thus, according to Tennant,

> before he even considers what is peculiar to any one discourse, the anti-realist will be committed to the tenet that truth is in principle knowable. That is, he will reject Knowledge-Transcendence across the board. For the principle of Knowledge-Transcendence is incoherent. Consider what it says: that there could be some truth ψ such that it be impossible to know that ψ. For the anti-realist, however, the truth of such ψ would have to consist in there being some truth-maker II for that ψ that we can recognise as such. Being able to recognise II as a truth-maker for ψ, we would therefore know that ψ. But precisely this knowledge is supposed to be beyond our reach! – a contradiction. In every discourse the notion of truth will be epistemically constrained. (Tennant, p. 50)

As I have said, Tennant goes further than most anti-realists – certainly further than Dummett – in allowing the force of various realist objections and counter-arguments. In particular he takes the point that any such claim for the knowability (even the 'in-principle' knowability) of all statements that are candidates for truth is one which goes flat against some of our most deeply held scientific and philosophical as well as everyday-commonsense convictions. After all, we have strong grounds for asserting (1) that we now know a good many truths unknown to earlier (less well-informed or scientifically advanced) enquirers; (2)

that those truths – especially as concerns mathematics and the physical sciences – must be thought to have held good objectively even at a time when nobody had the least idea of how to prove, ascertain, or perhaps even express them; and (3) that it is a strange kind of epistemic hubris to suppose that the scope and limits of our present-best knowledge are also the scope and limits of truth, properly (i.e., anti-realistically) conceived. Hence perhaps the most striking feature of Dummettian anti-realism: that it manages somehow to pass itself off as an outlook of due humility in this regard while in fact making knowledge – or the scope of human epistemic powers – the *ne plus ultra* of what counts as an instance of truth-apt discourse.

Thus the current debate is distinctly reminiscent of Socrates versus Protagoras on the question whether truth should be conceived as always potentially transcending our best state of knowledge or whether, on the contrary, 'man is the measure' in some no doubt suitably nuanced and qualified version of that claim. Tennant has a constant nagging sense of these problems with his whole line of argument and allows them to surface more forcefully than anyone else (Wright included) who has sought to maintain an anti-realist stance while acknowledging the various arguments that rise against it. Still there is a strong implication – as in the passage cited above – that he takes Dummett to have set the agenda for discussion of the realism issue and thus to have placed the burden of proof very squarely on those who believe that the realist case can be upheld without falling into various kinds of self-inflicted philosophical dilemma. This is why, as he says, 'truth is in principle knowable' and 'the principle of Knowledge-Transcendence is incoherent' (Tennant, p. 50). My own view, to repeat, is that such arguments are more like a classic *reductio ad absurdum*, since their full-strength versions cannot be sustained without involving a massive affront to all the principles of rational, truth-based enquiry while their scaled-down variants (like Wright's response-dispositional approach or Tennant's falsificationist account) achieve nothing more than a staving-off of the same endgame predicament. That they have come to exert such a powerful hold upon recent analytical debate is chiefly the result of Wittgenstein's influence, at least on that Kripkean reading of the 'private language' and 'rule-following' considerations which makes them absolutely central to discussions in epistemology and philosophy of mind and language.

V

McDowell is perhaps the most striking example of a thinker who has striven to negotiate a path between – as he is fond of putting it – the Scylla and Charybdis of full-fledged objectivism about truth on the one hand and, on the other, a 'sceptical solution' along Kripkensteinian (i.e., communitarian) lines. In his essay 'Wittgenstein on Following a Rule' McDowell comes out very firmly against any notion that correctness in such matters could amount to no more than conformity with communal practice.[59] Thus, in the case of correctly understanding a term like 'plus' and properly (consistently) applying it so as always to get the right answer for addition sums, there must be some criterion beyond the mere appeal to standard or received arithmetical practice. That is to say, there must exist a 'pattern of application that we grasp, when we come to understand the concept in question', a pattern (moreover) which 'extends, independently of the actual outcome of any investigation, to the relevant case' (McDowell, p. 325). Still one should not be driven to claim – and this is where the Kripkensteinian doubts kick in – that the defence of objectivity in rule-following requires the existence of some 'superfact' that would always and infallibly determine the correct answer for every arithmetical task, or some 'super-rigid rail' conception of reasoning which laid out the entire range of correct responses beyond any point on the numerical scale that we happened to have reached so far. For this would commit us to endorsing the (surely untenable) Platonist idea of an 'ethereal machine' – a kind of ghostly paradigm – that hovered above our various rule-following practices and somehow determined their objective correctness or otherwise quite apart from any question of what did or didn't count (among those qualified to judge) as a proper application of the rule. In which case, according to McDowell, we had much better seek an alternative, middle-way approach that can save us from shipwreck on either of those anfractuous rocks while not yielding ground to the sceptic (or the hard-line anti-realist) as concerns the prospect for redeeming some workable, since suitably scaled-down conception of objective truth.

Indeed McDowell thinks that one can have something very like a transcendental argument – an argument from the a priori conditions of possibility for thought and knowledge in general – that would justify our 'intuitive notion of objectivity' by showing how the anti-realist doctrine (at least in its strong form) runs into strictly unthinkable problems and aporias. This would demonstrate 'that there *must* be a middle position' because the only alternatives, as he sees them, are a slide from Dummettian anti-realism into Kripkean scepticism or an equally disastrous (since likewise scepticism-inducing) attempt to uphold the objectivist case by appealing to hopelessly deluded notions like those of the 'ethereal machine' or 'super-rigid rail'. According to McDowell's transcendental argument: '[u]nderstanding is a grasp of patterns that extend to new cases independently of our ratification, as required for meaning to be other than an illusion (and – not incidentally – for the intuitive notion of objectivity to have a use); but the constraints imposed by our concepts do not have the platonistic autonomy with which they are credited in the picture of the super-rigid machinery' (McDowell, p. 353). Whence his main objection to Wright's (as he sees it) over-readiness to meet Kripkensteinian scepticism more than halfway and thereby relinquish any viable conception of the normative character of rules, i.e., their possessing something more than the seal of communal approval.[60] For if one gives up the very idea of 'ratification-independence' then along with it goes any prospect of retaining the crucial normative distinction between 'true or correct as a matter of objective (non-practice-relative) warrant' and 'true or correct by our best communal lights'. That is to say, the chief problem for

Wright 'is to distinguish the position he attributes to Wittgenstein from one according to which the possibility of going out of step with our fellows gives us the illusion of being subject to norms, and consequently the illusion of entertaining and expressing meanings' (McDowell, p. 336). And again: 'the denial of ratification-independence ... yields a picture of the relation between the communal language and the world in which norms are obliterated' (ibid., p. 347). Where MacDowell's transcendental argument has its work cut out is in showing how our various epistemic practices, reasonings, rule-followings, and so forth can be subject to normative constraints of the relevant kind while nonetheless retaining sufficient connection with our usual (communally warranted) procedures so as safely to avoid any hint of evoking all that spectral Platonist 'machinery'.

However one may doubt that the argument goes through with anything like the required degree of transcendental (or even philosophically persuasive) force. Thus McDowell's firm resolve to steer well clear of any full-fledged realist conception that would open the way – so he thinks – to full-fledged Kripkean scepticism allows him no room for a more than notional idea of 'objectivity' or an other than vague and often rather tortuous specification of the normative standards involved. This is mainly because, like Tennant and Wright, he is in thrall to that Wittgensteinian notion which holds that objectivist conceptions of truth or correctness in rule-following are not to be had unless at the price of manifest self-contradiction. So what the transcendental argument amounts to is a strong sense, on McDowell's part, that the proffered alternatives simply won't do and that it *must* therefore be possible to navigate a course between the Scylla of objectivist realism and the Charybdis of Kripke's communitarian 'sceptical solution'. Yet when it comes to describing how that course should be steered McDowell has nothing more substantive (or nothing less Kripkensteinian) to say than that 'the key to finding the indispensable middle course is the idea of a custom or practice' (McDowell, p. 342). In which case one is surely entitled to ask what remains of 'objectivity' or 'normativity' once those values are taken as custom-dependent or practice-relative. After all, this is just the kind of lesson picked up from Wittgenstein by a good many 'strong' sociologists of knowledge, practitioners of 'thick' ethnographic description, cultural theorists, Rortian neo-pragmatists, and others for whom, quite simply, any notion of objective or practice-transcendent truth is one that should long since have been discarded, together with belief in God as the supreme guarantor of such values.[61]

To be sure, there are 'realist' readings of Wittgenstein (like that of Cora Diamond) which deny that his thinking has any such sceptical or cultural-relativist implications.[62] For does he not insist – against all its erstwhile grandiose revisionist claims – that philosophy when properly practised 'leaves everything as it is', including (one assumes) any realist commitments of an ontological or epistemological nature that might play a role in our received practices or customary modes of describing them? Yet this will scarcely satisfy the (non-Wittgensteinian) realist who takes it that the values of truth or correctness are in principle custom-independent or practice-transcendent. From her point of view any version of 'realism' defined in such terms is one that either dare not speak its name for fear of the standard sceptical rejoinder or has no wish to advance beyond the notion of truth as a matter of communal warrant. Thus when McDowell describes his 'indispensable middle course' as the 'idea of a custom or practice' it seems fair to say that he remains very firmly in the Wittgensteinian camp. Moreover he yields a crucial hostage to sceptical fortune since this opens the way for Kripke's admittedly 'wild', 'bizarre', or 'crazy' hypothesis that our standards of correctness in arithmetic, logic, and other such rule-following practices are incapable of rational justification save by recourse to (what else?) our received or customary ways of carrying on.

McDowell devotes some strenuous efforts of wire-drawn argumentation to the business of showing that his alternative 'middle position' doesn't lean over into scepticism, cultural relativism, or any other such inadequate (normatively deficient) account of what is involved in properly and correctly following a rule. This is where he takes issue with Wright on the precise significance of those passages in Wittgenstein which seek to disabuse us of the vain quest for meanings, reasons, explanations, and so forth beyond a straightforward acceptance that certain kinds of language have a certain role in certain communally shared practices or cultural forms of life. Such is the stage when, according to Wittgenstein, our 'justifications come to an end' and quite simply we have no choice but to acknowledge this fact, unless (that is) we are philosophers still hooked on those deluded habits of thought and thereby condemned to carry on aimlessly buzzing around in the fly-bottle. However this leaves McDowell somewhat awkwardly placed since he shows all the usual deference to Wittgenstein's authority and the usual compulsion to square his own position with Wittgenstein's, even though – as I have said – no philosopher has done more than Wittgenstein to encourage the kinds of radical meaning-scepticism and the retreat from normative values (such as those of objectivity and truth) that McDowell strongly resists. His answer – as so often in the secondary literature – is to claim that other exponents (Wright among them) have got Wittgenstein wrong whereas on his (McDowell's) account we can have all the proclaimed benefits with none of the supposed liabilities. That is to say, there is no ultimate conflict between a practice-based or communitarian and an adequately normative approach just so long as we keep 'objectivity' in the picture by treating it as the kind of corrective constraint that is exerted on our various reasonings, reckonings, and rule-followings by a due regard for the judgement of other, perhaps more expert or knowledgeable persons within our community.

Thus Wright's mistake, as McDowell sees it, is to under-estimate the extent of this corrective influence and its capacity to serve as an adequate replacement for notions of objectivity and truth that would somehow (impossibly) situate those values in a practice-transcendent realm beyond the scope of any saving appeal to communal 'agreement in judgement'. On Wright's account, 'there is nothing but verbal behaviour and (no doubt) feelings of constraint. Presumably people's dispositions to behaviour and associated feelings match in interesting

ways; but at this ground-floor level there is no question of shared commitments
– everything normative fades out of the picture' (McDowell, p. 341). Yet this
same objection could just as well be brought against McDowell's understanding
of Wittgenstein, and indeed against any treatment which claimed no more than
to elucidate the plain sense of Wittgenstein's words. For there is simply no
escaping what McDowell finds so unpalatable about Wright's exegesis, namely
the fact that Wittgenstein's idea of our justifications having an end in the
warrant of communal usage or customary practice is one that *inevitably* leaves no
room for the normative values of truth and objectivity which McDowell so
doggedly strives to uphold. That is to say, once those values are construed as
internal to some given language-game, community, or shared life-form then by
very definition they are incapable of exerting the kind of objective (practice-
independent) constraint that McDowell's argument plainly requires. This would
seem to be the intended force of his criticism that Wright reduces all language
to a 'ground-floor level' of 'verbal behaviour', a level at which there may be some
match between 'dispositions' and 'associated feelings', but where any constraints
that subjects might feel upon their sayings, reasonings, reckonings, and so forth,
can amount to no more than just that, i.e., 'feelings of constraint'. For if the
standards in question are ultimately those of communal 'agreement in judgement' then they can only be thought of as deriving from norms – from shared
ideas of 'objectivity' and 'truth' – which are felt to exert some directive or
corrective pressure but whose capacity to do so is entirely a matter of their
general acceptance among members of the community concerned. In which case
they are not so much 'objective' constraints in any genuine (non-belief-relative
or practice-independent) sense of that term but rather just the kinds of
inhibitory impulse or tendency to ratify some beliefs and reject or criticize others
that subjects normally acquire as a condition of precisely such communal
membership.

Hence McDowell's charge against Wright's exegesis of Wittgenstein: that it
fails to envisage any normative dimension to our various epistemic and other
(including moral) practices that would not come down to mere 'correctness' or
'truth' by certain communitarian lights. Wright, he goes on,

> hopes to preserve a foothold for a purified form of the normativeness
> implicit in the contractual conception of meaning, by appealing to the fact
> that individuals are susceptible to communal correction. It is problematic,
> however, whether the picture of the basic level, once entertained as such,
> can be prevented from purporting to contain the real truth about lin-
> guistic behaviour. In that case its freedom from norms will preclude our
> attributing any genuine substance to the etiolated normativeness that
> Wright hopes to preserve. (McDowell, p. 336)

Yet one could substitute 'McDowell' for 'Wright' in this passage and make just
as strong a case that his own argument fails to meet those basic normative
criteria – or requirements of objectivity and truth – which McDowell finds so

conspicuously lacking in Wright's treatment of the issue. What he takes to set their readings of Wittgenstein decisively at odds is the fact that Wright's 'denial of ratification-independence ... yields a picture of the relation between the communal language and the world in which norms are obliterated', whereas his (McDowell's) approach yields a different picture 'in which the openness of an individual to correction by his fellows means that he is subject to norms' (McDowell, p. 347). However those norms can scarcely be thought of as 'objective' or 'ratification-independent' if they require nothing more than a willingness to accept 'correction by his fellows' on the part of this or that individual for whom their corrective or normative force can itself be no more than a matter of communal warrant among members of the relevant (norm-prescribing) community. On this account – McDowell's as well as Wright's, since both take their cue from Wittgenstein – it is impossible to say how such norms might exist and exert their constraining influence except in so far as they played a role in our customary usages and practices. Yet it is just this sort of argument (or just this supposedly false interpretation of Wittgenstein) that McDowell so vigorously takes to task in his strictures on Wright and, even more, in his efforts to avert the looming threat of a full-fledged Kripkean sceptical paradox and a likewise sceptical, i.e., thoroughgoing communitarian 'solution'.

Thus McDowell's criticism of Wright – that he leaves the idea of normative constraint 'looking like, at best, an explanation of our propensity to the illusion that we are subject to norms' – is one that comes back like a boomerang when applied to his own argument. For as recent debates around anti-realism and response-dependence have made abundantly clear there is just no way that one can save the notions of objectivity and truth by adopting some 'moderate' anti-realist position, most often with reference to Wittgenstein, which claims to restore those notions to a sensibly qualified, non-objectivist, or practice-based conception of the truth-values concerned. What those debates bring out most forcefully is the fact that so much present-day philosophy in the analytic line of descent has been sidetracked – not to say hoodwinked – into taking its agenda from a range of pseudo-problems or false dilemmas with their source in Wittgenstein's later ideas abut 'private languages' and 'rule-following'. The result shows up in the above-cited passage from McDowell when he questions whether the 'basic level' (i.e., that envisaged in Wright's Wittgensteinian conception of communal usage as our last, best source of epistemic guidance) can be thought to contain 'the real truth about linguistic behaviour'. For where scepticism nowadays gets a hold it is precisely through this constant slide from issues of truth and normativity conceived in objectivist ('ratification-independent') terms to issues regarding the possibility (or otherwise) of knowing for sure that our meanings, reasonings, or reckonings are consistent from one occasion to the next. That is to say, it is at just the point where Wittgenstein's placid assurance that we need nothing more than communal warrant by way of epistemic 'justification' gives way to Kripke's ultra-sceptical rendition of that same argument, i.e., his contention – however 'crazy' or 'bizarre' – that there is simply no 'fact' about our rule-following practices that could determine whether we are right or wrong in any given instance.

So the charge that McDowell lays against Wright – that at this 'ground-floor' level of linguistic behaviour 'its freedom from norms will preclude our attributing any genuine substance to the etiolated normativeness that Wright hopes to preserve' – is one that rebounds with singular force when applied to his own argument. As soon as one takes the Wittgensteinian turn from questions of objective (e.g., mathematical, logical, or scientific) truth to questions concerning our certainty – or lack of it – with regard to what we now mean or meant in the past by concepts like 'addition' or 'following a rule' then we are launched willy-nilly (and Wittgenstein's contrary assurances notwithstanding) on the path toward full-fledged Kripkean scepticism. Yet this is just the kind of doubt-inducing philosophical confusion between truth, knowledge, and certainty that sceptics have always been quick to exploit and which emerges to particularly striking effect in the great volume of secondary literature that has built up around Kripke's ingenious yet stubbornly perverse lucubrations on the topic of 'following a rule'. 'Even now as I write', he confides, 'I feel confident that there is something in my mind – the meaning I attach to the "plus" sign – that instructs me what I ought to do in all future cases' (Kripke, p. 18). And again: 'if I intend to accord with my past meaning of "+" I should answer "125" [i.e., if asked "What is the sum of 68 + 57?"] . . . [since] the relation of meaning and intention to future action is normative, not descriptive' (ibid., p. 19). However, once again, this reduces normativity to a feature of our various introspectible *meanings* and *intentions* – along with our ('real' or supposed) state of certainty concerning them – rather than locating the relevant standards for correct (as opposed to deviant or erroneous) reckoning in a realm of objective arithmetical truths quite distinct from such no doubt fallible sources of private, apodictic, first-person, or 'inner' assurance. And then, having set things up in this skewed fashion – having made it appear (at least for those willing to play along, which includes most writers on the rule-following 'paradox') that correctness in such matters stands or falls on the issue of our *certainty* regarding the content of our meanings, past and present – Kripke can proceed to push right through with his sceptical paradox and arrive at his equally sceptical (i.e., wholesale communitarian) 'solution'. For is it not the case, as emerges very clearly from a reading of Wittgenstein on the joint topics of 'private language' and 'following a rule', that any such appeal to our convictions of correctness in this or that instance of rule-application is sure to be one that invites the charge of infinite regress or vicious circularity? And are we not thereby forced to conclude – even if 'crazily' and against our own better judgement in moments of relative sanity – that there is simply no 'fact' about what we now mean (or what we meant on previous occasions) that could serve to distinguish 'plus' from 'quus', 'addition' from 'quaddition', 'count' from 'quount', and so forth?

So we had best give up on this hopeless attempt to outflank the Kripkean sceptic by a mere transposition of terms, any of which he can treat as further proof of our total inability to know for sure that we are applying the 'correct' or the self-same rule from one instance to the next. After all, we should long since have learned from Wittgenstein that there is no such thing as a purely self-interpreting mental state, or a conviction with regard to some first-person, epistemically 'privileged' truth (e.g., about our own meanings or intentions) that requires nothing more than the guarantee of its own apodictic self-evidence. In which case, Kripke maintains, the sceptical paradox holds firm against any possible counter-argument and we are left with no recourse save the 'sceptical solution' which of course has Wittgenstein's blessing but which strikes even Kripke as failing to provide an adequate (philosophically reputable) answer. Yet it is wrong – indeed nothing short of absurd – to suppose that any standard of correctness in matters such as arithmetical addition or subtraction should depend on some inner state of certainty with regard to what we mean, meant in the past, or believe ourselves intending to mean in the future by terms like 'plus', 'minus', and 'count'. Just *how* absurd can be seen from Kripke's (again distinctly Wittgensteinian) idea that this point about the ultimate inscrutability of 'private' meanings and intentions – and hence about the lack of determinate criteria for rule-following correctness – can be made by analogy with 'private' sensations such as pains, visual or tactile impressions, 'inner states' of various (e.g., emotional) kinds, and other such presumptively subjective modes of experience. Thus it might be said that 'meaning addition by "plus" denotes an irreducible experience, with its own special *quale*, known directly to each of us by introspection' (Kripke, p. 41). In which case we could simply disregard Kripkean or other such forms of hypercultivated sceptical doubt since they possess no force against the kind of jointly intuitive and rational self-evidence that distinguishes our knowledge of the items concerned, whether qualia or the meanings we standardly attach to terms like 'plus' and 'addition'. However, '[n]o internal impression, with a *quale*, could possibly tell me in itself how it is to be applied in future cases. Nor can any pile-up of such impressions, thought of as rules for interpreting rules, do the job' (ibid., p. 43). This conclusion is strictly inescapable (Kripke thinks) if we have registered the cumulative impact of Wittgenstein's rule-following, private-language, infinite-regress, and vicious-circularity arguments.

Still one should not be too impressed by such a swift and (on its own terms) utterly decisive statement of the case for radical meaning-scepticism. No doubt, Kripke goes on, 'if there were a special experience of "meaning" addition by "plus" analogous to a headache, it would not have the properties that a state of meaning addition by "plus" ought to have – it would not tell me what to do in new cases' (ibid., p. 43). But then, who would ever think of drawing any such analogy, or of making the (surely absurd) suggestion that our grasp of arithmetical functions – or the sense assigned to certain basic arithmetical terms – could usefully be thought of as possessing something in common with our experience of suffering a headache? Least of all could this notion exert any hold upon thinkers in the Kripkean target-group (i.e., realists about mathematics or other truth-apt areas of discourse) for whom the appeal to private intuitions or 'inner states' of any kind – including that of subjective certainty – is totally beside the point, or just the kind of red herring typically trailed by sceptics in quest of an easy knockdown argument. The only exception within philosophy of mathematics is one that may be thought to prove the rule since it hails from the intuitionist quarter, that is to say, from the branch of strongly anti-realist (or anti-objectivist) thinking whose influence has spread – chiefly via Dummett – to a great many areas of present-day philosophic thought.[63] Indeed one finds Brouwer, its leading proponent, expressing the view that truth in mathematics is indeed some kind of 'inner feeling', an intuitive sense of conceptual grasp which accompanies the discovery of a proof and which must be thought not only to precede and enable but to constitute the very grounds of any such proof. Thus Brouwer firmly rejects the idea 'that mathematics, when it is made less formal, will pay for it by a loss of "exactitude", i.e. of mathematical truth'. On the contrary, '[f]or me "truth" is a general emotional phenomenon, which . . . can be coupled or not with the formalistic study of mathematics'.[64]

I should not wish to claim that Dummettian anti-realism in this or other areas of discourse can be traced back to an emotivist revolt against the rigours of formalist (or objectivist) truth-talk. More to the point is its close link with the debate around Kripkean meaning-scepticism – which he (Dummett) explicitly rejects while nonetheless taking certain of its cardinal premises on board – and the way that Kripke contrives to saddle the realist with a wholly implausible doctrine concerning the analogy between our sense of correctness in rule-following and certain 'private' goings-on like headaches, tinglings, sensations of warmth, and other such subjective qualia. This line of argument is among the most frequently exploited by anti-realists about mathematics who point to the manifest absurdity of thinking that we could ever have epistemic (by which they mean some kind of quasi-perceptual or sensory) contact with abstract entities such as numbers, sets and classes. However, as I have said, it is strongly denied by mathematical realists (from Gödel to David Lewis and Jerrold Katz), who respond by distinguishing the order of empirical, contingent, or 'might-have-been-otherwise' truths where perceptual acquaintance has a genuine, informative role to play from the order of necessary truths (e.g., those of mathematics or logic) where such issues of empirical warrant are clearly beside the point. Thus as Katz puts it (to repeat):

> In virtue of being a perfect number, six must be a perfect number; in virtue of being the only even prime, two must be the only even prime. Since the epistemic role of contact is to provide us with the information needed to select among the different ways something might be, and since perceptual contact cannot provide information about how something must be, contact has no point in relation to abstract objects. It cannot ground beliefs about them.[65]

Or again, in Lewis' equally forthright statement of the realist case: 'it's too bad for epistemologists if mathematics in its present form baffles them, but it would be hubris to take that as any reason to reform mathematics . . . Our knowledge of mathematics is ever so much more secure than our knowledge of the epistemology that seeks to cast doubt on mathematics.'[66]

Of course the anti-realist will come back at this point – like sceptics of various persuasion down through the ages – by simply denying the opponent's major premise. i.e., the claim (in this case) that our knowledge of mathematics, logic or the formal sciences is anything like as 'secure' as the realist naïvely supposes it to be. In so doing the anti-realist may well contend that this is not at all a version of scepticism – at least not a full-fledged version of the Kripkensteinian sort – but rather a means of holding such scepticism at bay by bringing mathematical and other kinds of knowledge within the compass of human epistemic attainment. Hence, as we have seen, the various suggestions for a scaled-down or suitably provisoed version of truth that would avoid both the Scylla of objectivist recognition-transcendence (placing it beyond our utmost cognitive reach) and the Charybdis of all-out Kripkean meaning-scepticism. These proposals range all the way from Dummett's original (agenda-setting) anti-realist conception of assertoric warrant, via Wright's somewhat strengthened (more discriminate) ideas of 'superassertibility' and 'cognitive command', to response-dispositional accounts of the criteria for knowledge in various specified areas of discourse. Then again, there is Tennant's falsificationist variant of the case for a moderate anti-realism, hedging that case around with as many doubts, reservations, and concessions to the realist as could well be managed without letting it go pretty much by default. Yet none of these approaches has the least chance of meeting – or defeating – the Kripkean challenge. For what they all share, despite some otherwise very marked differences of view, is a basic willingness to argue their case on ground which the sceptic has staked out in advance and been careful to plant with all sorts of tripwires and explosive devices.

VI

This is why no version of anti-realism, even when supplied (like Tennant's) with a maximal range of intuition-saving caveats or escape-clauses, can possibly come up with a statement of the case that would protect it against the kind of all-out sceptical attack that Kripke is so adept at mounting. Thus, for instance, he is able to make short work of the dispositionalist challenge which holds that 'to mean addition by "+" is to be disposed, when asked for any sum "$x + y$", to give the sum of x and y as the answer (in particular to say "125" when queried about "68 + 57")', while 'to mean quus is to be disposed, when queried about any arguments, to respond with their *quum* (in particular to answer "5" when queried about "68 + 57")' (Kripke, pp. 22–3). On this view the fact that I had not up to now been set any task in the given numerical range is nothing to the point – no grist to the sceptic's mill – since I might (indeed must) have been *disposed* to come up with one or the other response in so far as I had grasped the operative rule and had the question been asked. 'By hypothesis I was not in fact asked, but the disposition was present none the less' (ibid.). However this response once again falls plump into Kripke's sights since it assumes – after Wittgenstein – that any adequate (non-question-begging) answer to the sceptic will have to go by way of our state of *certainty* or our assenting disposition with regard to the answer and the process by which we arrived at it.[67] At which point the Kripkean sceptical machinery gets back into gear and shows that such 'certainty' is based on (what else?) the mere fact of our being thus disposed, but without the least reason to credit this fact with any kind of normative or justificatory force. 'Well and good', Kripke says: 'I know that "125" is the response I am disposed to give (I am actually giving it!), and maybe it is helpful to be told – as a matter of brute fact – that I would have given this same response in the past.' All the same, '[h]ow does any of this indicate that – now *or* in the past – "125" was an answer *justified* in terms of instructions I gave myself, rather than a mere jack-in-the-box unjustified and arbitrary response?' (Kripke, p. 23). And of course if the question is framed in these terms then it can only elicit a negative response, i.e., that if issues of truth and falsehood finally come down to issues of certainty or of how we are disposed to answer in this or that case then the sceptical argument goes straight through and the realist is once again played off the field.

As I have said, this is a conclusion strongly resisted by most anti-realists (Dummett included) who take a less pyrrhic view of the prospects for attainable human knowledge and who often advance their own arguments as a means of resisting – rather than endorsing – such an ultra-sceptical upshot. Nevertheless, it is one that lies at the end of the road that all these thinkers are travelling and which cannot be avoided by any strategy for bringing truth within the compass of our knowledge or optimal epistemic powers. That is, unless those powers are so defined – as sometimes they are by exponents of the Euthyphro Contrast – in such a way as to make it simply *impossible* that the verdicts of best judgement should come apart from the range of valid statements in this or that area of discourse.[68] However this lets the whole issue go by default since it amounts to no more than a somewhat shifty acknowledgement of the realist position, or a means of deferring to the strong hold upon us of certain objectivist beliefs while nonetheless retaining some notional role for best judgement or optimized warrant. Thus one finds McDowell doing his utmost to show that there is a 'real application' for our 'intuitive notion of objectivity', one that goes beyond anything redeemable in straightforward communal terms, i.e., as a product of Wittgensteinian 'agreement in judgement' among members of some given socius (McDowell, p. 351). Yet one also finds him, in the same article, proposing 'the idea of a custom or practice' as the key to discovering that 'indispensable middle course' that will offer a solution to all these problems (ibid., p. 342). Or again: it is our 'shared membership in a linguistic community' that provides us with the requisite normative criteria, including (presumably) our grasp of those objective, 'ratification-independent' truth-values. Where the Kripkean dilemma takes hold, according to McDowell, is through the notion that following a rule must involve some element of *interpretation*, that is, some scope for variant understandings or divergences in the import ascribed to that rule by various followers. Yet do we not have it on Wittgenstein's authority that 'there must be a way of grasping a rule which is not an interpretation, but which is exhibited in what we call "obeying a rule" or "going against it" in actual cases'?[69] From which McDowell draws the appropriate lesson, namely that 'we have to realise that obeying a rule is a practice if we are to find it intelligible that there is a way of grasping a rule that is not an interpretation' (McDowell, p. 339). For we shall otherwise have no answer to the Kripkean sceptic when he lays down his standard challenge to the realist, i.e., that of assigning any normative content to our usage of terms like 'plus', 'addition', or 'count'.

However it is hard to see that this advances the discussion one iota beyond the 'sceptical solution' which Kripke proposes in answer to his own 'sceptical paradox'. After all, what could such a 'practice' consist in if not the kind of communally warranted procedure that disposed individual rule-followers to perform this way rather than that? In which case 'going against it' – Wittgenstein's phrase – could only be a matter of contravening some accredited communal norm rather than failing to meet the requirements of objectivity and truth. And again, what else could such 'objectivity' amount to if not some more or less widespread 'agreement in judgement' among members of the epistemic community concerned? But at this point we are faced – precisely as Kripke would have it – with the problem of explaining on *just what grounds* we can count one such procedure 'correct' and any other 'deviant' or off the rails except by reference to that same communal norm. And if the norm in question is considered to derive from our membership of a 'shared *linguistic* community' then one may doubt that McDowell's talk of 'practice' or 'custom' can avoid reintroducing the idea – the fatally scepticism-prone idea – that rule-following must involve some element of interpretation. Unless, that is, we are to posit the existence of some logically perfect (unambiguous, crystalline, or ideally perspicuous) language such as Wittgenstein once envisaged – along with other thinkers like Leibniz and Frege – as a cure for all our philosophic ills.[70] Yet of course this idea is a main target of Wittgenstein's later writing and one that is routinely rejected by most participants in the rule-following debate. So if McDowell's argument is to work then there must be some way of squaring his claims (1) that rule-following consists in obedience to shared linguistic (or communal) norms; (2) that those norms are nonetheless 'objective' for that; and (3) that despite being based on 'practice' and 'custom' they involve no recourse to 'interpretation' since their correctness consists in their endorsement by standards which are simply not subject to Kripkean or any other form of sceptical doubt. Thus, according to McDowell, 'shared command of a language equips us to know one another's meaning without needing to arrive at that knowledge by interpretation, because it equips us to hear someone else's meaning in his words' (McDowell, p. 350). That is to say, 'interpretation' thankfully drops out and we are somehow granted privileged access to 'someone else's' (as well as our own) meanings through a mode of understanding that manages to bypass all the problems thrown up by Kripke's perversely sceptical take on Wittgenstein. Yet nothing could more plainly invite all the standard charges – of circularity, vicious regress, and belief in a realm of self-evident 'inner' or 'private' goings-on – that have since become the veritable stock-in-trade of post-Wittgensteinian and (in particular) Kripkean philosophy of mind and language.

Thus McDowell's purported middle-way solution to the rule-following paradox is one that falls straight into all the traps set in place not only by a downright sceptic like Kripke but also by Wittgenstein himself. That Kripke's is a highly ingenious yet somehow perverse and mistaken rendering of Wittgenstein's thoughts on this topic is a belief shared by just about every contributor to the current debate. For many, like McDowell, the conviction persists that by simply going back to the passages in question and at last – after so many failed efforts – managing to read them aright one can make good on Wittgenstein's so far unfulfilled promise to release the fly from the fly-bottle and thereby 'give philosophy peace'. However, if one thing emerges with striking regularity from the various commentaries by Dummett, McDowell, Tennant, Wright and others it is the fact that no such happy deliverance can be had on the terms laid down by Wittgenstein himself, and merely pressed to their logical (ultra-sceptical) conclusion by Kripke. What they involve is the basic triad of anti-realist premises: (1) that the appeal to 'practice' or 'custom' is in some (however specified or provisoed) sense the furthest one can get in matters of epistemic justification; (2) that issues of truth or knowledge come down to issues of 'certainty', for instance with regard to our own and others' meanings, intentions, assurances of rule-following correctness, and so on; and (3) that this certainty must have to do with the kinds of assertoric warrant offered by the Wittgensteinian appeal to communal 'practice' or 'custom'. Beyond that there is the more specific anti-realist claim (4) that the truth-value of any given statement cannot be conceived in objectivist terms which would entail the possibility of that value somehow being fixed quite apart from our best proof-procedures, investigative methods, or evidential sources. Nor is the issue decisively affected by particular differences of view within the anti-realist camp, as for instance between Dummett's programmatic and Wright's more epistemically nuanced version of the case, or again, between Dummett's (however refined) verificationist approach and Tennant's proposal for a 'moderate' form of anti-realism with its basis in a falsificationist (Popperian) account of knowledge and the logic of enquiry. What they all have in common is an order of priorities whereby truth-values are taken as dependent on truth-conditions, these latter conceived as coterminous with the scope and limits of assertoric warrant, and such warrant then defined (after Wittgenstein) as a matter of our *certainty* regarding those empirical facts or truths of reason that we just cannot doubt unless at the cost of wholesale scepticism.

Yet one need not subscribe to anything so *outré* as Kripke's version of the case in order to see that this notion of certainty as an ultimate or bedrock ground of appeal is one that lies wide open to sceptical challenge. Moreover, as Kripke was quick to perceive, that challenge can be mounted to best or most telling effect precisely on Wittgensteinian grounds, i.e., by application of the 'private language', 'vicious circle' and 'infinite regress' arguments as a means of dispelling any such delusion with regard to the privileged, self-authorizing status of first-person epistemic warrant. So if we cannot be *certain* even as concerns the meaning and consistency of our past or present usage of terms like 'plus', 'addition', 'count', and so forth, then the only alternative – so Kripke contends – is the 'sceptical solution' that falls back on communal assent as our last, best hope in such matters. However this putative solution is still very much a part of the problem, as we have seen repeatedly in various efforts (by McDowell, Wright, and others) to square it with some viable, that is to say, some Wittgenstein-compatible notion of 'objectivity' or 'truth'. For there is just no way of conserving such values in any more than a notional or ersatz form if one treats them as subject to ratification only by the standards of some shared practice, custom, or communal life-form. Of course it may be said – again taking a cue from Wittgenstein – that certain concepts are so deeply entrenched in our everyday or other, more specialized practices that we should think of them as like the bed of a river that pursues its course wholly undisturbed by the swirls and eddies of shifting cultural belief.[71] However this metaphor clearly fails to make the intended point if it is supposed to reconcile the practice-based or communitarian approach with one that would respect what McDowell calls 'our intuitive conception of meaning and objectivity'. For it is a central feature of that default conception – as most of these thinkers readily admit – that truth should be regarded as a matter of objective (rather than communal or practice-based) warrant, and that objectivity should likewise be conceived as always potentially transcending the limits of best-attainable knowledge. Moreover there is an equally strong presumption that mere *certainty* – or force of conviction – is neither here nor there when we move beyond issues of belief to issues of knowledge and (even more) to questions of truth.

Thus, reverting to Wittgenstein's fluvial metaphor, one can scarcely conclude from the *relative* depth of the river-bed and the *relatively* steadfast course it follows over *relatively* long periods of time to the notion that it constitutes a permanent feature of the landscape *entirely unaffected* by any surface or middle-depth perturbations and currents. Perhaps this is to place an undue weight of philosophical significance on what is offered merely as a passing analogy or illustrative trope. Still it is one that has attracted the notice of many commentators and which does seem to convey rather aptly what Wittgenstein has in mind when he talks about 'certainty' as the furthest we can get by way of rational justification or epistemic warrant. So the fact that it doesn't work out quite as he (or the more fideist) interpreters would have it is a point of some importance when we come to assess the implications of Wittgenstein's later thinking for philosophy of mind and language. That is to say: Wittgenstein substitutes an ill-defined and (even on his own terms) deeply problematical notion of 'certainty' for any realist or objectivist approach that would draw a sharp distinction between that which we *believe* – with whatever strength of subjective, psychological, or doctrinal conviction – and that which we are *justified* in so believing since it meets the requirements for veridical knowledge.

Moreover it reverses the intuitively self-evident order of priority between truth and knowledge so as to make its case for the notion of truth as epistemically constrained and of any such constraint as ineluctably subject to the scope and limits of 'certainty', thus conceived. This is where the Kripkean sceptic is able to insert his knowledge-devastating wedge and where anti-realists of a non-sceptical persuasion – among them McDowell, Tennant, and Wright – come to grief on the plain inability to square their Wittgenstein-influenced approach with their strong countervailing intuitions. What has so far managed to pass itself off as a remedy for all our 'metaphysically' induced problems and per-plexities is in fact a chief source of those chronic doubts that continue to plague philosophical enquiry and whose single most striking manifestation is the rule-following debate.

If there is a lesson to be learned from all this it is one that has been evident at least since Hume and which Kripke himself is apt to acknowledge in off-guard moments when his sceptical defences are down. That is to say, it is the lesson that all such arguments against the existence of recognition-transcendent (or falsification-transcendent) truths will at length – when pushed to the 'logical' extreme – turn out to constitute a *reductio ad absurdum* of the case for main-taining precisely that anti-realist thesis. If I have somewhat belaboured this negative point through my lengthy commentary on various thinkers of a more or less sceptical persuasion then I trust that this will seem not so much an exercise in purely destructive criticism as an effort to show what truly emerges in consequence of all their often exceptionally sharp and perceptive arguments. No doubt there is a sense in which the sceptic will always (inevitably) have the last word if he chooses to stick it out by deploying the range of, on his own terms, strictly indefeasible counter-arguments developed to a high point of logical sophistication by philosophers from Hume to Kripke. However he will then be in the surely difficult position of denying that certain truths would hold good irrespective of whether there were sentient perceivers or rational enquirers around who happened to possess the requisite (i.e., knowledge-constitutive) powers of perceptual, cognitive, or epistemic grasp. Among them would be the truths of elementary arithmetic, the most basic axioms of logic (like non-contradiction), and the fact that we must be either right or wrong – objectively so – when we advance some well-formed even though unprovable proposition such as 'Goldbach's Conjecture is true' or 'there exists an as-yet undetected subatomic particle with the following (precisely specified) charge and spin characteristics'.

The whole debate around anti-realism can best be understood as a range of more or less resourceful attempts to make sense of these and other such likewise (on the face of it) truth-apt statements while paying due regard to the pre-sumptive veto on truth-values that would somehow transcend the limits of proof or verifiability. Yet that solution is simply not to be had, as emerges with striking regularity from the various, often heroically dedicated efforts to achieve it examined in the course of this chapter. Least of all can it be had – so I have argued here – by confronting the widely acknowledged scandal of all-out

Kripkean scepticism with a different, supposedly salvific reading of those self-same passages in Wittgenstein that Kripke was himself able to exploit to such powerful and disturbing effect.

NOTES

1 See especially Ludwig Wittgenstein, *Philosophical Investigations*, trans. G. E. M. Anscombe (Oxford: Blackwell, 1953) and *On Certainty*, ed. and trans. Anscombe and G. H. von Wright (Blackwell, 1969).

2 For examples which fairly leap off the page despite his biographer's marked reluctance to draw any such unseemly conclusion, see Ray Monk, *Ludwig Wittgenstein: The Duty of Genius* (London: Jonathan Cape, 1990).

3 Wittgenstein, *Philosophical Investigations* (op. cit.), Sections 201–92 *passim*; Saul Kripke, *Wittgenstein on Rules and Private Language: An Elementary Exposition* (Oxford: Blackwell, 1982); also Alexander Miller and Crispin Wright (eds), *Rule-following and Meaning* (Chesham: Acumen, 2002); Paul Boghossian, 'The Rule-following Considerations', *Mind*, Vol. 98 (1989), pp. 507–49; Bob Hale, 'Rule-following, Objectivity, and Meaning', in Hale and Crispin Wright (eds), *A Companion to the Philosophy of Language* (Blackwell, 1997), pp. 369–96; John McDowell, 'Wittgenstein on Following a Rule', *Synthèse*, Vol. 58 (1984), pp. 325–63.

4 For further discussion of this curious tendency, see Christopher Norris, *Truth Matters: Realism, Anti-Realism and Response-Dependence* (Edinburgh: Edinburgh University Press, 2002) and *Philosophy of Language and the Challenge to Scientific Realism* (London: Routledge, 2003).

5 See, for instance, Cora Diamond, *The Realistic Spirit: Wittgenstein, Philosophy, and the Mind* (Cambridge, MA: MIT Press, 1991).

6 See especially Michael Dummett, *Truth and Other Enigmas* (London: Duckworth, 1978) and *The Logical Basis of Metaphysics* (Duckworth, 1991).

7 See Note 6, above; also Norris, *Truth Matters* (op. cit.); Michael Luntley, *Language, Logic and Experience: The Case for Anti-Realism* (London: Duckworth, 1988); Neil Tennant, *Anti-Realism and Logic* (Oxford: Clarendon Press, 1987) and *The Taming of the True* (Oxford: Oxford University Press, 1997); Crispin Wright, *Realism, Meaning and Truth* (Oxford: Blackwell, 1987) and *Truth and Objectivity* (Cambridge, MA: Harvard University Press, 1992).

8 J. L. Aronson, 'Testing for Convergent Realism', *British Journal for the Philosophy of Science*, Vol. 40 (1989), pp. 255–60; Aronson, R. Harré and E. Way, *Realism Rescued: How Scientific Progress is Possible* (London: Duckworth, 1994); Richard Boyd, 'The Current Status of Scientific Realism', in Jarrett Leplin (ed.), *Scientific Realism* (Berkeley and Los Angeles: University of California Press, 1984), pp. 41–82; Gilbert Harman, 'Inference to the Best Explanation', *Philosophical Review*, Vol. 74 (1965), pp. 88–95; Peter Lipton, *Inference to the Best Explanation* (London: Routledge, 1993).

9 Cf. Larry Laudan, 'A Confutation of Convergent Realism', *Philosophy of Science*, Vol. 48 (1981), 19–49.

10 See especially Paul Benacerraf, 'What Numbers Could Not Be', in Benacerraf and Hilary Putnam (eds), *The Philosophy of Mathematics: Selected Essays*, 2nd edn (Cambridge: Cambridge University Press, 1983), pp. 272–94; also Michael Detlefson (ed.), *Proof and Knowledge in Mathematics* (London: Routledge, 1992); W. D. Hart (ed.), *The Philosophy of Mathematics* (Oxford: Oxford University Press, 1996); Philip Kitcher, *The Nature of Mathematical Knowledge* (Oxford: Oxford University Press, 1983); Hilary Putnam, *Mathematics, Matter and Method* (Cambridge University Press, 1975).

11 Kurt Gödel, 'What Is Cantor's Continuum Problem?', in Benacerraf and Putnam (eds),

Philosophy of Mathematics (op. cit.), pp. 470–85; also Jerrold J. Katz, *Realistic Rationalism* (Cambridge, MA: MIT Press, 1998).

12 Cited by Michael Williams, *Unnatural Doubts: Epistemological Realism and the Basis of Scepticism* (Princeton, NJ: Princeton University Press, 1996), pp. 43 and 226.

13 Ibid., p. 56.

14 See entries under Note 7, above.

15 McDowell, 'Wittgenstein on Following a Rule' (op. cit.).

16 Thomas Nagel, *The View from Nowhere* (Oxford: Oxford University Press, 1986).

17 See, for instance, Hilary Putnam, *Reason, Truth and History* (Cambridge: Cambridge University Press, 1981).

18 Wright, *Truth and Objectivity* (op. cit.), p. 48.

19 Ibid., p. 103.

20 Ibid., p. 61.

21 Ibid., p. 48.

22 Ibid., p. 61.

23 See entries under Note 3, above.

24 Kripke, *Wittgenstein on Rules and Private Language* (op. cit.), p. 16. All further references to this work given by 'Kripke' and page number in the text.

25 Wittgenstein, *Philosophical Investigations* (op. cit.), Section 265.

26 Wright, *Truth and Objectivity* (op. cit.), p. 228.

27 Ibid., p. 228.

28 See Wright, 'Moral Values, Projection, and Secondary Qualities', *Proceedings of the Aristotelian Society*, Supplementary Vol. 62 (1988), pp. 1–26 and 'Realism, Antirealism, Irrealism, Quasi-Realism', *Midwest Studies in Philosophy*, Vol. 12 (1988), pp. 25–49; also Mark Johnston, 'Dispositional Theories of Value', *Proceedings of the Aristotelian Society*, Vol. 63 (1989), pp. 139–74 and 'How to Speak of the Colours', *Philosophical Studies*, Vol. 68 (1992), pp. 221–63; Philip Pettit, 'Are Manifest Qualities Response-Dependent?', *The Monist*, Vol. 81 (1998), pp. 3–43 and 'Noumenalism and Response-Dependence', *The Monist*, Vol. 81 (1998), pp. 112–32.

29 Wright, *Truth and Objectivity* (op. cit.), p. 5; also *Wittgenstein on the Foundations of Mathematics* (Cambridge, MA: Harvard University Press, 1980).

30 Michael Dummett, *Elements of Intuitionism* (Oxford: Oxford University Press, 1977).

31 See entries under Note 28, above.

32 Norris, *Truth Matters: Realism, Anti-Realism and Response-Dependence* (op. cit.).

33 Plato, *Euthyphro*, in *The Dialogues of Plato*, Vol. 1, trans. R. E. Allen (New Haven: Yale University Press, 1984). For discussion see Wright, *Truth and Objectivity* (op. cit.) and 'Euthyphronism and the Physicality of Colour', *European Review of Philosophy*, Vol. 3 (1998), pp. 15–30.

34 See Note 28, above; also Jim Edwards, 'Best Opinion and Intentional States', *Philosophical Quarterly*, Vol. 42 (1992), pp. 21–42; Richard Holton, 'Response-Dependence and Infallibility', *Analysis*, Vol. 52 (1992), pp. 180–4; Mark Johnston, 'Objectivity Refigured: Pragmatism Without Verificationism', in J. Haldane and C. Wright (eds), *Realism, Representation and Projection* (Oxford: Oxford University Press, 1993), pp. 85–130; Mark Powell, 'Realism or Response-Dependence?', *European Review of Philosophy*, Vol. 3 (1998), pp. 1–13; Peter Railton, 'Red, Bittter, Good', *European Review of Philosophy*, Vol. 3 (1998), pp. 67–84; Ralph Wedgwood, 'The Essence of Response-Dependence', *European Review of Philosophy*, Vol. 3 (1998), pp. 31–54.

35 Neil Tennant, *The Taming of the True* (Oxford: Oxford University Press, 1997), p. 49.

36 Michael Devitt, *Realism and Truth*, 2nd edn (Princeton, NJ: Princeton University Press, 1991); also Norris, *Philosophy of Language and the Challenge to Scientific Realism* (op. cit.).

37 For some acute commentary on the relationship between 'old-style' verificationism and

these latest variants on the theme, see C. J. Misak, *Verificationism: Its History and Prospects* (London: Routledge, 1995).

38 Tennant, *The Taming of the True* (op. cit.), p. 246. All further references given by 'Tennant' and page number in the text.

39 Dummett, *Truth and Other Enigmas* and *The Logical Basis of Metaphysics* (Note 6, above).

40 David Lewis, *The Plurality of Worlds* (Oxford: Blackwell, 1986), p. 109.

41 Katz, *Realistic Rationalism* (op. cit.), pp. 36–7.

42 Devitt, *Realism and Truth* (op. cit.).

43 Wright, 'Kripke's Account of the Argument against Private Language', *Journal of Philosophy*, Vol. 81 (1984), pp. 759–78; p. 771.

44 Wittgenstein, *Philosophical Investigations* (op. cit.), Sections 201–92 *passim*.

45 For further discussion see Wright, 'Realism, Antirealism, Irrealism, Quasi-Realism' (op. cit.); also Paul Boghossian, 'The Status of Content', *The Philosophical Review*, Vol. 99 (1990), pp. 157–84 and 'The Status of Content Revisited', *Pacific Philosophical Quarterly*, Vol. 71 (1990), pp. 264–78.

46 J. L. Mackie, *Ethics: Inventing Right and Wrong* (Harmondsworth: Penguin, 1977).

47 See entries under Notes 10 and 11, above.

48 For two sharply contrasting views on this topic, see Paul Churchland, 'Eliminative Materialism and the Propositional Attitudes', *Journal of Philosophy*, Vol. 78 (1981), pp. 67–90 and Jerry Fodor, *Psychosemantics* (Cambridge, MA: MIT Press, 1987).

49 See especially W. V. Quine, *Word and Object* (Cambridge, MA: MIT Press, 1960) and 'Epistemology Naturalized', in *Ontological Relativity and Other Essays* (New York: Columbia University Press, 1969), pp. 69–90. For opposing arguments, see Noam Chomsky, 'Quine's Empirical Assumptions', in Donald Davidson and Jaakko Hintikka (eds), *Words and Objections: Essays on the Work of W. V. Quine* (Dordrecht: D. Reidel, 1969), pp. 53–68 and John Searle, 'Indeterminacy, Empiricism, and the First Person', *Journal of Philosophy*, Vol. 84 (1987), pp. 123–46; also – for some illuminating commentary – Gary Ebbs, *Rule-following and Realism* (Cambridge, MA: Harvard University Press, 1997).

50 See Notes 6, 7 and 30, above.

51 Scott Soames, *Understanding Truth* (Oxford: Oxford University Press, 1999).

52 Thus according to the realist, as Dummett puts it, 'mathematical structures, like galaxies, exist, independently of us, in a realm of reality which we do not inhabit but which those of us who have the skill are capable of observing and reporting on' (*Truth and Other Enigmas* [op. cit.], p. 229).

53 See Soames, *Understanding Truth* (op. cit.).

54 See especially Dummett, 'Can an Effect Precede its Cause?', 'Bringing About the Past', and 'The Reality of the Past', in *Truth and Other Enigmas* (op. cit.), pp. 319–32, 333–50, 358–74.

55 Christopher Norris, 'From Copenhagen to the Stars', in *Quantum Theory and the Flight from Realism: Philosophical Responses to Quantum Mechanics* (London: Routledge, 2000), pp. 231–62.

56 John A. Wheeler, 'Delayed Choice Experiments and the Bohr-Einstein Dialogue', paper presented at the joint meeting of the American Philosophical Society and the Royal Society, London, 5 June 1980. My source here is F. Selleri, 'Wave-Particle Duality: Recent Proposals for the Detection of Empty Waves', in W. Schommers (ed.), *Quantum Theory and Pictures of Reality: Foundations, Interpretations, and New Aspects* (Berlin: Springer Verlag, 1989), pp. 279–32. See also J. A. Wheeler and W. H. Zurek, *Quantum Theory and Measurement* (Princeton, NJ: Princeton University Press, 1983).

57 See Note 54, above.

58 Dummett, *Elements of Intuitionism* (op. cit.).

59 McDowell, 'Wittgenstein on Following a Rule' (Note 3, above).

60 Wright, *Wittgenstein on the Foundations of Mathematics* (Note 29, above). See also Cora

Diamond (ed.), *Wittgenstein's Lectures on the Foundations of Mathematics* (Chicago: University of Chicago Press, 1976) and S. Shanker, *Wittgenstein and the Turning-Point in the Philosophy of Mathematics* (Albany, NY: State University of New York Press, 1987).

61 See, for instance, David Bloor, *Wittgenstein: A Social Theory of Knowledge* (New York: Columbia University Press, 1983); Clifford Geertz, *The Interpretation of Cultures: Selected Essays* (New York: Basic Books, 1973); Derek L. Phillips, *Wittgenstein and Scientific Knowledge: A Sociological Perspective* (London: Macmillan, 1977); Richard Rorty, *Consequences of Pragmatism* (Brighton: Harvester, 1982).

62 Cora Diamond, *The Realistic Spirit: Wittgenstein, Philosophy, and the Mind* (Cambridge, MA: MIT Press, 1991).

63 Dummett, *Elements of Intuitionism* (op. cit.).

64 L. E. J. Brouwer, *Collected Works*, Vol. I, ed. A. Heyting (Amsterdam: North-Holland, 1975), p. 451. Cited in Karen Green, *Dummett: Philosophy of Language* (Cambridge: Polity Press, 2001), p. 92.

65 Katz, *Realistic Rationalism* (op. cit.), p. 37.

66 Lewis, *The Plurality of Worlds* (op. cit.), 109.

67 Wittgenstein, *On Certainty* (op. cit.).

68 See Notes 28, 33 and 34, above.

69 Wittgenstein, *Philosophical Investigations* (op. cit.), Section 201.

70 Wittgenstein, *Tractatus Logico-Philosophicus*, trans. D. F. Pears and B. F. McGuiness (London: Routledge & Kegan Paul, 1961); also Gottlob Frege, *Conceptual Notation and Related Articles*, trans. Terrell Ward Bynum (Oxford: Oxford University Press, 1972).

71 Wittgenstein, *On Certainty* (op. cit.), Sections 95–9.

Index of Names

Abelard, Peter 23, 25
Adorno, Theodor W. 125, 129n
Allen, Barry 127n
Anscombe, G.E.M. 152n
Aristotle 12, 23, 47, 62, 76, 85, 94, 103, 108, 114
Aronson, J.L. 38n
Austin, J.L. 94, 145, 146, 153n

Bacon, Francis 63
Bellarmine, Cardinal 80
Benacerraf, Paul 128n
Berkeley, George 109
Bernstein, Richard J. 71n
Bhaskar, Roy 71n, 71n
Bloor, David 202n
Boghossian, Paul 199n
Bohm, David 100n
Boyd, Richard 38n, 71n, 99n, 199n
Brandom, Robert 1, 152n
Brouwer, L.E.J. 22, 192, 202n

Carnap, Rudolf 25, 55, 63, 73n, 87
Chihara, Charles S. 126n
Chomsky, Noam 51–3, 65–6, 72n, 201n
Churchland, Patricia 141–3, 153n
Churchland, Paul M. 62, 73n, 141–3, 153n, 201n
Code, Lorraine 74n
Coffa, J. Alberto 129n
Copernicus, Nicolaus 80, 119

Dalton, John 79
Darwin, Charles 47, 62, 85, 114, 118
Davidson, Donald 1, 5–6, 23, 28, 30, 39n, 56–7, 59, 64–5, 67–70, 74n, 83, 86–7, 89–95, 97, 101n, 102, 106–21, 124, 134, 141
Derrida, Jacques 2, 3, 7, 11, 145, 147, 148, 151–2, 153n, 154n

Descartes, René 12, 52, 68, 96, 141, 142
Devitt, Michael 39n, 71n, 82, 83, 88, 96, 168, 173
Diamond, Cora 98n, 186–7, 199n, 202n
Duhem, Pierre 42, 44, 80, 84, 99n
Dummett, Michael 1, 4–6, 9, 10, 12, 18, 25–34, 37n, 39n, 48, 60, 75, 73n, 82–5, 87–9, 96–8, 100n, 123, 157, 161, 165–7, 169–70, 173–4, 179, 181–5, 192–4, 196, 201n

Ebbs, Gary 201n
Einstein, Albert 47, 57, 79, 85, 99n, 118
Euclid 125
Evans, Gareth 73n

Fermat, P. de 20, 165–8
Feyerabend, Paul K. 80–1, 99n, 115
Field, Hartry 38n, 57, 73n
Fine, Arthur 99n
Fodor, Jerry 73n, 201n
Føllesdal, Dagfinn 37n
Frege, Gottlob 1, 4–6, 9, 10, 12, 14, 16–28 *passim*, 31–6 *passim*, 37n, 38n, 82, 83, 87, 94, 97, 100n, 123, 148, 152, 154n, 169, 195
Freud, Sigmund 14
Friedman, Michael 39n, 71n
Fuller, Steve 81, 99n

Galileo 61, 62, 80, 94, 108, 109
Gardner, M. 99n
Geertz, Clifford 202n
Gibbins, Peter 71n
Gibson, J.J. 38n
Glover, Jonathan 148
Gödel, Kurt 22, 48, 124, 129n, 159, 192, 199n
Goldbach, C. 26, 60, 123–4, 157, 166, 181, 198